Twinflame

Twinflame
Awaken to Self Discovery

Shananda

LitPrime Solutions
21250 Hawthorne Blvd
Suite 500, Torrance, CA 90503
www.litprime.com
Phone: 1 (209) 788-3500

© 2020 Shananda. All rights reserved.

No part of this book may be reproduced, stored in a retrieval system, or transmitted by any means without the written permission of the author.

The characters in this book are purely fictional. Any relationship to anyone living or dead is purely coincidental.

In reading this book, please do not try any of the practices without proper guidance. This writer does not accept responsibility for the results of what may happen with or without the proper guidance.

Published by LitPrime Solutions   12/03/2020

ISBN: 978-1-953397-41-6(sc)
ISBN: 978-1-953397-42-3(e)

Any people depicted in stock imagery provided by Thinkstock are models, and such images are being used for illustrative purposes only.

Certain stock imagery © Thinkstock.

Because of the dynamic nature of the Internet, any web addresses or links contained in this book may have changed since publication and may no longer be valid. The views expressed in this work are solely those of the author and do not necessarily reflect the views of the publisher, and the publisher hereby disclaims any responsibility for them.

A Special dedication:
Twin Flame

Thank you for coming into my life to
show me the clock is ticking …
That it is time to heal and move forward …

Contents

Chapter 1. The End 1

Chapter 2. Rude Reality 31

Chapter 3. Goodbyes 45

Chapter 4. Dream Lover 58

Chapter 5. Affairs of the Heart .83

Chapter 6. It's Christmas!—Show's Over! 123

Chapter 7. Awakening 146

Chapter 8. Looking Within 162

Chapter 9. Righteous Anger 179

Chapter 10. New Realities 204

Chapter 11. Moving Forward 222

Chapter 12. The Beginning 232

CHAPTER ONE

The End

He looked deep into my eyes as we made love. I could feel him within every fiber of my being. Yes, this was love, and I'd loved him forever. I smiled up at him as though I would burst. This was the love I'd waited lifetimes for.

The hands that knew my body caressed me as if we were one, and my passion mounted again. He rolled onto his back, taking me with him. I rested on his chest while looking into his eyes, taking a moment to study this familiar face: the beautiful brown eyes that were so deep one could get lost in them—so much like mine. My finger traced his face as if to memorize every inch, including the Roman nose and high cheekbones. My finger lingered on his full, well-defined lips. His was a face I'd never seen yet knew so well.

His strong hands held me, pulling me closer as he continued with kisses that reignited the fire within. Again, I looked into his eyes and smiled while noticing his beautiful, rich, dark hair that I brushed away. As our passion deepened, my thoughts strayed. "Never leave me," I said

"I never will," he murmured. We were so synchronized. His hand slid down the contour of my body, touching me ever so lightly.

Abruptly, rudely, I was awaked by that damned alarm clock screaming in my ears.

I slapped the snooze button, desperately hoping as always to recapture the dream. But as always, it wasn't going to happen. I knew this scenario. I'd lived it many times before. I pulled the sheets over my head while moaning for him. *Please, just five more minutes.*

Breep! Breep! Breep!

"Okay!" I blindly reached for the alarm and managed to turn it off. Time for *this* reality—to live in the real world.

I dragged myself from the bed and made my way to the shower, sighing regretfully as I prepared for my workday. I turned on the faucet, stepped into the warm water while still half asleep, and stood under the steady stream of water that coursed down my body. The sensory input of the dream returned to overwhelm me. His smell—soft yet masculine, pleasant, and strictly his own—filled my senses. I felt the firm velvet of his skin yielding to my touch, against my cheek, under my tongue as I ran it down his torso. The memory of being pressed against his muscular body revived the appetite that was unsatisfied fifteen minutes ago.

"Enough already!" I insisted to myself, though a bit too loud for my small bathroom.

Reaching for the soap, I shook my head vigorously to shake him out. But he never really left. He was always there in some corner, nook, or cranny, rooted in the deepest parts of my brain. The residual emotion of the dream was most confusing. It was the love that was so sublime, tranquil, and intense for a man I'd never seen.

While I dried my hair, it struck me how much alike we looked, he and I. Was this male persona somehow symbolic of me? Was he really some aspect of my own psyche? That rang true to me, and at the same time, I knew he was a separate person. This reflection caused a weird feeling in my solar plexus. I feel a distinct pull. I embrace my stomach as if it were to fall from my body. I found myself staring into the mirror, looking into my own eyes and seeing his. Yet again I'd fallen into another daydream.

"Kate, stop this! Wake up, girl! Man, this is weird." The dream had never lingered this long. "Damn!" I exclaimed, hoping it would snap me out of this trance. "I've got to get ready for work!"

Hmmm. I wonder if it's going to rain today. I looked out of my apartment window into a beautiful Monday morning. A few people were already out and about. I felt a smile sneak across my face as I speculated just what Bill would think of my mystery man. A little giggle even escaped my lips as I realized he wouldn't be too thrilled! I felt excited as though I was privy to some illicit secret. This stranger was so real to me, and my life was so tangible.

I turned on the stereo and poured a cup of coffee. "Dream Lover" was playing on the radio. "Dream lover, come rescue me," I sang, but not quite in tune. "Yeah, I wish he would. Ooh, there's that tug in the pit of my stomach again."

I came to an abrupt stop and held my stomach. After the feeling passed, I looked at my clock and realized I had dreamed the morning away.

I stepped into the bedroom for one last look, making sure nothing was amiss, and quickly fixed my hair while admiring myself in the full-length mirror. *Not bad. All the right stuff in all the right places.*

It had taken me years to get over being self-conscious about myself and start appreciating the fact that I was blessed with good looks and a small but nice figure. Oh well. I still saw quite a few heads turn when I walked by, even though Joe had us wear these silly uniforms. They were *pink,* for heaven's sake, and so unflattering. They were eerily reminiscent of the cafeteria women's dresses of our elementary school years. Not the sexiest fashion in design history.

It took a couple of minutes to braid my thick, red hair. I'd worn it long all my life, but it got in my way when I worked, and as a waitress, the health department required this. Like Joe's hair doesn't get in the food as it was. At the rate it was falling out, it wouldn't be long before that balding Italian head finally reached the point where he wouldn't have to wear that awful ball cap.

I ran through the apartment to make sure everything was turned off, poured the last cup from my two-cup coffee maker, grabbed my coat, and flew out the door. I would be late once again for work. Joe was never on time anyway.

Walking to work, I pondered why my "dream lover" had begun to visit me every night. It was also odd how the dreams were never the same yet featured the same man—plus each night I received more details of his appearance. The same perfect man. This guy said all the right things, held me just right, and was a better lover than any man I'd ever had in real life.

The problem was I was obsessed with my dream life, and that wasn't normal or healthy. I had to admit that I wasn't too concerned about normal. But healthy—I really wanted to maintain that state in my life, especially concerning the mental part.

I finally reached the Corner Diner, where the bell on the door announced my arrival. I hung my jacket on the same hook as I had most days for the past three years. Joe came out of the kitchen to greet me. "Hey, Kat-*ie!* Late as usual! Doin' okay? Do you possibly think you could get to work now? Or can we make an appointment? It's meat loaf day, and we're gonna be slammed!"

"Yeah, Joe, let's rock and roll."

Incredible but endearing. The Monday lunch special had been meat loaf since I started working here, and yes, we would be busy. Joe's meat loaf wasn't too bad, his prices were reasonable, and he had been here since the beginning of time. I believed he and Moses are on a first-name basis.

I couldn't be too upset. I was blessed to even have this job. It was a block from my apartment, an easy walk since I didn't have a car. The place was a little old-fashioned, short-order diner with a high turnover, and the tips were pretty good. Hey, it paid the bills and kept me from having to move back home. Joe had taken pity on me when I first arrived, taking me under his wing and helping me find a place to live.

It wasn't a secret that I'd hated living in Flint. When I couldn't handle it any longer, I'd packed my small suitcase and headed to Chicago. No way I was going to be stuck there like Mom. Poor Mom. Fifty-five going on ninety-five.

Joe walked over to the front door and turned over the open/close sign, even though we had ten more minutes before opening. Joe couldn't stand to have any customer waiting outside.

"Beth, get the lead out! You gonna stay in that damned toilet all day? We got customers waiting!" he bellowed from the order window. His expression changed from a frown to a smile as he acknowledged his favorite patrons. "Good morning, Mr. and Mrs. Robertson! Go to your usual table, and Katie will get your coffee!"

He nodded toward the coffee, signaling me to get to work.

I was getting decaf coffee when Beth finally emerged from the bathroom. "Papa, you know I started my period this morning! Leave me the hell alone! I'm not in the mood today, and you know damn well Kate hates being called Katie!"

Beth stood in front of her father, who came running out of the kitchen to shut her foul mouth up. It wasn't too long before they were in an argument. It was quite comical watching Beth shaking her finger at her father and him shaking his in return.

Beth met her father in height and had the same frame: small and thin. It was difficult to tell she was the mother of a fifteen-year-old girl. She looked to be in her twenties. Her hair was ebony black, cut short with wisps of hair accenting her face. She was large breasted, and her uniform fit her very well. It was a bit too short, but it made up for the tips she received daily. She had a very outgoing personality, and everyone here loved her deeply. In fact, she could do no wrong. Hell, even her ex-husband was still in love with her. He is what's currently referred as an "absentee parent." Beth was pure Italian from head to toe—with a temper to match. Man, I envied her.

I let them argue and returned to things at hand. I walked over to James and Dee Robertson, who were regulars. Most of our customers were. A longtime friend of theirs, Ed Franklin walked in and Jim waved him over to the table. All three of them were retired and came every morning for the senior special. The Robertson's were a cute couple, the typical "Mom and Pop."

Ed was really nice, a widower of six years. He and Jim were friends since WWII. Dee sat between them smiling and listening to the same conversation they had every morning. I walked over and poured their de-cafe when Jim said, "Now that's de-cafe—right, dearie?"

Dee placed her hand over his and replied, "Ignore him Kate. You know very well it's de-cafe Jim, now leave the girl alone."

"Come on, I was only having fun. I know what it is." Jim winked at me and laughed. I placed the filled coffee cup in front of Jim as he proceeded to tell Ed the latest joke he heard. He prides himself on being quite the comedian. Naturally, I laugh as though it's the funniest joke I've ever heard. Dee just smiled, as she always does and probably has for the last thirty-five years of their marriage. I'll bet she's heard everyone of his jokes at least a hundred times.

"I'll be right back with your orders," I said on my way back to the kitchen to turn in the order and get my apron. "Three senior specs". I yelled at Joe who had already started them. He already knew what everyone was going to order.

Beth came into the kitchen to refill the shelf over the stove with cleaned dishes, "Hey, girlfriend! You awake yet? It's obvious I'm not. I was up late with Lisa. Thought you were going to come over and help with that damned prom dress? You should see her—man it's scary! She's gonna have tits like me. Poor thing!" Beth laughed and returned to her prep work.

"Beth! You watch your mouth in front of the customers! I've told you before …" Joe was shaking a spatula at Beth.

"Oh, Papa, if they don't know what these are (she held her breasts in her hands facing Joe) then they better go back to school and relearn their hygiene!—Get it?" Beth chuckled as she ducked the flying spatula and ran back to the sink, "Man, you'd think after all these years, he'd develop some kind of sense of humor!" She pretended to brush her brow with her arm and then made an obscene gesture from her chin towards Joe.

Things were never dull here. Beth's a real clown sometimes, but that's the personality trait I treasure most in her. I tend to be a bit of a pessimist. I can always count on her to inject humor into any given situation.

"Well sweetie, you haven't answered me. You okay today?"

"No, Beth, I'm still dazed and confused. Bill came over and we went to a movie. He acted weird all evening—like he had some kind of secret and wouldn't tell me."

Beth rolled her eyes at me and made a face of discernment.

"Look, I know you two don't get along. It would really help me if you would just lay off him a little—okay?"

"I can't help it if he leaves himself wide open as a target for rebuttal. But for you sweetie, I'll try." She pinched my chin between her fingers shaking my face.

"So, 'ole' Bill's got a secret. Hmmm ... I wonder ..."

Beth wasn't able to wonder about it for long, the Monday morning crowd started filing in and the place was swamped. The bell on the door announced the arrival of more patrons; I looked up to see Bill walking in. He stood in the doorway for a moment, allowing his eyes to adjust to the inside lighting. His slender physique looked great in the expensive suit. The deep color of the material setting off his clear blue eyes which now seemed to sparkle a little more than usual.

He spots me and a smile breaks out across his fair face. I noticed he had one hand behind his back as he walked toward me. "Hi, love", he said as he produced a huge bouquet of roses mixed with wildflowers from behind his back. The feeling of surprise was overwhelming. I stood awkwardly with a huge tray of food staring at the flowers.

Quickly thinking, Beth ran up to me grabbing the tray from my hands making it easier to receive this wonderful gift. Caught up in his thoughts, Bill held me by the shoulders, pulling me close when he realized where he was. His look quickly changed from one of love—to embarrassment, turning beet red to the top of his scalp. His blonde hair couldn't hide the red blush. "I'm sorry Katie, I hope I didn't embarrass you. These ... are for you." Bill stuttered, dropping his head and running his hand through his hair. This caused it to become disheveled, which made his embarrassment look even a bit more comical. Sometimes I found it hard to believe he was an up-and-coming executive for an advertising agency. Nevertheless, his eyes were twinkling as he stood before me with so much pride in his accomplishment,—I thought he was going to burst.

"Bill, they are beautiful ... But why?" I didn't hear his answer. The flowers captured my full attention. I was enveloped by the fragrance of the roses—I love the *smell of roses!* The fragrance permeated the air and I was lost in deep thought my mystery Dream Lover pushed his way to the front of my thoughts. *Would he bring me flowers?* I immediately answered myself in the affirmative, remembering how perfect he is. However, I scold myself, *he isn't real! Bill, on the other hand—is real.* I suddenly become aware of the fact that Bill was talking to me.

"Katie, are you listening to me? Did you hear me? I am trying to tell you something." He was starting to look a bit disgruntled.

"Bill, I'm sorry. I was drifting again. The flowers threw me. Go ahead. I'm listening now." I hate it when that happens.

Bill can be so sensitive and sometimes I inadvertently hurt his feelings by my wool gathering. Strangely enough he seemed to be in very good humor today and was actually laughing about my behavior.—*Man! This must be important.*

"Now that I have your attention, I do have it?—Good. I got the position of Executive Vice-President of Sales with The Cannon Group!" He said while proudly straightening his tie, "Don, the head man himself, called me in with the congrats! You know what this means? I'll be able to stay here! No more extensive traveling for weeks at a time!" I must have had that wandering look again, "Katie, don't lose me again. Look, I need you sit to down for a moment—please? This is important." *Does he have tears in his eyes?* I got it together for what was about to happen ... *Think clearly Kate—focus on Bill.*

"Baby, you have been a real trooper—so patient and understanding these past two years", he held me by the shoulders. "I know I can be difficult at times, but you have always been there for me in so many ways; as a friend, lover (he was bright red then), and confidante. Katie, surely you know how much I love you,—don't you?"

As I nodded my head in response, this strange numbness creeps over me when I realize what he was about to say. He reached into his jacket pocket and produces a small black box. A million thoughts run through my mind at once. I felt confused and out of touch with reality and my present confusion must have been showing in my facial expression …

"Oh, Katie, this must have been the wrong time. I hope this wasn't a mistake all together … I apologize …" His facial expression quickly changed to one of confusion.

"No. No, Bill", I interrupted. *I do love Bill. I must be going insane, thinking about my imaginary man as my real-life lover of two years proposes to me.* I reached for Bill's hands and carefully took the small box out of his hands. "Let me see …" Inside the small black box was a marquise solitaire diamond, at least full carat. *My god, it's flawless! I've - never -in-my wildest dreams!*

Then he soft and lovingly said, "Katie, will you marry me? I love you."

I leaped into his arms and held him tightly saying, "Yes, yes, I'll marry you and *love* you so very much". Now I was the one with tears in my eyes.

Bill looked around beaming with delight as I came back to reality realizing that our audience was sharing in our happiness with applause. From the corner of my eye, I saw Joe, hiding behind the counter, wiping his eyes.

It wasn't long before Bill had me quit my job at the diner. His excuse was, "No wife of mine will ever have to work" and wanted us to live together until the wedding. I thought, what the hell? I was tired of working at the diner anyway.

"I'll take care of everything. All I want you to do, is take whatever time you need to plan our wedding." He said proudly.

It was difficult to believe that I was becoming a woman of leisure. I guess I was so wrapped up in being independent, I never thought Bill would ask me to quit working. I found it difficult to understand at first. I even questioned us getting married. *Oh, come on, you're just having premarital jitters. You love Bill and he loves you—that's why he doesn't want you to work. He loves ya and doesn't want ya working in an old greasy spoon. Let's face it girl, you left home before you finished college. Just two years in and realized it was impossible to work full time and go to school. You couldn't handle living with Mom and Dad, so off you went to the big city without any type of skill. Maybe after the marriage settled in, I can go back. Who knows what could happen;* I tried to convince myself?

As a wedding gift to me, Bill decided to have a garden room added to the back of his condo along the side of the atrium. His house is nothing short of grand. It's in a rather exclusive suburb and of contemporary design.

I couldn't help but admire Bill. He had a rather tragic past. His parents were killed in a car accident when he was a child. His father's family took him in and raised him. Although he was grateful for their love and support, he told me that he never felt like part of their family. Bill quickly learns how to manage his inheritance to sustain him as he went through school. With his drive and ambition I can easily see him achieving his goals for success.

It didn't take us long to move everything from my tiny apartment. Mrs. Logan was in tears when I left. I had to promise to invite her to the wedding and stay in touch. I was very grateful for this woman's kindness, taking me into the tiny apartment two years ago with only a word from Joe. I bought most of my furniture from area garage sales to fill the tiny flat. I had only my suitcase with the few items I had taken when I left Flint. Mrs. Logan could see the fear in my eyes when Joe brought me to her door.

She allowed me to pay rent by the week and gave me her son's old twin bed for a start. I decided to leave all my furniture in the tiny room and told her to rent it furnished to the next frightened person who came to her door, which left me again with a few personal items and a few boxes left to retrieve. Bill told me I could take whatever I wanted, but looking into the apartment as I left; I knew in my heart that this was where they belonged. With one last look, I closed the door and handed Mrs. Logan the key.

Mrs. Logan held me tightly and I pushed a small piece of paper into her hand with my new phone number. I walked to Bill's car without looking back.

I was going over some wedding plans when I suddenly came to the realization, I hadn't had the dreams anymore. This was the first time I had given any thought to my "dream lover" since Bill proposed. I wonder where in the recesses of my mind he's planted himself? Maybe this was for the best. *I'll definitely take this as a good sign that maybe marriage is the best thing for me.* Maybe I needed emotional stability in my life.

The wedding would be a small, informal one. Neither Bill nor I have many relatives, and he doesn't really stay in contact with the few he has … My folks couldn't afford to come. Bill offered to pay for their trip, but my father refused to "take charity" from anyone. If truth be known, Dad was still pretty angry with me. He still hasn't forgiven me for retaliating about his behavior with Mom, so this was his way of getting even. I know my mother was heartbroken, but Bill promised we'd go visit them later.

My brother Mike would be the only one here and he promised to be Bill's best man only after Bill surprised me with the tidbit of information that he asked Mr. Cannon to give me away before I could talk to Mike. I didn't want to make a scene about it, but I know it hurt Mike terribly. Mike couldn't understand why I didn't just say no to Bill and proceeded to spell out the true political reason for Bill's behavior. I found myself defending Bill and trying to soothe Mike's feathers at the same time. Little did I know this would be the first of many encounters I would have during the next few years.

We set the date for April fourteenth. It was to be a Catholic ceremony since Bill belongs to the church. I didn't have a problem with confirmation classes since I don't believe that I ever went to church as a child. In fact, I don't believe we were raised in any type of religion. I remember Mom saying that her family was Catholic, not to mention Dad's. Father Flanders took me in with open arms and helped with my lessons.

Of course, Beth was my maid-of-honor, and Lisa my bridesmaid. Beth introduced me to her cousin Estelle who had been safely keeping Beth's wedding dress. Beth had inherited a beautiful wedding dress that had been passed around the smaller family members and been redone countless times. I know Bill would have paid for a new one, though when I saw the dress, I knew it was me. It was of an Italian design with very little lace; Nostalgic, reminiscent of the late thirties. Estelle had me stand on a stool, walking around, looking me over while trying to decide the best way the dress should be altered. I found myself taking inventory of the characteristics of this very Italian family.

Estelle was a large beautiful woman, who carried the air of command when she entered the room. I am sure her overlarge breasts would send many a young boy running for fear of becoming caught in their loving grasp when hugged. When any of these women walked into a room, I am sure that the mood of the room changed because of their personalities. From Beth's brashness to Estelle's overly boisterous laughing,—Lisa was a blend of them both. For now, the world had to deal with Lisa's teenage sarcasm. When she blossoms—look out world!

Estelle gave me the once over, "You are not very big … Hmmm … I believe you will be the last to wear this dress. After I take it in, well … I don't believe it will fit anyone else in the family! Most of us are—I guess you can say … Well, you know?" she said while giving them a shake, then bursting into a fit of laughter, "What can I say? Hmmm, Beth, are you sure you want to do this? Lisa may want to get married and need this dress." Estelle gave Beth a look, "You missed getting this dress. Someone in our family needs to wear it—right?"

Looking from Beth to Lisa, it wouldn't take too much of a genius to understand Estelle's concern for the antique dress. I don't believe that I would ever fall into that "well endowed" category unless I got a major boob job. I'm sure puberty hit Lisa at a young age, from looking at this fifteen-year-old in a body that would send any woman of twenty-five into fits of jealously. I watched quietly as these women of beauty assessed the situation.

"I don't ever want to get married!" Exclaimed Lisa. "Besides, should I decide otherwise, I don't want some hand-me-down. This dress looks like it came from a thrift shop! See it's starting to turn a little brown.—Yuck!" Lisa looked at the dress in disgust.

"Nice way to insult Kate, Lisa. The dress doesn't look that bad, it has a small history behind it." Beth said sternly through the pins in her mouth, "Your great, great- grandmother was married here in that dress. She brought it over from Sicily … So, you think you're too good to wear this dress." Beth was shaking her hand at Lisa. "Well fine. I am not planning to be married any time soon and if I do, I don't believe it will be in white. The dress was handed down to me and I believe that Kate should wear it—if she wants to," said Beth looking in my direction seeking my approval.

"Of course, I'll wear the dress. I'm just sorry we'll have to make so many changes to it." I was exasperated from their indecision and constant pulling on me. "Beth, are you sure you want to do this to the dress?"

Beth was half listening to me and working on the dress, "I don't have a problem. Have you decided what you want me and Lisa to wear? Remember to be careful. One wrong move and we could look like misfit hookers!"

Estelle burst into laughter, "It's nice for you to finally decide this, from the way you dress with your dresses around your ass! This isn't so good of a role model for your daughter! Oh, Jes—sus!" Estelle dramatically shook her fingers in the air.

"Well, I have a couple of patterns I would like Estelle to see downstairs", interrupting what could have been a major quarrel. I knew Beth well enough by now to know there wasn't any place too sacred to voice her opinion. "I was thinking of a mid-drift cut a bit low—not too low, fitting loosely at your waist and then falling straight to the floor. Sort of V-shaped around the front and back of the neck. The sleeves would be long and tapered like the wedding dress. Yours, Beth would be in a very pale pink and Lisa's would be in a soft lavender."

Lisa took a deep breath of delight, "Thank God … No puffy sleeves and thousands of petticoats! Yes!—I can do this!"

"I still have to get the flowers ready. Oh!—And someone to pick up Mike at the airport. Beth, could you? I know you have a lot to do … He'll be here the night before the ceremony. You can bring him by here before he has to go to Bill's bachelor party." I went down the list of things I had left to do as Estelle and Beth worked steadily on the dress.

I began to fidget after being held hostage on the stool for quite some time. At first Beth and, Estelle ignored me. Lisa came to my rescue. "Look guys, Kate's worn out. Can we stop now?—Please?" She pleaded.

Beth looked at her watch and realized how long I was on that stool. "Sorry, Kate, I guess we just got on a roll." Stepping back, taking one last look, she was very pleased. "Kate, you're going to be beautiful. Oh, I almost forgot, Pops sent you a bottle of vino! Why don't we go downstairs and relax with a glass?"

I nodded in relief, "Sounds good to me, I'm afraid a glass may be just enough to put me to sleep. So just one glass for me. Lisa, if you would take Estelle with you, I'm sure she's just as worn out, go get things ready; Beth can help me get out of these pins and we'll meet you downstairs in a few."

Beth helped me off the chair and carefully out of the dress. I wrapped myself in the robe I had brought up earlier. Beth noticing my silence, "Kate, you okay? I didn't mean to keep you up there so long."

There were tears in my eyes as I held the fragile dress in my arms. I was so overwhelmed from the love Beth had always extended me. We were more than sisters. I never had anyone treat me with such kindness. I burst into tears and Beth held me in hers arms–pins and all. We didn't have to say a word. Beth knew about my life in Flint and understood what I was going through.

"I wish she would leave him. I want her here, Damnit! She should be here! Why does she take his abuse like that?" Wiping my nose on the sleeve of my robe.

Beth rolled her eyes and handed me some tissue, "You're worse than Lisa! Here, use this. It's a good thing one of us is using her head. I remembered my wedding, there were enough tears to flood the city of Chicago! Ugh! You ain't seen tears until you've been to an Italian wedding!" Beth, said softly, "Don't worry so much, I'm sure your mother wanted to be here. Mike did tell you she was pretty upset."

I giggled, "I guess you're right … God! What am I thinking? If Mom were here, she would have sat over there like a little mouse and not said one word. I would have become frustrated and our continued fight would once again begin." I was crying uncontrollably awhile Beth held on lovingly stroking my hair until I finished.

"You feel better, sweetie? Now, if you could do me one small favor, I would be forever in your debt." Beth was trying to pull back a bit and I looked at her rather puzzled. "These damn pins are poking the hell out of me! We can continue the moment, but it will have to be without that dress.—Okay?"

I turned a deep red but was happy for the intervention of Beth's stand by humor. I wiped my eyes with my robe and placed the dress by the sewing machine. "You know, I'm ready for that glass of wine. I'll leave this here for Estelle and start on the rest of the wedding plans tomorrow. Tonight, let's just relax.—Kay?"

After I regained my composure, Beth slipped her arm into mine and we headed downstairs to see what Lisa and Estelle had gotten into. While Lisa was pouring the wine, Estelle was raiding the fridge. There were already the makings for any type of sandwich on the counter. Estelle finished retrieving the last of the sandwich meats and turned her attention to making our snacks, "Hope you don't mind me making myself at home, but my payment for working for the family isn't much, a little vino … A little food …" She said as she shrugged her shoulders and smiled.

"Only if you don't mind making a ham on rye for me.—Heavy on the mayo …" I replied between yawns.

Beth was leaning on the counter watching Estelle and sipping the wine, "Kate, I can't help but notice that the fridge is full of food. I know that you *must* have gone shopping. As I remember, Bill only had two beers and a bottle of pickle relish in there last week. It was scary. How do men do that?"

I giggled, "Well, the two bottles of beer are still there hiding behind the food. I knew you and Lisa were going to be here, so I threw out the leftover Chinese I have been nibbling on, decided that I had better have something to feed you guys. I guess my days of eating restaurant leftovers are over. I'm going to have to learn how to cook or Joe will have to start doing takeout!"

"Yeah, my fridge is full of leftovers from Pops' place too. I remember he wouldn't let you leave unless you took something home with you. He didn't want you to starve. He thinks it's his job to make sure the neighborhood doesn't go hungry—even the stray dogs! We got this damn old mutt now that hangs around every day at four P.M.

Expecting his evening meal! Je-sus!" Beth looked sullen for a moment and looked at me, "Man Kate, I know it's only been a few months, we sure do miss you around there. I mean, we really didn't expect you to spend the rest of your life there or anything. You were the first person to last as long as you did without wanting to kill Pops or run out screaming cuz they couldn't take any more of his temper. The new girl lasted three weeks!"

"I have to agree with Mom, it hasn't been the same, Papé has decided he needs to get closer and now believes it's his place to inspect my boyfriends! Mom isn't a lot of help. She needs more of your guidance,— give the kid a break, she's only having fun,—you know? By the way, did you get any of this Mom?"

Beth rolled her eyes and sipped her wine appearing to ignore the teen's subtle comments.

"Hey, your grandfather loves you. Whether Ka-*tie*' is there or not, little one, your grandfather would have nosed into your life more because of your age. He did that with your mother. Whew! You should have seen the boys run!" Estelle pointed at both with her sandwich, "You still want to believe he didn't know when you started sneaking off to meet Anthony? Think again. He just knew there wasn't anything he could do to stop you. So, *you*, Miss know-it-all, just bring a boy around every now and then to make him happy, and most of all learn from your mother's mistakes—*No* sex until after you are married!" After saying her peace, Estelle gave her wine and sandwich her full attention.

I snuggled deep into my favorite chair, quietly listened to Beth and her family reminisce. It wasn't long before the wine hit my head and made me drowsy. The last thing I remember was Beth covering me with my Afghan, giving me a quick kiss on my head and letting herself out.

I could hear Beth's car in the driveway. *Funny, I haven't had butterflies in my stomach in a long time. Hey, there's no need to be nervous, it's just Mike.* I ran down the driveway to meet him.

"Hey Red!—Long time no see-Yo—P!" I jumped into his arms before he could say another word and he swung me around as he did when we were kids. "You're getting a little big for this, aren't you? No, I guess you'll always be my little Red." He said, affectionately rubbing the top of my head for good luck.

A flood of memories swept through me. I felt safe, protected, in spite of the flutter in the pit of my stomach which was familiar yet strange. *Why should I be feeling this now?* I shrugged it off as Mike slipped his arm around my waist leading me to the front door. He stopped, looked over his shoulder at Beth, who had just walked around the car after opening the trunk, he said, "Don't worry about it Beth, I'll get it later."

"I wasn't. If you had any idea that I would bring in your luggage; you're in dream land buddy." Beth said comically.

Mike stopped so abruptly that I was jarred. His face was beet red, "Beth, I-I didn't mean ..."

"Hey, I was just kidding! Man, I can see where Kate gets a lot of her personality ... Lighten up!—Kate, I'm thirsty. Did you drink the rest of the wine?" She was shaking her head as she strolled passed us and went into the house first. I watched Mike's eyes linger as she strolled by.

"Is there something I need to know big brother?" I grinned.

"What? No. I guess I'm tired from the trip. Beth's right about one thing, you got anything to drink?—Beer maybe?" He asked avoiding my question.

"Yeah, there might be one left in the fridge. I don't think Bill's touched them since he moved into the hotel." I looked at him in wonder. Mike never shows his feelings, much less says anything.

I asked Beth to stay for dinner. It didn't take a moron to pick up that Mike wanted to be in her company as long as he could. "I thought you were going to the bachelor party tonight?" I teased.

"Nope,—wasn't invited."

"Oh, yes you were, and you know it. I called you about it more than a month ago." I rebuked.

"Look sis, Bill and I have never seen eye-to-eye on much of anything and I'm still fried about not being able to give you away," Mike hesitated when he saw the look on my face. "I don't want to start anything the night before your wedding. I'd rather be here with you anyway. It will be good to catch up on things."

Beth interrupted, "Man. I can tell this is going to be a bundle of laughs. It's no big deal whether Mike was invited to that damn party or not. I'm not going to get in the middle of this … But if memory serves me, Anthony, my *ex*," she made quite clear, "Was so hung over the next day, he could barely remember what to do during the ceremony.

Father Flanders had to nudge him a couple of times to wake him up. When the time came for the Communion, Anthony took the wineglass from the Father, tossed the Sacrament aside and asked for a refill. I thought Pops was gonna kill him! Looking back, I should have taken *that* as an omen. Let's hope Bill is the better for it and behaves himself tonight so tomorrow he'll remember what to do."

"I guess we won't have that problem with Bill. Don will be there, so he'll be too busy brown–nosing, to concern himself with what is even going on." Mused Mike.

I ignored him and said, "Let's eat. It's not much, but it will have to do." I set the pot of stew on the table, looked around making sure I had left nothing behind.

"Hell Kate, I didn't know you knew how to cook? What's the number for poison control—911?" Mike conveniently ducked the flying potholder and was rolling with laughter. Kate, you remember that time when you tried to cook for some boyfriend?" He was laughing hard, "Beth you should have seen it!"

Beth watched Mike roll with laughter and duck from the second potholder flying in his direction. "So, tell me. Kate doesn't indulge in her childhood very often."

"Mike, I warn you! Be quiet!"

"Sorry sis, I can't pass this up … It's too damn good. See Kate was trying to impress this jock, okay? Well, she invited him over for dinner one night … Not scary yet, but wait, she told him she'd cook for him. He said sure fine. Well, the big night came, man were we scared! Kate told Mom she wanted to do it all herself—no help!

So, the guy came in, sat nervously waiting for his meal *and* getting the third degree from Dad … The moment came and, we all sat down for dinner …" Mike looked as if he were going to burst into a fit of laughter, "The only food on the table was a plate of potatoes!—That's it, nothing else, just potatoes! No, No wait! She baked the potatoes. What made these potatoes different from *most* baked potatoes? Was she peeled them! All that poor sap had for dinner was peeled baked potatoes!"

Mike stood deep in thought. After a moment he said, "You know, I bet that was one of the few times, Dad was ever funny. He had put up a huge sign by the phone; In case of an emergency, dial—911!"

I leaned against the stove hiding my face from embarrassment. I looked up to find him still laughing, I flung a wooden spoon, smacking him right on the head. "What the hell did I know? I was only fourteen at the time. I panicked and figured there was no way I could possibly screw up potatoes!"

"Didn't you *ever* pay attention to Mom while she cooked our meals? You know, meat, veggies … That sort of thing …" Snickered Mike while rubbing his head, "Well one thing is for sure, you still have that temper! Bill better watch out!"

Beth stared at me in disbelief, "I can now understand why you lived on take out, missy.—Wait a minute, what do you mean temper? I don't believe I've ever seen Kate even raise her voice … Is there a side that no one here knows about? This has got to be good."

"Mi-i-ke, don't go there." I said sternly trying not to laugh. "We don't need to revive our childhood, now do we."

"Why not? It wasn't all that bad, there were some good times. If I remember correctly, you told me that you and Beth were very close—so what's it gonna hurt?" He asked with a devilish grin.

"Come on." Beth pleaded, "I need to know that there is another side to this girl".

Mike looked at me with a familiar smirk on his face. I knew I was in trouble. He got that look when there was something juicy about to happen or he was about to get someone with one of his wild jokes. Something told me I was about to become the recipient of both.

I reluctantly said, "Well, if this torment is going to happen, let's do it while we eat. That way I'll have something tangible to throw at you in my defense." I winked at Beth and plopped into the chair knowing there was no stopping him.

"Well, my favorite one to tell was the time Kate beat the hell out of a friend of mine." His eyes beamed at the prospect of having a secret. He leaned in closer to Beth and began:

"Down the road from school there was a vacant lot surrounded by a small cluster of trees. In the middle of the trees, was a slab of cement an old fallen house had once stood I guess the owners of the property had cleared away the house some time ago, the trees had grown over the slab so you couldn't see it. Kate discovered it and shared her secret with me. Against Kate's better judgment, I brought my friend Mac to help fix it up. It became a sort of fort or, hide out. Kate and I used it whenever Mom and Dad were at each other's throats. It wasn't hard to pretend being so far away from the road no one could hear what was going on. The trees were so close together they were like walls, they aided in hiding our secret. Well … This place became very personal to Kate. She had it fixed it up really nice. She was always combing the streets for junk. It wasn't too long before she had a table and a couple of chairs. Mac and I helped by putting up a few shelves between any two trees that were close together."

"One morning Mac and I decided to play army. Kate was already there when we arrived. She had other plans. She had brought some empty jars from home filling them with rocks and dirt; pretending they were sugar and flour—you know—girl stuff. Mac firmly told her that we were going to play army, and this was no place for girls. Kate said that she was there first. I suggested if she would play with us, we would help her clean up when we were through. She saw right through us," Mike chuckled, "Kate knew damn well when we were finished, that we'd head for the hills and leave the mess to her.

Mac took his rifle and broke some of the jars in retaliation when Kate said no. She stood in front of the jars that were unbroken with her hands planted firmly on her hips. I got nervous and told Mac we should leave; agreeing Kate was there first. Man, Mac got *right* in her face Kate stood her ground. Nothing could budge her when she was angry. You could almost see smoke starting to rise from Kate. I started backing away, I knew better than to force Kate into anything. The guy wouldn't stop yelling. He told her to get out and if she didn't–he'd wreck her like he just did to the place. I told him to forget it and get out of there. He just laughed and said that wasn't afraid of no girl! Before Mac could get the next word out—Kate was all over him like flies on rice!" Man, I *have* never seen anything like it. Mac's hair was flying all over the place. Kate was beating the hell out of him. I will never forget looking at this poor sap on the ground trying to cover his head and yelling at me to call her off. As soon as I pulled Kate away, he was gone in a flash." Mike dropped his head and shook it; "Poor bastard made one fatal mistake … Stopping just short of the fort yelled out some obscenities about our dad. Which sent Kate back out in the street throwing stones at the guy. One smacked him right on the head. I believe Mac never talked to me after that." Mike grinned at me, I can't understand why."

Giggling, "That asshole said some pretty bad things about Dad. Don't you remember? What was it?—Something about us being the bastards of that Irish drunk. I was glad he didn't say anything bad about Mom, I'd have had to kill him." *Brother Mike, you would have killed him years later if you only knew the whole truth about him.*

"Oh, hell Kate, Dad was the topic of conversation for most of the people in our neighborhood. You felt like it was your obligation to protect him."

"Didn't it bother you to know that everyone in town knew our problems? Dad knew all police on a first name basis? I don't know why you stay there. I was sure you would have been in Toronto by now. Mike, why are you teaching in Flint?" I turned to Beth, "You know Beth, Mike could have gone pro playing hockey. It paid his way through college. Hell, he had offers."

"Kate, you know why I stay there. Someone has to watch after Mom. So, now I coach. Besides, after four years of school playing, I was beat all to hell. There are not many who can get out and still have all their teeth." Mike scooped up the last bit of stew and winked at Beth.

"It's kind of hard to believe that our quiet little Kate was once a feisty little thing. Makes one look at you in a whole new light. So … What happened?" Asked Beth.

"I don't know, I guess I got tired of the fighting and it was easier to stay quiet and leave when I did. Hey, enough of this depressing talk. I'm getting married tomorrow. Bill left a bottle of Riesling in the fridge for me. Why don't we open that puppy up and toast my future?"

After the bottle was finished Beth said, "Well, it's that time. I better get going so I can get back here with my teen early in the A.M. We will have a lot to do. Boy I am glad you hired someone to take care of the church and reception. That eased up the stress quite a bit. So, tomorrow morning we can focus on you. Bye sweetie, I'll see you later." Beth kissed me on the cheek and picked up her jacket.

"Let me walk you to the car. Are you okay?" Asked Mike in concern.

"No problem, Mike. Remember … I'm Italian! I had watered down wine as a child like every good Italian should. We're weaned on wine—not milk. Sure, you can walk me to my car." Beth waved good night and left with my brother following her like a puppy.

I watched from the window as Mike said good night. I was just a bit jealous to see Beth teasing him. Mike wasn't too tall; almost six foot—but not quite. His stature was strong and solid. He still worked out although he doesn't play much anymore. He didn't look Irish, taking after Mom's Spanish side with the dark hair. He did get Dad's blue eyes, and against his olive skin, they dazzled. Funny how that worked out with me inheriting the auburn hair and brown eyes, in fact, we really didn't look like we were related, yet we had our tempers in common.

I had to tease him when he returned. "Big brother, you're not fooling me. You're wild about Beth! To think, I never thought anyone would be able to turn your head.—Especially one with a temper! I thought you liked them quiet and timid?"

Mike's face turned bright red. Shaking his head, "Sis, I don't know what it is about her, but I've been crazy about her since I first met her. Remember when I visited you at the restaurant? I know, I know ... You don't have to say anything ... She just nodded at me and returned work after you introduced me—Man! When she smiled, it was like rockets! I don't know what to do Kate ... And please! I know you Kate ... Don't play matchmaker!"

"Don't get defensive! I know better with you. No, I won't say anything to Beth, but what are you going to do? It's not like you to play the role of shy boy." From the desperate look in Mike's eyes, I knew better than to pursue this subject any further. "Look, sweetie, it's getting late, why don't you go to bed. I still have a few things to do before *I do*.—No pun intended!"

Mike's old humor returned, and his eyes lit up, "Kate, please tell me something." The smile turned serious, "Are you sure you want to do this? I know you and Bill aren't rushing this and you have known him little more than two years ..."

I interrupted him, "What, what are you getting at now? You know I love Bill." I started to raise my voice, "Sure he's a little ambitious, but look at the work he does. To stay on top and get where he is, you have to be a little aggressive! Please don't start this now. What is this about? The fact he didn't give you a personal invitation to the bachelor party?—Or is it that Don is giving me away? I thought we worked this out!" I flopped into the chair and started to cry.

Mike rushed over and held me tight. "I'm sorry sis. I didn't mean to … I guess I am still a little protective about you. I–I don't know why I don't like Bill. I'll tell you what; I'll really give it a try. Okay? He lifted my chin, "Now, show me where I can sleep, and I'll see you in the morning … I love you so much Kate, I don't want anyone hurting you—that's all."

I ran my fingers through his dark hair and smiled, "Sure, Let's get going." *We sure have been through a lot together. There is no reason for me to become angry with him for something as stupid as this. It must be the jitters.* Mike kissed me good night and went to bed.

Taking a hot bubble bath to relax, I reflected on Mike's concern for Bill. The few times that they were together weren't very pleasant. It didn't take much to set off a fight between them. Reclining deep within the bubbles, my thoughts drifted to my first meeting with Bill.

Beth talked me into going to a restaurant/bar she frequented, called Cliff's. I was wearing a very short red dress; it was the first daring thing I bought for myself. Beth and I were standing at a table by the bar when I observed a tall slender man with blonde hair, watching me. As he approached us, he told the bartender to put our drinks on his tab. Of course, Beth had to comment about how we could take care of ourselves in her "get lost buddy voice." Bill ignoring her, leaned closer to me and asked me to dance. It was strange, the way I was drawn to him. It seemed so natural for me to just get up and dance with him. We melted into each other's arms as we danced in silence. Strange, it was as though we have always been together. When the dance was finished, Bill walked me to my table and didn't sit with us. The only other words spoken that evening between us was Bill asking for my phone number, he reminded the bartender to put our drinks on his tab and left the bar.

It was a week later when he called me. I didn't mean to be rude, but I forgot who he was! He quickly refreshed my memory and asked me to a cocktail party. I had never been to one and had no plans, so I agreed. It was the first of many dates to come. Over the next two years Bill and I saw each other off and on.

His job required a lot of traveling. He even paid for my flights to visit on some weekends, allowing me to see places I've never been. It seemed to amuse him watching me. He was amazed how I saw things with innocence. When we'd returned home, he would stay at my place. I always thought it strange that he would stay with me, in my dump of a place instead of staying at his condo. This place was like a palace compared to my old apartment.

Beth pretty much stayed on his nerves. He didn't appreciate her sense of humor. She couldn't understand what I saw in him—neither did Mike. I couldn't then and still cannot explain why we are so drawn together. It's like we were supposed to be. I mean, are you supposed to have all these answers? Sure, Bill could be demanding times. But no one was able to see the times where he was loving and kind. I guess the bottom line is that I'm happy and for me, that's all that matters. I giggled. Hmmm … *Tomorrow I will be Mrs. Kate Sawyer … Hmmm, sounds nice.* I inspected my ring and noticed that I had been in the bath way too long.

"Kate are you up yet" yelled Mike from the living room. "I've got to go. I have a few things to do before the wedding. Bill is waiting outside. Of all things I never figured, was him breaking the rule of not seeing the bride before the wedding. I could be wrong though, he does have on his sunglasses and his head is resting on the steering wheel." Mike burst out laughing, "Man, it's time to have a little fun with the 'ole' boy." He was wringing his hands as he peered out of the window. "You know—break him in right. …"

I ran down the stairs pleading with Mike, "Mike, no! Not today, please help me! Don't upset him." I looked out the window and started to giggle at the sight. Poor Bill took everything he had to get out of the car. He staggered a tiny bit grabbing the edge of the door to keep from falling. I chuckled into my hand as I watched this man, I was about to wed try to act cool, adjusting his sunglasses, lick his parched lips as he waited for Mike.

"Don't worry sis, I'll get some coffee into him and get him to eat something. Poor bastard. ... I'll see you at the church." Mike hugged me and said, "I am happy for you Kate. I want you to be happy, okay?" He touched my nose with the tip of his finger and with a peck on my cheek, hustled himself out the door to abuse his prey.

Bill could barely wave at me! The sight was hilarious to watch as Mike eased Bill into the passenger side of the car. I'm sure Mike suggested that he drive if they were expected to get to the church today. There was no telling what Bill was in for; Mike was still pretty steamed with him. I quickly closed the door, noticing the chill in the air.

I rushed to the kitchen and poured a cup of hot tea, Beth and Lisa will be here shortly. I knew I had better put my makeup on fast before Beth arrived, or she would want to do it. I loved Beth dearly but our taste on certain things was quite different. She loved everything in life to be bright with lots of color, including her makeup. Myself, I liked things very simple. As I started to apply the base, my hands were shaking–not to mention my entire body. In the pit of my stomach, I started to feel queasy and my face became flushed. I staggered backward trying to find the edge of the bed, taking deep breaths, trying to catch my breath when the doorbell rang. I said loudly, "Door's open!" I took another deep breath and a sip of my tea, pulling me together as Beth and Lisa came up the stairs, carrying their dresses.

"How's it going sweetie,—time to bust a move! Where's Mike?" Beth rambled, "I guess he's already gone to the church?—Hey, you okay?" Beth sat down next to me, looking concerned.

"Looks like she's gonna hurl to me." Said Lisa.

Beth stared at Lisa and shook her head, "I don't think *hurl* is the way I'd put it. It's probably wedding-day jitters. We all get them. How about a little brandy to calm your nerves?"

"No, I don't think so. I'm afraid that *will* make me sick." I said weakly.

"Listen to me. Lisa, go downstairs, make some coffee and fix it the way Pops does,—add a touch of Brandy to it, then bring it here … While you are at it, make me one.—I know what you are thinking and *no*, you cannot have one. The coffee maybe,—but no liquor!—Now!" She snapped her fingers.

"Okay!—Okay! Man, don't have a cow!" Lisa left still mumbling under her breath, "You'd think I was going to drink the whole bottle!"

Beth watched Lisa as she left to carry out the demands, as it were. "Teens, you know I love 'em. She's been a little out of control today. She made a liar out of me at the salon this morning when I firmly told Merna she wouldn't like her hair up and—look, there it is! All of it on top of her head—Kind of scary! It makes her look twenty-five. Yep, fifteen going on twenty-five and man is *she* loving it! Je-sus!" she exclaimed melodramatically.

Before Lisa made it back with the coffee, another wave fluttered through my stomach. I ran into the bathroom, soaked a bath cloth in cool water, and placed it on my flush face as I leaned against the toilet. *What the hell is wrong with me? I can't believe this is even happening. My thoughts drifted to the dream. It can't be that dream. I had it last night for the first time since Bill proposed. Why is my subconscious playing tricks on me?—Why now?—Why the night before my wedding? Why doesn't he just go away? No living man can compete with him and I can't live forever with this frustration … Maybe I shouldn't get married.* I shook my head and threw the cloth into the sink and dried my face. *I'm seriously beginning to wonder if I'm not a little off my rocker.—Whew! Let's get back to reality! Beth was right; this is just a case of wedding jitters. Maybe Bill has it better than me. All he has on his mind is a hangover!* I giggled—*and Mike there to torture him! Great! What a mess I just made! My makeup is smeared! What next!*

"It's about time, I thought I was going to have to come in and get you. Look what you've done to your make up." Seeing the concerned look, I had, "Don't worry, I'll take it easy with your face … Let's get cracking, Lisa brought up your coffee, and she made you something to eat. If I know you—you haven't even thought of food, much less feel like you can hold it down. I know, Father Flanders told you not to eat anything before Communion.—Everyone eats a little something. It is impossible to stand there long, nervous, with nothing in your stomach. Hell, the small sip of wine will go straight to your head. That's all they'll need is the bride to pass out before she even says her vows. I'm sure Mike will make sure that Bill will eat something too." Beth chattered on as she repaired my smudged make up.

I tried to eat the toast and took a few sips of the coffee. I had to admit, after a few sips, I started to loosen up and the dream worked its way to the back of my mind and now I could concentrate on what was at hand.

The limo was outside waiting for us. The driver came in to help us with our clothes and other little needs. It became obvious that he was the only one with his head on straight and also evident that he had assisted in at least a few of these events. Beth, noticing that he had his eye on Lisa, didn't take too long to tell him that Lisa was only fifteen. Lisa rolled her eyes in classic teenage fashion. I had to hold back the giggle as Beth played the possessive mom. We could almost see the steam coming from Lisa's ears.

The driver parked by the antechamber adjacent to chapel where Bill and I were to be married. I grabbed my stomach the feeling was so strong again. I leaned against the doorway and Beth's sixth sense was ahead of everyone. Anticipating this, she was already by my side to help me to a small couch. The feeling was frightening. I wanted to turn and run until I couldn't run any more. Beth and Lisa picked on me, saying it was only cold feet. She poured me a small glass of wine Estelle had slipped into the room.

Estelle was there before us, now excitedly bellowing her orders to

Beth and Lisa as they dressed. The dresses were wonderful and the colors just right. I knew Beth, and even Lisa, would be able to wear these again, if they ever wanted to. Beth was relieved Lisa's dress wasn't as revealing as she first thought it would be. It wasn't difficult to see, Lisa was. "I don't know where your mind could have been, if you thought otherwise, Missy!" Commented Estelle. She fussed and commented on their dresses until she decided they were just right, then ordered them to sit down until she had me dressed.

My gown was so beautiful. Estelle and Beth were both in tears. It was very simple with straight lines that just barely hung away from my body. The back wasn't too low and the V–shape came up my back just covering my shoulders and draping across the front of my neck. The sleeves were long and tapered to a point at my wrists. The veil was the only thing that didn't go with the dress. It was made from Spanish lace a gift from my mother. It draped my head and shoulders, and cascaded to the floor. I was so pleased that it was sheer enough to see the back of the dress.

While Beth and Estelle were doing final once overs, there was a knock at the door. Before I could say anything, Mike slipped inside, "I had to see you before you went down the aisle …" He smiled and said softly, "Kate, *you* are so beautiful! Mom should see you! Let me take a picture—Okay?"

Everyone stepped away so that Mike could take his picture, when the usher knocked, stating they were about to start. Don was outside, waiting patiently, when I stepped out of the room. There was an awkward moment between Mike and Don … Mike was wonderful. He bent over and kissed me on the cheek and placed my hand into Don's saying, "I need to get into the church. Bill will think his best man deserted him. I leave my precious sister in your hands sir." With a wink, Mike was gone.

A sigh of relief from Don, and everyone else relaxed. Don held out his arm for me take, "You are certainly beautiful my dear. I am very sorry your father couldn't make it. I am sure he regrets not seeing you for himself. I am very honored you asked me to take his place in absentia." Said Don rather formally. Clearing his throat, "I guess it is time to start, I hear the music." Beth ran up to me and gave me one last hug and Estelle did the final pulls and fusses ... I turned to Don smiling, nodded, then took my first step forward ...

CHAPTER TWO

Rude Reality

I don't recall when Bill's behavior started to change. The first year of our marriage was wonderful. I seemed to be totally oblivious to everything around me. I spent most of my time planting flowers, making the small garden in the back my own area. I secretly enjoyed this the most. I filled most of the area with roses and added a makeshift pond—with Bill's help. We soon found out that tools weren't his forte.

I didn't see much of Beth, except for the occasional lunch. It became difficult to see her with Bill's attitude towards her. He didn't make it a secret about his feelings. I found that it was best to see her without him knowing anything about it.—Especially lately. He seemed to snap about everything. His patience hadn't been the best and no one could talk to him. I couldn't say anything to appease him. It really didn't help matters with me being sick so much lately. That seemed to get on his nerves the most. He hated being around anyone ill. Some days I would be fine and then others—I couldn't get up in the mornings for the queasy feelings.

Bill finally suggested I go to the doctor. I agreed deciding to call Beth and make a day of it. I had to admit I was about to go nuts not having anyone to talk to.

Ever since Bill and I have been married, my social life hadn't been on the top of my "to do" list. The people I did know were from Bill's job or the never-ending dinners we had. I hated those the most. I would spend most of the time by myself, being ignored. Playing the pleasant wife doing her wifely thing.

It was wonderful walking into Cliff's. I felt free. What a weird feeling. To think that I felt cooped up—I love my house ... I have a lot to keep me busy ... *Man! What is happening to me? I feel as though I'm close to tears!* This thought quickly exited my head as I grabbed a chair next to the door, my head reeling from the smell of food. A waiter promptly came to my rescue and helped me to the table with Beth leaping from her chair to assist him.

"Sweetie, you okay? Sit down—You there—please get her some water!" Beth was shouting her demands and causing quite a stir.

Embarrassed and flustered from the attention, I stuttered, "Beth, I'm fine. Just let me sit here for a minute and I'm sure everything will be fine ... Is it hot in here to you? Yeah, please help me with this jacket ..." It wasn't long before the restaurant finally settled back down and directed their attention to things at hand. I was able to regain my composure and take a deep breath. "Whew! Sorry about that! This is why I am going to the doctor this afternoon. It doesn't happen every day—but when it does ..."

"Sounds like you're a bit pregnant, Kate," Beth laughed. "You okay now?"

"Pregnant? No! Well I'll be damned! I knew the rhythm method wouldn't work. Especially when Bill won't take *no* for an answer! Well, well, well, I guess I'll be busy now." I stared into my glass of water. I was stunned. "I don't believe I'll have the wine with lunch. Just a salad please."

"I'll have the same, except *I'll* have the wine, and give her a bowl of soup with that,—kay? Thanks." Beth turned to me; "You've got to have more than salad. This is no time to be concerned about your figure! So, how long have you been this sick? Have you been ill in the mornings? When did you have your last period?" Beth asked with controlled excitement.

"For a couple of months now ... I-I don't know when my last period was … Let me think … wait-three months ago! See I don't ever think too much about it, I have never been regular. Sometimes I can go six months at a time." I shrugged my shoulders rather indifferently.

"Kate, let me get this straight … You and Bill are having sex with the rhythm method and *you* don't have a regular period?" Beth was stupefied.

I didn't know what to say, "You know Bill is a Catholic, Beth. He won't let me go on the pill.—I didn't even think to tell him since he was so adamant about it. Besides, there is nothing wrong, he'll be very excited about it. Maybe this is what we need. Bill has been so—so edgy lately. He needs a bit of good news right now."

"I don't believe what I am hearing. Kate, where is your mind? You don't have a baby to make someone happy … You know that—don't you? And what does Bill's behavior have to do with a baby?" Beth leaned across the table closer to me. "Kate, is there something you are not telling me?"

"No, there isn't any secret. It's just that Bill gets very angry at the drop of the hat. I think work is just a bit much for him right now. He works late and is up all night sometimes in his office. I don't know. It's not the same …" I said sadly, "I walked into his office at the house once and he went nuts about not knocking on the door first or something … I don't know what I said, but we ended in an argument and … and …" I realized that I said too much by the look on Beth's face.

"And what, Kate, what?—Did he hit you?" The look of rage was so intense; I jumped when she hit the table demanding an answer. The waitress quietly placed our orders on the table and left without a word. I was grateful we had to pause when our food arrived. This gave me time to regroup my thoughts and for Beth to settle down.

"He didn't mean to hit me, Beth. He was very sorry afterwards," I said in his defense. "He even brought me a kitten as a gift. Besides, I know he won't do it again. He promised—and I promised to stay away from his office," I added quickly. "That's all over and everything is fine." Now was the time to change the subject, "You should see the kitten. I named him Jazz. He's so tiny …" I rattled on for a time about the cat and noticed that Beth was just patronizing me. The look on her face was still deeply concerned. She lightened up after lunch when I promised her that I'd let her know as soon as I left the doctor's office.

On the way home from the doctor's office, I was trying to decide how to tell Bill about the baby. I was so excited that I completely forgot to call Beth. Apparently, my mind was racing as fast as the car; I didn't see the police officer behind me until it was too late. He was very kind to me and let me go with a warning. A cute idea came to mind from the sobering stop, on just how to reveal to Bill the tiny package I held within. Now lost in this thought, I found myself heading in the wrong direction and found myself scrunching behind the steering wheel as I three-fingered waved at the officer watching me in astonishment from the absent-minded illegal U-turn.

I prepared a wonderful dinner. Thank God Bill's taste in food was simple; I could barely keep my attention on what I was doing. I went into our dining area and set the table. On Bill's plate I set a small teddy bear with a card in between its paws with our secret message written on it. I was making the final touches when the phone rang.

"Hi, Katie. It's me." Before I could reply, "Baby, I'm sorry, but work is a bitch looks like I'll be here a bit longer. I should be out of here in a couple of hours—give or take. Will you keep dinner warm for me? I'll make it up to you. That's my girl, love you baby … Bye."

Sadly, I put the receiver back and sighed. I looked at the tiny bear patiently waiting, holding the news, "Well, we'll just have to wait a little longer before he knows—that's all."

The few hours turned quickly into very late. Jazz jumped into my lap asking for rubs. I rubbed his little head and finally decided to go to bed. I was very disappointed as I looked at the dining room table to see the bear sitting there waiting patiently for someone to pick him up and make the discovery. I placed my hand on my stomach, rubbing it as I did Jazz and went to bed.

I was awakened at two in the morning by Bill as he gathered me into his arms, crushing my body against his while mumbling some apology for not coming home sooner. I could smell the liquor on his breath and there was a strange, glazed look in his eyes. His excitement about the baby made me forget about asking him why he was so late and I becoming caught up in his emotions instead.

I awakened the next morning to the sound of furniture being shoved around. Bill, up before me, was already upstairs rummaging around. I grabbed my robe and proceeded upstairs to find him tearing his office apart. I patiently stood at the door remembering his earlier warnings. Bill heard me and turned, "Katie! Look, I've given it a lot of thought and *what* are you doing standing out there?—Come here!"

He placed his arm around my shoulder drawing me into the room already in deep discussion, explaining in detail what his plans were and how he intended to do them. He thought the office would be better for the baby and would turn my sewing room into his office. I stood beside him patiently, listening to him excitedly babble on. It was obvious he wasn't talking to me anymore. I found it comical he started referring the baby as "he" (I guess most men do). "I know I'm going on and on about this. Tell me Katie, what do you think? I really want to know your ideas about this. I can get a contractor in here. I don't have the time to move all this stuff out of here, much less have you do it.—What?" Bill looked at with so much love in his eyes … A look I have not seen in some time.

"Your ideas are great. You're right, this would be a better room for the baby than the sewing room … Just one small problem …" I replied with tears filling my eyes.

"What? Problem? What kind of problem?" His excitement turned to genuine concern.

"What if it's a girl? Don't you think it would be better if we did the room a different color? You know, not the traditional blue and pink?" I answered with a soft joyful chuckle.

"Yes … Maybe you're right sweetie." He slipped his arms from behind me and held on tight. "Maybe you're right."

For the moment I was in a bliss, I had not been in sometime … I closed my eyes and said a soft prayer of thanks. *See? Maybe Beth was wrong this time. Maybe a baby was just what we needed to bring Bill and I back together again as a loving couple.*

Bill's attention to me was lighter and happier. Things seemed to be right back on track. We were behaving like a happily married couple again. He hired a decorator come in and assists on all the preparations with the room. A tall dark-haired slender woman with designer glasses that just stood balanced on the tip of her nose strolled into my home and began taking over my home. She had my sewing room boxed up and put away while she another group of assistants cleaning and painting the baby's. She and her entourage bullied me for my own good until Beth put her foot down and reminded her this was my baby and she was working for me. From Mrs. Fisher's reaction to Beth's comment, I thought Beth was going to do her bodily harm.

"Excuse me Kate, I cannot possibly do my job while this, this disputable person insists on interfering. I feel that I must leave," rebuffed Mrs. Fisher. Funny, she was on a first name basis with me from the first, I only knew her as Mrs. Fisher. Not at all the type of person I would have chosen for the project at hand; but on second thought, this is not a project, this is my baby.

"Mrs. Fisher, I guess you will have to leave. It is very clear to me, you don't like any of my ideas, and it is obvious that you have no plans to cooperate with any suggestions we have to make.—Please, you and *your* entourage know the way out." I said curtly.

"I hope *you* understand that I must call your husband about this. He is the one that hired me—not you." She replied a bit miffed.

"Well, *I'm* the one who is firing you." I demanded defiantly.

Mrs. Fisher stormed out of the room, her little group obediently following. I started to giggle when we heard the door slam behind them. I was relieved. The last couple of months were starting to take their toll. I couldn't handle the daily upheaval of my home. She no longer asked for my opinion on final decisions.

"Don't let the door hit you in the ass on the way out! Man am I glad that she is gone! Can you believe? This is only a baby's room not the Queen of England's State room," declared Beth. "Some people."

"Yeah, some people." I muttered as I paced the room. I was in doubt how Bill was going to react to this. Beth picked up on my thoughts.

"Don't worry, sweetie, Bill has been a prince lately," she patted my arm lightly. "I can't believe he would get too upset about some decorator. It's easier to let him yell it out and you just deal with it. Once he lets out all his steam, tell him there isn't too much left to do and between the two of us, we can get it done.—And I won't charge him a cent!" Beth laughed. It made more sense and was easier to relax with her logic. "Well, sweetie, I need to get my butt home and take care of my teen. She's starting to believe we're more like roommates rather than Mother–daughter. I raised her to be way too independent. I'll call you tomorrow. Don't fret, everything's goin' to be fine."

After Beth left, I went back upstairs to clean up some of the mess. I guess I got pretty involved because I didn't hear Bill come in.

"Katie, where are you?" He yelled up the stairs.

"Up here, in the baby's room." I started to become nervous. His voice sounded irritated. I guess Mrs. Fisher ran to her car, picked up her little car phone and promptly called Bill. D*amn it! I don't need this.* I patted my tummy. I was pretty proud that I was already showing—well not much. But to me, it was enough for me to run out and buy maternity wear. I wanted to give this little guy all the room she or he needed.

"Hi, sweetie," Bill gave me a quick kiss on the cheek and looked puzzled. "What are you doing? Where is Mrs. Fisher? I thought she'd still be here helping you."

"She's not here. I—uh … fired her." Flinching after I told him, in fear of that immediate blow.

Bill's puzzled look turned to rage. "Why in the hell did you fire her? Do you know what she is costing me? Shit! Katie, what possessed you to fire her? Man, that's why she left three messages for me. Damn!

This is all I need to end this God damned lousy day!" He flung his coat on the floor.

"Don't get upset honey, Beth and I can finish …"

"Beth? Beth! It's always God damn Beth! I'm tired of her being around Katie!" Bill shouted as he stormed about the small room.

I stood quietly, jumping as each box or toy hit its new place from Bill's misdirected blows. I hopelessly tried to change the subject. "What happened to you today?"

Bill slumped into the rocking chair with a heavy sigh. His fingers running through his hair, eyes cast in a daze; he replied in a tired irritable tone, "Don, hired this guy from Canada to come in and *assist* me with new accounts. He *says* I need help, somehow, I've fallen behind. Rich-*ard* is a trouble shooter for our rival company. Cannon's paying big bucks for this guy to come in and straighten up my mess!—Damn it! Everyone falls behind sometimes. I can't understand why he can't give me more time." He slammed his fist on the arm of the chair. "Damnit! I'll make sure *Richard* will have his hands full of nothing when he arrives next month!"

I could not understand why every time Bill said Richard's name; my stomach went into knots. "I'm sorry you've had a horrible day," I replied softly. I reached over and gently touched his shoulder to comfort him; he pushed me away.

"Leave me alone." He got up from the chair pushing passed me heading for the baby's bathroom and slammed the door behind him. I heard the strangest thing—the sound of the lock turning over—he locked it. I stood there on the other side, confused, staring at the door. I couldn't believe how angry he was about things at work, much less locking me out.

I started to become very nervous. He was in there for quite some time and in the state, he was in,—I just didn't know what to think any longer. I decided my best course was to get him to talk to me, so I apologized for firing Mrs. Fisher. "H-Honey, if you want," I yelled through the bolted door, "I could call Mrs. Fisher tomorrow and ask her to come back …"

No answer.

I continued nervously, "Look, why bother her? I really thought Beth and I could finish the room … I mean, I know you don't want Beth here, but she is cheap … She said she'd work for free," I laughed lightly. "There isn't a whole lot left to do and to be really honest, I really did enjoy working in the room by myself today," I babbled, "Beth could help me put the finishing touches and help me with the crib—it can't be that hard." I was becoming frantic when the door finally swung open with Bill looking at me with glazed eyes. I stepped away from the sight. *What was wrong with him?* I've never seen him like this before. His nose was runny.—Like he just developed a cold. I went numb inside. "Bill, are you okay?" My voice was shaking.

"Yeah, I'm fine." He pushed past me wiping his nose and left the room.

I had to know what he was doing. I went into the bathroom and looked around. It looked normal, nothing out of the ordinary. Maybe I'm losing my mind. I sat on the toilet seat feeling rather relieved. Hell, I didn't even know what I was looking for. As I stood up, from the corner of my eye, I saw a rolled up twenty-dollar bill. I carefully picked it up, looked at it rather puzzled, rolling apparently purposely rolled twenty-dollar bill between my fingers. I unrolled the tube to find a film of powder residue inside. I numbly walked out of the bathroom still inspecting the powder and was met by Bill, standing in the doorway with a surprised look on his face. Startled, I wadded up the bill and my hands went quickly behind my back. Bill slapped the slide of his jacket cursing under his breath.

"Katie, it's not what you think!" He said in a panic. His eyes watched me hide the bill behind my back.

"What *do* I think, Bill? I-I don't understand …" I replied in defensive confusion. I didn't understand what had come over him. This wasn't from drinking,—it was different. The wild look in his eyes scared me. I found myself taking a step back, just out of his reach.

Bill stopped, his eyes glistened as he softly spoke, "Poor Katie, she lives in her dream world. I bet you don't even know what that is! You see everything through the eyes of a Pollyanna.—All pure and perfect." He wickedly mocked. Again, he wiped his nose and sniffled. If I didn't know better, I'd believe he just developed a cold.

"I *do* have an idea. I am not that stupid," I frantically lied. The fact was—I was that stupid. It was like a bolt of lightning that struck hard. I knew … *No!—Not Bill! Not this?—Why? This explains why he would get so angry at the drop of a hat. How long was he doing this?* Panic hit me. The usual flutter turned into a heavy sick feeling in the pit of my stomach as if the baby knew the answer too. "My God!—My baby! Bill how long.? I desperately clutched my stomach. The thought was frightening.

"Katie, it's not like that! Jesus! Katie, don't! I wouldn't do anything to hurt you or the ba—" He leaped for me as I slipped from him.

"You ass! I've been putting up with all of your shit! Believing *I* was doing something wrong! It's been *you* all along! Why?" Anger filled me at the thought of the harm he may have caused me and my child much less the abuse I had endured these past months; I slapped him hard across the face.

He wasn't the least bit stunned from the slap, instead his facial expression turns to one of pity, "Katie, the pressure has been so much as work, I have to keep up! You don't understand! Come on, Katie, please!"

"I don't know what pressures you're going through, I don't care! My God, my baby!" I held my swollen stomach tight. "I've put up with so much! I-I defended you with Beth—even Mike! Damn you!—I'm getting out of here!" I turned quickly to run down the stairs, but not quickly enough. Bill sprung at me grabbing me by the long braid.

"Oh, no you don't! *You,* my dear, are staying here with me! You belong here! You're mine. You have to listen to reason!" He ranted as he jerked me back to face him.

"Bill, stop!—You're hurting me! Please, I have to leave. I can't live like this." I struggled to get away from his hold. "Let … go … of … me!"

It seemed, the harder I struggled to get away, the harder he tightened the grip in my hair. His eyes still glowed. Bill tried reasoning with me; I was not about to listen. I couldn't. I had to do something. I blindly threw out my fist hitting him as hard as I could in the stomach, knocking the wind out of him causing me to fall on the floor. Bill tried to help me up; I started to kick at him to keep him away from me. I was hysterical. I don't know how I got on my feet, it proved to be a huge mistake because Bill grabbed me by the elbow and slapped me in the face with the butt of his palm.

I fiercely tried backing away from him as he began to strike me across the face when I realized I had run out of hallway—so did Bill. In slow motion, eyes wide, I watched Bill hopelessly grasped for my hand as I fell backwards down the stairs to the bottom.

I laid there in a pool of blood. Bill ran down the stairs and cradled me in his arms. He was sobbing for me to forgive him.

"Katie, please, I didn't mean to!" He became frightened and gently shook me, "Sweetheart, please, can you hear me?"

"Yes … I can hear you." I weakly replied. "Bill, please call an ambulance. Something is terribly wrong." I was afraid to move.

"Yes … Yes sweetie …" He gently laid me on the floor and was suddenly filled with horror when he finally saw the blood all over the floor and all over him. He ran to the phone and called for the ambulance.

I woke in the hospital and noticed a police woman standing by the door. When she saw I was awake, she opened the door and informed the nurse I had come around. I looked at her curiously, and then I remembered what had happened and why I was there.

"Did I lose the baby?" I asked. I wildly felt my stomach and sighed deeply. The sensation of my child was gone.

"Ma'am, the doctor will be here in a moment. I know this isn't a good time to ask, but you must understand that I have to ask. I need to know what happened. Did your husband do this to you?" She questioned composedly.

I didn't care about what question she had to ask I wanted to know about my baby. Deep inside I knew, but I wanted verbal acknowledgment, "Did–I–lose my baby? Why can't you tell me?" I screamed in panic. *Oh God what has just happened? Please let me be wrong. Please. Please don't take my baby.* I cried in silence.

There were tears in the police woman's eyes as she nodded her head yes. She cleared her throat; started to ask me the question again when the door opened, and the doctor appeared. Bill was in the hallway trying to fight his way in. Another police officer was doing his best to hold him back.

"Katie, please tell these people I can come in! I told them I tried to catch you as you fell down the stairs ... Katie, baby, please let me come in!" He wailed.

Clutching my head in agony, I continued to cry, not only from my loss, but from the fear that Bill's hold on me was so tight.

The doctor quietly came over and placed his hand gently on my shoulder, "You're going to be fine Kate. I gave you a sedative to calm you down. It should take effect shortly." There was such sadness in the doctor's eyes. He didn't have to say anything, I already knew the answer, "I am very sorry we couldn't save your baby. I know this doesn't sound so rational to you now, there is good news ... You can still have more."

The doctor continued, "Now, the thing at hand is, will you answer the police officer's question? Did your husband do this to you? Kate, you are pretty beaten up. I am very concerned about some of the bruises around your face. You are very lucky he didn't break any of the bones in your face. We can have him arrested for this if you want to press charges."

I laid there deep in thought wondering what to do. My feelings were torn between love and hate for Bill. I couldn't understand what was happening, much less why it all happened. It was as though I didn't have any control, I couldn't stop the words. Through the tears I quietly mumbled, "I fell down the stairs." Bill did try to grab in time, b-but he was too late." I closed my eyes to try to keep the tears back, but to no avail. They slid down my cheeks and my body shaking as if there were tremors erupting from deep within.

The police woman furiously insisted, "Ma'am, we know there is no way you could have sustained those bruises from just falling down those stairs. We have programs that will protect you from him—keep him from ever hurting you again … All you have to do is tell me what happened, and I'll do the rest."

She almost had me convinced. The door opened again, and a nurse came in to consult with the doctor. I could hear Bill's cries, pleading for me to let him in. I thought I was going to go mad.

I burst out, "I told you what happened! Why are you interrogating me like this? I fell down the stairs! That's it! Now—let my husband in!" I fell back into my pillow and cried hysterically. *Jesus make this stop! I cried from within. Make it go away! Why didn't you take me? Why leave me in this hell?*

The doctor looked at the police officer and nodded. She slammed against the door, cursing under her breath. As she entered the hall, she paused and glared at Bill–blocking his way. Bill pushed her out of his way and ran to my side. He cupped his hands around mine and pulled them to his lips kissing them repeatedly–mumbling and sobbing into them, "Katie, I'm so sorry I couldn't catch you. I am so very sorry."

He turned to the doctor and said, "You said she was going to be fine—right Doc?" He didn't listen to the doctor's answer, turning back to me, brushing my hair from my face and saying, "Sweetie, the doctor assured me we could have more children later … you know, when you get better. We could try again. You'd like that wouldn't you, my sweet Katie …" I nodded my head in response knowing he wasn't really speaking to me. He was only reassuring himself for what he had done. Bill laid his head on my side still holding on to one hand while crying and reassuring us both—everything was going to be just fine from now on.

I watched him lying there with his head resting against my side; my heart ached from the sight. He looked so much like a very sad and helpless little boy. I was confused with anger and pity for this man. I didn't know him anymore … Or did I know him at all. My last thought as I faded into a deep sleep was wondering what held us together; what was the tie that kept me there with him. I couldn't turn him in for the insane thing he had just done to me. Somewhere, deep, inside I felt I had to protect him no matter what ...

CHAPTER THREE

Goodbyes

While in the hospital, Mike called Bill with news of my father's death. Bill explained that we would be there as soon as I got out.

Bill was very quiet and sullen on the plane which was a relief to me. I really didn't want any comfort from him at this moment. This wasn't the way I wanted to see my family. I hadn't had time to grieve for my small child yet and my own childhood emotions were filling my head. I was very confused about how I felt for my father. The rage that filled me turned quickly into helplessness. I didn't have anyone to turn to. I knew I couldn't tell Mike about this. He would murder Bill and I really didn't want this burden on Mom ... It wasn't as though she would really listen to me. She would try in her own way, but her answers were always framed to not rock the boat.

I sighed; yep she would handle this problem in the same damn way she handled all of our problems, without getting herself involved. She would see this situation as just a mishap and that I must realize I had it good, so why upset things any further? Be quiet and it will go away. I remembered this technique as a child, she would ask me not to say anything to my father, dismiss it, and rattle on about something else. To this day, I truly believe Dad stayed pretty much in the dark about a lot of things. I guess I had to agree with her on some things, it kept him from verbally thrashing us about whatever the problem was. *God!*

I wanted to crawl under a rock! I started to whimper and turned to the window to keep Bill from seeing my distress.

Bill's hand softly touched my elbow. "Katie, I want you to hear me out. I know I don't have the right to talk to you but please, please listen to me. I didn't mean to hurt you! I–I don't know what has gotten into me lately. I know there's no excuse for my behavior … I really need you to forgive me. I am so sorry. You– you know I would never deliberately hurt you." He was sobbing uncontrollably. "Sweetie, I love you so much … God! The thought of you ever leaving me!" He took a long deep breath, "I don't believe I could ever deal with you out of my life. Please forgive me, please Katie—my sweet?" He wiped his eyes and looked so forlorn, desperately waiting for my answer.

My heart ached at the sight. Filled with my own grief, I gave way to forgive him. I couldn't be alone right now. Maybe it was an accident. Even Beth couldn't believe that he could outright push me down the stairs. She was livid at the thought that he would strike me in my condition. My rage again flared up, "Bill, you can't patch this up with another kitten! I don't know what has gotten into you lately, but it's not the same. I don't know you anymore. You seem to be so angry about something and won't talk to me anymore! I don't know what to do." I hid my face in my hands and started to cry.

Bill tried to pry them away, "I know I can't make up for it. I'll try, if it's the last thing I do, to–to make it up to you. You'll see. You know the doctor said that we could have another. Remember? Look at me Katie. I want things the way they were before, don't you?"

"I remember," I said sadly and searched in my purse for more tissue. I knew I was a mess and frankly, right now, I didn't care. I also remembered what Beth had said to me in the hospital and decided to use this anger to my benefit. "I–I don't want to have another baby right away Bill. I think I should go on the pill for a while, you know, until I can get my body regulated. I'm sure Father Flanders would understand under these circumstances."

"Yeah, sure, baby. Whatever you say. We can try later. I think you're right not rush into this." With a sigh of relief Bill gave me a sincere hug and chatted about things that were happening in the office until the plane landed. It didn't matter to me. I was in sheer delight of my small victory. At least now I would have the upper hand about when we would have another child.

Mike met us at the airport looking rather haggard. I ran to him and held him as tightly as I could. I found myself sobbing in his arms. I didn't know what I was crying about. Whether it was for my lost baby, my father or even for the fact I felt safe knowing that he was here with me. It was at that point I became so hysterical with grief Mike had to pick me up and carry me to the car. Bill barely keeping up behind us, was babbling about the strain being too much for me.

Bill had to retrieve our luggage and meet us at Mike's car then drive us from the airport. Mike held me not saying a word. He allowed me to cry myself out. I was exhausted when we arrived at Mom's house. Bill tried to help me, but I couldn't let go of my brother. Something inside wouldn't allow me to leave Mike's protection, "It's no big deal, I'll carry her upstairs." Mike was very distressed at my appearance, sighs, "She looks so frail."

Mother was at the door. Seeing the look on Mike's face, she too became nervous and ran down the sidewalk to my side. "Is she all right? Mike, take her to your room and I'll call the doctor. She's bleeding all over you! Should we take her to the hospital?"

"No, Mom, I'll be fine," I replied. "Just let me get cleaned up.—Bill, I guess you will have to help me." I said, weakly.

Bill followed Mike up to the bedroom and proceeded to help me with my clothes as Mike went to get fresh clothes from my luggage. He made one mistake; he opened Bill's first and stepped back with a small vial in his hand.

Bill rushed towards him snatching it from his hand and tossing it back into the suitcase. "That *one* is Katie's." He pulled out a nightgown and brought it to me. When I returned from the bathroom,

Bill and Mike were standing eye to eye with clenched fists not saying a word.

Totally whipped from the trip and all that had happened, I watched them for a moment, "What's wrong with you guys?" I decided that I really didn't want any more news—no matter what it was. I crawled into bed; all I wanted to do was sleep. I couldn't wait for the doctor to arrive so I could get something to put me out of this insanity.

"Nothing. Nothing's wrong," snapped Mike. "I'm going downstairs to see if Mom has called the doctor. I'm glad we still live in a small town. Doctor Samuels still makes a few house calls." He looked down at the blood-stained shirt and jeans. Mike tried his best at a bad joke, "I guess I'd better change, I don't want Doc Samuels to think *I'm* the one with the problem!" Mike's eyes filled with tears as he choked, "I'll be back in a bit Is. You need anything?"

I shook my head no then closed my eyes; hoping this would send Bill out of the room with him. Bill sat by my side until the doctor arrived.

Mom stayed in the room with me after the doctor left. I could hear the soft mummers in the hallway.

"This has been way too much for her. May God bless her—poor thing, to have lost both her child and father within days. I gave her something to sleep for a while. She really needs her rest, or she will have to return to the hospital. I hope it will be a while before she has to go back home. I don't want her to start bleeding again," explained Dr. Samuels.

"I have to leave tomorrow, I'm sure she won't mind staying a few more days visiting before coming home. Thanks for everything Doc," said Bill.

"Good, if she needs me, please call and I'll be right over. Mike, please walk me out, I want to go over a few things with you about the funeral."

"Sure, Dr. Samuels, I'll be with you in a minute." Mike turned around and glared at Bill, "Man, you're smooth."

Bill leaned against the hallway wall staring at the opposite wall. Mom came out of the bedroom and said, "With all of this excitement, we seemed to have forgotten you. I'm sorry Bill, I am sure you are just as upset about the baby as Kate. Why don't we go to the kitchen and find you something to eat? There's plenty of food. All of our neighbors have been stopping by with something. As soon as I see that Kate is asleep, I could meet you downstairs and put something together."

"No thanks Carmen, I'm fine. I am sure Katie needs you right now more than I do. I'm not really hungry. Maybe I'll find something to drink. Thanks anyway."

"If you want, there's some Irish whisky in the cabinet. Doesn't look like we'll need it any longer." She sighed heavily and went back into the bedroom.

Bill was settling in the living room with his drink when Mike returned from his visit with Dr. Samuels. Mike watched him for a moment and said bluntly, "Well, I see it didn't take you very long to find what you needed from the liquor cabinet."

"Look, I am not in the mood to deal with you. If you must know—asshole, your mother told me where it was, I'm tired ... So, I checked out the 'ole' cabinet and found this ..." He rocked the glass back and forth.

Mike jumped right in his face, "Oooh! And you believe that is going to impress me? Don't you have enough drugs to keep you from being so ti-*red*? The big executive from the big city trying to come down to the level of us poor hicks ... I don't know what is going on in your life, and I don't give a shit if you try to kill yourself with whatever was in that bottle, but you hear this, if you ever—or have ever hurt my Kate ... I just had a long talk with the doctor and he's pretty damned upset about those bruises," He paced like a wild lion, "Just how did she get those bruises? If Kate's miscarriage was caused by you in any way ... So, help me! I ... will ... make you dread the day we ever met! Mike was in such a rage that he was physically shaking as he yelled at Bill who sat in the chair with a blank expression on his face and feeling numb from the drugs and alcohol. This angered Mike to the point that he jerked Bill out of the chair and started shaking him. Mike's hand rested on Bill's throat.

"I'm sooo scared ... and what do you think you're going to do?—Asshole? Hurt me?—Right that's all your Katie needs now—more grief. Let's face it buddy, she's with me now—not you." Bill stabbed his finger into Mike's chest as his eyes were glazed with a spark of evil. With an over confident sarcastic tone, "I take damned good care of her." He then shrugged and with cocky justification, "Besides, she fell down the damn stairs. It was her fault ... "

Mike stared at Bill in disbelief. He couldn't believe what he was hearing. His only thought at that moment was to take his hands and squeeze the very life out of this man. He wouldn't struggle too much, plastered as he is. The picture of this man abusing Kate was too much for him. His fingers began to grip Bill's throat and he began to squeeze watching Bill just stand there glazed, not caring ... hate ... *Yes ... It would be so easy ... This bastard. ...* The anger flooded Mike to the core ... His nostrils flared as his strong hands slowly tightened their grip ... Before he went totally out of control, Mike was brought back to his senses by the scream from upstairs ...

"Michael Jonathon Perry! My God! What *are* you trying to do? Have you lost your senses?" Mom ran down the stairs and jerked numb Bill away from Mike, "Please forgive him. There has been so much grief around here. He doesn't know *what* he's doing. Please sit-down Bill, I'll get you something from the kitchen," while turning to Mike whispering sharply under her breath, "You,—come with me! I need help in the kitchen!"

Mike took one look at Bill slumping back into the chair and sipping from the drink as though nothing had happened. Bill looked up and with a mock toast chuckled and continued his drink as Mike turned abruptly to Carmen knowing what was about to befall him; following her obediently like a scolded child into the kitchen. He was still shaking uncontrollably as he searched the refrigerator pulled out and opened the last beer. "I need to get out of here for a while. Is Kate asleep? How is she doing?"

"Well, she's doing better than you! I don't know what has gotten into you, to-to attack that boy like you did ... Mike, please, I do not need this grief right now!" Carmen rubbed her aching head as she watched her son lean against the sink … "I don't know how much more I can take. Please try to control yourself … W-what has gotten into you?" Her sad tear-filled eyes looking at her son with frustrated concern.

Mike threw his beer into the sink and held back the words as he looked into his mother's eyes. She was so tiny and frail. He didn't realize how frail until now. Both of the women he loved so dearly looking this way broke his heart. "I think it's best for me to leave now. Kate is asleep. I'll head back to my place. Call me if you need me for anything." He kissed her on the forehead and said, "I'm sorry Mom.—I love you. Please get some rest yourself. Tomorrow is going to get hectic. You'll need your strength."

"Don't worry about me, the worst is over. He's in the ground and finally at rest. I'll be just fine." Carmen replied smiling.

I pulled the covers under my chin flinching as I heard the door slam. I couldn't bring myself to find out what went wrong downstairs. I glanced around the familiar room. I couldn't explain why I felt so safe here. I couldn't remember too many happy memories from this place.—Hell, I couldn't get out of here fast enough.

In the corner of the room, a small rocking chair held my favorite rag doll. I walked over ever so quietly, I did not want the family, much less Bill, to know I was up and about; carefully picked her up. "Hello Emily. Long time—no see." I sat in the rocker looking lovingly at my old friend and confidant, gently pulled her hair into a pony-tail and re-tied the bow. I held her close the tears filled my eyes as the memories came flooding back.

I could feel Father in our room. His anger seemed to overwhelm the house … It was late when he arrived at the door. Another night with whiskey heavy on his breath. He would proceed to yell at Mother because dinner was cold. She tried to keep it warm as long as she could and finally giving up before it was ruined. As she ran to the kitchen to reheat it, he would pour another drink. Mike and I would stay in our rooms, quietly listening, praying he would just eat and pass out on the couch. That would be a blessing. Usually, he would find something wrong with his dinner and throw the plate across the room hitting the wall. Mother would sit quietly. It didn't matter, he would slam his drink on the table, the obscenities would fly, and the next blow would be for Mom. I would sneak into Mike's room and we would sit on the floor huddled together with Emily tightly, embedded within my arms. Tears quietly ran down my cheeks as Mike tried to soothe my fears and hiding his own, flinching each time we heard our mother cry out from his blows. I shuddered as I remembered Father dragging Mother around by the hair. The screams echoing throughout the house as Mike and I dug deeper into the dark corner of the room for sanctuary. A memory Mike and I carried for a long time with deep quilt knowing there was nothing we could do to save her from this wrath.

Suddenly, the bedroom door would fly open and he would stand in the doorway to find us awake, huddled in the dark corner. Seeing this would send him in into another fit of rage. Mother would hang onto his arm, pleading with him to please leave us alone. Her face held a look of desperation and pain. Mike would hold me tighter, I couldn't breathe from his grip and the fear that flooded my body. Mother would somehow manage to get Father away from our room taking on whatever was needed to keep him from lashing out at us. Mike and I would crawl into his bed. I would stay there feeling safe as Mike stroked my hair, "Don't worry Kate, everything will be fine. One day we'll be free … One day he'll be dead."

I woke in a daze, Emily in my arms, the memory was only a dream, one I seemed to have had replayed over and over most of my life. My mind was filled with thoughts from the dream. I couldn't understand how Mother could continue to live with him. *Oh well*, I sighed, *I guess that's water under the bridge.* He's gone now, I guess she'll breathe easier now whether she realizes it or not. I'm sure she doesn't even have a clue why he stopped beating her … No, Mike wouldn't tell her what he told dad. Mike quietly explained to the old bastard that he would kill him if another finger was laid on her again. No, Mom couldn't handle that.

I had Mike take me to Dad's grave. I was very grateful to have missed the funeral. I don't know how I would have handled the emotions I've held for so long around the whole lot of Irish friends and enemies. Funny how you become a friend to everyone once you're gone. I asked Mike to give me a moment alone with Dad. Mike wanted to stay with me, but I assured him that I would be fine.

I looked at the newly covered grave finding it impossible to cry for his death, until from deep inside, I felt an emotion I could no longer keep as it swelled in my throat. My throat ached as I spoke, "Well, funny seeing you like this; never thought you would die first. Hell, I thought you would never die old man. No matter how hard I prayed for it as a child, they were never answered,—just–to–drop–dead." I sighed deeply, "I guess your prayers were answered. My sin has been paid in full and you will never know about it to gloat. I lost my baby. You damned me when I wouldn't tell you who the father of my child was. All you could think of was your honor, calling me a whore and a tramp. Did you think that I wanted to be married at sixteen? You would never believe I was raped."

I braced myself for my own confession, "Well, I guess I can tell you now, you remember that nice boy that you liked so well? Mac? Well, that nice boy raped me in an act of revenge for me beating him up when we were kids. Something about making him look stupid. Yeah, he had to finally show me who was boss. He played you for a fool to get to me. You wouldn't have ever believed it was him. Not the boy who kept you supplied with your booze." I laughed hysterically, "Oh no, you handled it just swell, like the wonderfully caring father you were. Instead of being there for me, you sent me to a home so I could have this *sin* in private, without any further stain on the family name. Good 'ole' Mom, she just stayed in the background allowing you to do your worst. She stood there as you told them to give up my baby.—You remember," I choked and spat, "For the good of the child …" I wiped my eyes and took a deep breath, "Maybe it's just as well my child was adopted. That was the only good thing you ever did for me. Why would I want my child to put through the same physical and mental torture you put us through? I can imagine the lies that ran rampant while I was stuck away in that home."

"Poor Mike, I left him alone to deal with your wrath for my sin. My sin,—my sin, and what about *your* sins?"

I cleared my throat, "I guess I am the one with the last laugh. You will finally have to face all your sins.—Or will you be able to talk around those too?—No, I think not." I turned to walk away stopping abruptly looking at the mound of soil, "Oh, yeah, there *is* one more thing … I started to laugh; "I still think it's hilarious you wouldn't come to my wedding.—You know, finally making my life, right? You'd love Bill; he's just like a chip off the old block.—Same backhand and everything … Well old man, this is it. Time to say good bye. I *am* sorry about one thing … I can't forgive you right now … I don't know if I ever will.—I do want you to know I don't hate you. I can't. I don't know why … Maybe it's the same reason why I can't hate Bill. Maybe one day I'll even cry for you. But not today … Today, I cry for my baby … Good-bye Daddy."

The drive home was quiet. I was relieved Bill had to head back to the office. We stopped by the house to take him to the airport. I couldn't help noticing the tension between Mike and Bill. The silence between them was deafening. Mike didn't even glance at us in the back seat as Bill fussed over me.

"Are you going to be all right while I'm gone? I don't want to leave you here. Are you sure I can't arrange for you to come on home?" Fussed Bill.

"Yes, I'm sure. Besides, remember what Dr. Samuels said about too much moving around. I haven't had time to be alone with Mom much less help out with the final details of Dad's funeral. I'll be home in a couple of days." I patted Bill's hand and gave him a quick kiss as I pushed him out the door.

Watching Bill reluctantly leave his quilt in the car, I slid next to Mike in the front seat, leaned back sighing deeply. "Sounds like you're glad to be rid of him too," said Mike.

"No, it's not that," I started to defend, "I need to be alone for a while,—that's all.—No big deal. Don't go there, Mike, I'm not ready to talk about anything right now. Okay?" I smiled, "Let's just go home."

That evening I was trying to sort through Dad's things when Mom finally burst into tears. I didn't know what to do for her. I just stood frozen staring at her. Mike ran to Mom, as he always did, to comfort her. I was still frozen in my spot when Mike spouted at me in shock, "What is your problem Kate? Can't you see that she's in pain? My God, her husband is gone! A-and you stand there like a lump on a log!" Mike held Mother in his arms and continued to comfort her.

I couldn't help feeling the way I did. I was confused. It wasn't long before the confusion turned into anger. I wanted to walk over to Mike and knock him into the next country. I couldn't believe that after all we had to endure growing up with that–that monster of a Father, Mike comforted Mother's pain. "I don't understand what your problem is. Mike, don't you remember what he did to us? It's enough to have her stay in la–la land denying what he did, but it's another for you …"

"Shut up Kate! Don't you talk about Mom like that! Of course, I remember. *You* have got to stop thinking about yourself and understand what she is going through. You need to get over it. It was a long time ago. Her pain."

The anger was about to turn into blind rage when my mother's comment stopped me dead in my tracks. "Don't blame her, Mike. She has every reason to feel the way she does. She's still holding the pain of both her babies and has no–one to turn to in her own pain." Mother looked at me with a mixed pain/love as she continued, "Oh yes Kate, do you believe for one minute we weren't hurt by the decision you made at sixteen?"

I was dumbfounded. How dare she talk about the pain they felt while I watched them stand in the background while I signed the life of my child away. They turned away and left me alone in that room without any comfort for my decision. How could I keep that child when my doctor told me they didn't want him? They were so ashamed of me for what I had done. I couldn't get my mouth to open to yell at her about my anguish. I became sick to my stomach and felt me drop to the floor weeping.

Mother came to my side and held me close. Mike stood over us watching with tears in his eyes. Mother cradled me and in a soft voice, "There, there now. Shhh. Everything is going to be fine."

"What do you mean everything is going to be fine, Mother? There you go again, ignoring why I'm so damn angry! Can't *you* get angry about anything?"

God, you sound just like Bill! I thought. My head was swimming, yet somehow the words kept flowing from my mouth, "What you and Daddy did *was* unforgivable. You … You just stood there … Watching!"

The look on Mother's face was priceless. IT quickly turns from love to deep heart felt pain and horror, "Kathleen, you really believe that we were that horrible? We couldn't talk to you about this because the doctor told us you didn't want the child. He explained that you were so angry with us, he even thought it would be in everyone's best interest for us not to say anything. He-he told us where to stand and not to say a word about our feelings. He also knew that if I had stayed in the room, I would have talked you out of this decision. So, he made me leave. Your Father was devastated. He just didn't know what to do or say. You know he was never one to express his feelings. He didn't know how." Mother covered her face and began sobbing into her hands … The truth was finally unloaded from her shoulders too. One both she and I carried for years, not spoken until now …

I couldn't believe my ears, "Mom, the doctor told me you and Dad didn't want the baby, that you and Daddy were very disappointed in me and didn't want my baby around."

Now it was Mom's turn to stare in horror; Mike was beside himself, "That bastard!" He said under his breath. "He probably had some family ready for your baby! Jesus Christ, Mother Mary of God!"

"Mike! Do not blaspheme our Lord and his Mother!" Scolded Mom returning her attention back to me. "There's nothing we can do about it now but pray that he's in a wonderful home and loved. Kathleen, I am truly sorry for what happened. I have no one to blame but myself. I just didn't know what to do." She continued to stroke my head, "Please believe he was much better off in the new home."

For the first time in my life, my mother did the most inconceivable thing. She looked deep into my eyes and said, "I love you Kathleen. I am so very sorry that I was not there for you and Mike as children. Yes, my time was greatly spent trying to avoid your father's wrath. Maybe I should have left him; we might not have missed so much life together … Well, what's done is done. I do want you to know that I love you both so very much."

I couldn't believe it took the death of my father for my family to finally start working towards healing our feelings with one another. When Mike took me to the airport, I couldn't let go of Mom. The last few days had been wonderful. I didn't believe I had ever heard my mother laugh much less joke. It made it even more difficult to forgive Dad. He took so much away from us. Mother went on the band wagon about forgiving him. I told her to give me time. Maybe she did see something in him that was hidden from us as kids. It's hard to see a good side when you are always in fear. I guess there is one good thing about all this, it took my father's death for me to finally hear the words I have never heard from either parent, I love you … Maybe there is hope … Maybe someday I'll find it in my heart to forgive …

CHAPTER FOUR

Dream Lover

Bill strolled into the bedroom and monotonically said, "We have an invitation to the Cannon's summer party. Don feels he's killing three birds with one stone. One—to impress my clients, two—he wants to introduce this new guy from Canada, and three—get his wife's summer party over with. By the way, it's today. I didn't tell you because I am tired of your damn sick headaches. This way you can't conveniently arrange one. The dress is casual—so get ready to go. "I'll be ready in a few."

It was useless to argue with him anymore. Well, at least it was casual. I hated going to these things all dressed up. I've been keeping myself busy around the house since returning from Mom's. I know it's been three months. I don't know, maybe the change will do me some good. It sure beats staying here with the baby's room still not taken apart. I don't know what I could have been thinking to believe Bill would find someone to take care of it while I was still at Mother's.

Walking into my closet, I stopped short and grabbed my stomach. It was a weird sensation making me want to drop to my knees. My legs shook like jelly. I leaned against the closet door for support.

"Hey, sweetie—you okay?" Said Bill, rushing to the closet to help me. "What's the deal? Man, Katie, I didn't mean what I said before. I know you've been under a lot of strain lately. I'm worried about this continual brooding around the house. It can't possibly be healthy. Should I call the doctor?" The look in Bill's eyes was of genuine concern. *Was Mike wrong? Could all of this have possibly created some kind of change in him?*

"No, I don't think so. I don't know what it was.—It was weird. Let me sit down for a minute." He gently guided me to the bed, sitting next to me with his arm around my shoulder. There was a deep feeling in my heart that wanted to reach out to him. Yet, still in the front of my mind, there was still deep remorse for that horrible day. I so terribly wanted to curl up into a ball somewhere and hide for the rest of my life. I desperately longed for my secret haven I played in as a child. Deep down I knew there no longer was such place for me to hide. I walked past it while I was at Mother's, someone had bought the property and built a nice house nestled in the middle of those safe wonderful trees. I sighed and realized again I went into one of my trances as Bill realized I wasn't listening. His concern turned quickly into frustration.

"Damn it! Katie, are you all right? Do you want to go to the party? Don would understand." He pleaded in frustration.

Tears filled my eyes as I shook my head; the startled look shook them free, "No. I mean, sure, I want to go. I-I'm fine now. Go get ready, Bill, I'm fine." I patted his knee in reassurance. *Whew! I don't know what that feeling was; I haven't felt it in a very long time. Maybe it was something I had to eat. I mean had not eaten … Who cares?* I absent mindedly ran my fingers through my hair as I continued to get dressed. *Jeans and a white shirt can't get more casual than that. I'll grab a sweater and tie it around my waist. My waist, it's now back, small and flat.* I fought back the tears. "Besides," I said half under my breath, "I don't want to be around alone with that room still intact."

Bill came out of his closet patted my bottom and responded in a sing song tone, "Oh, I thought we'd keep the room like it was. I figured we could try again soon. You know, when the doctor gives us the okay."

There are no words to explain the stunned feeling that slapped me at that moment. "I–I thought *we* agreed to wait a while before trying again.—Remember the plane?" I was dumbfounded. I stared in disbelief at this man/monster before me ...

"But sweetie, I had to say something to calm you down. You weren't yourself. I knew once this was all over, you'd come back to your sweet Katie self and see reason," he said, pinching my cheek in delight.

"Oh ... I'm going to the bathroom." *So, I can throw up.* "I'll meet you downstairs. I need to check myself before we head out the door." I choked out as coolly as I could manage with a twisting stomach.

Bill gave me a quick peck on the cheek, headed for the kitchen, whistling that singsong tune. I grabbed my purse and went into the bathroom. Still in a state of shock, I sat down facing my small vanity. I stared into the mirror in horror. I opened my purse pulling out my small makeup kit that held my birth control. Dr. Samuels gratefully filled the prescription with several refills.

I decided it would be in my best interest not to leave these about for Bill to see. There was no way I would have another child with Bill until things have calmed down and I've had time to think. I lied to Mike and Dr. Samuels about knowing Bill was taking drugs—and now I'm lying to myself that he would ever accept me being on the pill. I guess it is difficult to admit failure in your own life ... and with that, I looked into the mirror. With a deep sigh of sadness, I placed my next lie back into the safety of my purse.

Don's parties haven't changed; all the usual people were there, including all the company puppies lapping up every word he had to say. I'm sure if Don said run, heel, and roll over; they would comply without hesitation.

His home was a remarkable sight, a large summer home befitting a king. It had a majestic view of a lake, every detail tended to, and not a thing out of place. The eerie thing was, it was all decoration. I don't believe I have ever seen anyone in his family ride any of the horses in the stables –much less take advantage of anything, except the family cars.

Marion Cannon, a tall slender woman with brilliant red hair

accented her sparkling blue eyes, walked up to us with her usual insipid greeting and inviting us in, leading us to the bar.

"I'll get something later. Sweetie, I have to meet with Don before our new clients get here. Be sure to get something in your stomach, maybe you'll feel better." Bill gave me a quick hug and was out of sight.

Marion turned and looked at me, "Are you well, dear?" She said in her overly sweet monotone voice, playing the proper host.

"Marion don't worry about me; I haven't eaten today, that's all," I turned towards the buffet. She really didn't like to get involved with anyone—not even her kids ... *There it was again, that feeling in the pit of my stomach.* It came over me like a wave of nervous emotion. I grabbed my shirt and realized that Marion was staring at me. I decided to leave it alone and tried to straighten out the wrinkle I made then; asked the bartender for a drink instead. "I'll have a Canadian Mist straight up with a Coke back, please."

"Are you sure you should be having that dear? I mean with an upset stomach—well it's none of my affair ... If you'll be all right, I have more guests to greet." She smiled and turned away, already greeting another guest.

I took this as my cue to leave. I left my Coke on the counter and walked outside. It was a beautiful day. I shaded my eyes, looking over the grounds to observe the rest of the guests. I had determined there wasn't anyone I knew when I heard a low roar coming from the path just behind the stables. I was looking in the direction of the sound when I realized that gnawing feeling in the pit of my stomach was there again. *What was the deal?* The answer hit me like a ton of bricks. Well, it almost ran over me. Around the corner of the stable a motorcycle appeared, heading towards the driveway–having no regard for the beautifully manicured lawn. He made his way through the awed guests allowing him to get to his destination. I covered my mouth trying to hide the giggle while watching the valets run up to this guy. It was like watching the "Three Stooges" running around him trying to explain the errors he just committed. He dismounted the bike, handing his helmet to the valets. Totally oblivious to their chatter, as though no one was there to witness this blunder. My stomach continued to flutter as if this man had connection to what was happening to me. I moved in closer to see what had my insides in such turmoil.

I wasn't the only one who was interested in this mayhem; Don was making his way towards this dark headed wonder, laughing loudly as he held out his hand to shake. Don slapped him on the shoulder, pointing him in the direction of the party. Everyone else relaxed, going back to their chatter –after seeing Don's indifference to the incident.

It was all I could do to keep my startled look hidden while staring into the face of the *man* in my dreams! Don mistook my look as one of disapproval and walked up to me saying, "Now, Katie my dear, everything's just fine. Richard likes to stir up feathers wherever he goes. That's why I paid an arm and a leg to steal him from my competitor. As for the lawn—that's what I pay these damn fools around here for—right?" Don patted my shoulder in comfort, not really paying attention to me and walked off with Richard in deep conversation. I stood there boggled from what I had just seen.

Yeah,—what I have just seen! What did I just see? Those eyes, you could get lost in them! *My God—Where in the –hell did he come from!* I swallowed my drink in one gulp believing this would bring me back into reality. However—this was real, and he was *just* standing in front of me ...

My thoughts were rudely interrupted by Maggie's squeal of delight, "Yum! Doesn't he look delicious Katie? Yep, he's for me!" She held onto my arm and continued to squeal into my ears. "Don't you think so—Oh I'm sorry Ka-*tie*!—*You* belong to Bill!" Before I could respond to her remarks, she bounced off to her father and this magnificent stranger.

Poor guy, he doesn't e-ven have a clue what he's in for! I laughed silently at the sight of Maggie holding on to Richard for dear life. Maggie was beautiful with strawberry blonde hair; her green eyes just a batting away at her latest potential conquest. I looked down at my empty glass, deciding to head back to the bar for a refill. Maybe I should get that bite to eat before my head starts to really spin.

I don't know whether the buffet looked great or I was finally hungry.

I was nibbling on some cheese, not caring for a plate or what anyone thought about my manners, when that feeling recurred in my stomach. "Damn! What *is* going on?" I said aloud.

"I guess what is going on, is a party—a pretty dead one from the looks of it. Hello," said the most unbelievably deep voice. I turned around to find the most incredible deep brown set of eyes looking into mine. "Hello. Richard's the name, and yours is Katie—right? We met …" He pointed outside to acknowledge our previous meeting.

It took me a moment to regain my composure, remembering the startled look before was a bit embarrassing, "Hello,—the name is Kate—not Katie." I deliberately pushed out my hand to shake his.

Instead of a quick hello handshake he held my hand smiling, "Well, hello Kate,—not Katie. It's nice to finally meet you … You're Bill's wife. Hmmm," Looking me over, "I see that Bill has very good taste."

I felt an electrical spark running from his hand directly into mine. Jerking my hand from his, I realized he was startled by my reaction, "Sorry, I was eating from the buffet—and my hands are—" wiping them on my jeans.

"No problem. I understand." He said while gazing deep into my eyes. He was so close I caught his scent—so familiar.—Intoxicating. I wanted to breathe him into me.

Panicked, I turned to the bartender and ordered another drink. I did notice the nervous feeling was gone from my stomach while he was next to me. *This doesn't add up. Why was this feeling gone –now that he was so close to me?* I must have been pale from my thoughts—or my stomach.

"Kate, you don't look well." Richard reached for my arm which almost sent me to the floor. "Do I need to send for Bill?"

"No—, whatever you do, *don't* get Bill. "I sounded a bit taken back and after a moment of regaining my composure, I laughed and said, "Look, I am brought to these damn parties and left alone to fend for myself—okay? Don't take what I am saying to heart, but don't worry about me, I will be just fine. It's no big deal. By the way, where is Maggie?" I looked around the party pretending there was someone

I knew that I could run to in a moment's notice, but let's face it there was no one here I even wanted to strike up any kind of conversation with much–less run to. I resigned myself to my situation when I saw Bill heading our way. *What did he want?* I was becoming agitated about pretty much everything at this point and now the *ass of my dreams* was approaching.

"Look Kate, I'm sorry if I've done something wrong. But it seems to me your husband must be out of his mind to leave you abandoned at any party. I certainly wouldn't leave your side …—and as for Maggie—she can definitely take care of herself!" Laughed Richard.

God, his laugh was contagious. No wonder Don thinks he can't do any wrong. Hmmm, be careful Kate—This is Bill's competition. I started laughing, "That is the one thing you're absolutely right about, Maggie has always been able to take care of herself. Especially—."

"Especially what?" Interrupted Bill.

"Nothing, we were talking about Maggie," I replied irritably.

"Oh, careful Katie. Let's give Maggie a break and not scare Rich here. It will take a guy with a whip and chair to ever gain control over that one." Said Bill with a smirk. He stretched his hand towards Richard's for a handshake. "I see you've met my wife, Katie."

"Yes, I met *Kate*. It's *Richard*, and no she hasn't scared me off. I find Maggie a delight. She is quite beautiful. I believe that it would be a sad day for anyone to harness that kind of energy, in fact to harness anyone in a matter of control is rather sad.—Don't you think? If you will excuse me, I believe I better get something to eat before Don starts his toasts to your clients, Bill. It was wonderful meeting you *Kate*, I hope we'll meet again." Said Richard in an aloof manner, smiling as he left. The look in Bill's eyes was of steaming rage—not to mention he was squeezing the hell out of my arm.

I knew the continued reference to the correct pronunciation of my name drove Bill nuts, "Bill, sweetie, don't let him bother you. He thinks he's the man of the hour.—That's all. He'll soon find out who Don's best man is." *He could be my man of the hour any time.* Bill took my smile in thought as a final gesture for him to calm down and returned the smile, but you could tell it wasn't for me. His mind was definitely elsewhere.

"Katie let's go home. I've talked to Don and finished my negotiations with our clients. They left twenty minutes ago. There *won't be* any toasts for them. I have to be at the office early to get with Martha and finalize the contracts. Let Rich-*ard* have his fun—for now," his look was serious. Richard would soon know not to cross Bill. "Meet me at the car, I have to make a pit stop before we head for the house."

I had just given the valet the receipt for our car when I heard the deep roar of the motorcycle start up. I noticed Maggie had already tried to make her claim on the new conquest. It was comical to watch her hang on trying to get that good night kiss as Richard tried just as hard to pull away. The valet was behind him in our car which, to Richard's relief, was his only rescue from Maggie. He paused far enough ahead in the driveway so the valet could park our car and hand me the keys.

"I see you're leaving the party early. You and Bill had enough?" Asked Richard.

"Bill only stays at these things long enough to get what he needs done. It looks like you have your hands full," I said as I looked in Maggie's direction.

"Nothing I can't handle," he shrugged.

"I guess not. I gather you have this problem often." I said jokingly.

"No,—that's not ..."

With the look of agitation, "Appears as though I keep interrupting your conversation," Bill shot angrily.

"No, I was saying good night. I guess I'll see you tomorrow, Bill, and it was nice to meet you, Kate. Good night." Said Richard in an overly courteous tone. To add to Bill's anger, he worked the gears until the bike became louder and louder.

Over the roar of the bike Bill yelled, "What the hell did he want? Shit! Get in the car!" Slamming the door in disgust.

I thought it was best to stay quiet noticing Bill's hands gripping the steering wheel. His knuckles were white as he rocked them back and forth. I leaned against the window, pretending to be asleep. I thought this would allow him to calm down and ignore me. When unexpectedly I felt the back of his hand levels me, slamming my face against the damn window. My head bounced off so hard, I hit it again from the reeling motion.

I grabbed my head and cried, "Why in the hell did you do that for?" My face was pounding from the pain.

"I'll tell you what it's for! I leave you to do one thing and I find you flirting with Rich!" Screaming at the top of his lungs, while slamming his hands against the steering wheel.

"Flirting! Since when is it called flirting when someone just stops to say 'nice to meet you and good night? I was only standing there—he stopped to talk, I didn't flag him down!" I shouted in my defense. "It wasn't a reason to hit me." I rubbed my aching head.

"To hear you tell it, Maggie saw otherwise. She grabbed me as soon as I left the house. She was talking to Rich, when he jerked away from her and went straight to you."

That bitch, no telling what she told him. I sank deeper into the seat and mumbled, "His name is Richard."

"What are you ranting about now?"

"Nothing, I said his name is Richard, not Rich, that's all." *Shit!* My head ached.

Bill burst out laughing as we pulled into the driveway. "Katie, I swear, you're crazy!" Bill leaned towards me and pinched my chin, "Let's forget it. Maggie can take care of herself. She can get this Rich dude all by herself. If I know her, it won't take too long before her claws are set in deep." Bill shook his head and grabbed my purse. "Come on Katie, I'm hungry."

Once inside, Bill tossed my purse at the couch causing it to hit the armrest and fly open—discharging everything inside. I ran over to gather it all up while he stood in the doorway of the kitchen laughing. I looked inside to make sure that all the contents were safely back where they belonged. At the same time both of us focused on the same thing. A small pink package on the floor under the edge of the coffee table. I rescued it, but as I was putting it back into its safe place, Bill was snatching it out of my hands.

His face grew hard as he stared at the small package. "What the hell is this?" He opened the package to find some of the pills missing. This added to his rage. "I don't fucking believe this! You've been doing this behind my back!"

"Bull shit! I haven't exactly been keeping it a secret. If you remember, we discussed it on the plane. I told you I was going to do it." I nervously explained.

"You were upset! I thought you were just ranting! What is Father Flanders going to say!" He replied furiously.

"I'm not going to buy into this Bill. I don't care what Father Flanders has to say about this! I am sure he'll be rather upset with you and *your* little tantrums before he'll say anything about me being on the pill! Hell, he will probably be grateful that I am!" I defiantly stood my ground.

"You wouldn't dare!" He retorted. "The hell I won't!" I defied.

It was in slow motion. I saw Bill's hand move from his side. In my head I knew I had better get the hell out of there. I couldn't move. It was as though my feet were nailed to floor.

I woke up on the floor. My face ached. I leaned on the couch for assistance as I pulled myself up. I sat on the edge of the couch, looking around the room. It was trashed. Everything was knocked over. After a moment I realized I was rubbing my throat. I picked up my purse and pulled out my compact to inspect for damage. Staring into the mirror, the whole scene flooded back into memory. Bill exploding like a bomb. The last thing I remember was passing out with his hands around my throat. Well, I guess that explains the fingerprints. My face was bruised around my eyes and mouth. I weakly got up and went to the bathroom to clean the blood from my mouth.

My eyes flinched from the daylight. *Shit, how long was I out?* I looked at the clock, 9:30 a.m.! "Shit!" I said aloud.

The doorbell rang. *Who in the hell is that?* "Who is it?" I squeaked out. The pit of my stomach went into a massive butterfly surge.

"Richard." Answered from the door.

Oh Jesus! Not now! "Richard, I don't think Bill is here. He should be at the office." I barely yelled at the door. My throat ached horribly.

"No, he hasn't shown up for work this morning. I needed to get his John Hancock on some paper work. His clients are waiting in his office. I'm told this isn't like him. May I come in? It's difficult speaking through the door."

"I'm sorry, please give me a minute." I grabbed some tissue and moistened it with spit, then cleaned around my mouth. *Well, there's no hiding a fat lip.* I pulled my sunglasses from my purse to cover my eyes and buttoned my shirt around my neck. I tried to pull myself together as I stumbled for the door kicking that little pink packet across the room.

I opened the door peaked from behind it just enough to block him from entering shading my sore covered eyes with my hand as I blinked from the sunlight. I pretended to adjust the glasses trying to cover my face. "Hi, Richard. I don't know where Bill is." It was all I could do to keep from dropping to my knees. "I didn't see him leave this morning. I assumed that he headed for the office. As you can see, his car isn't in the garage. Sorry, I can't help you."

Richard's face went pale. I lowered my face so that he wouldn't stare. "Kate, are … are … you don't look well … are you okay?" He stepped closer.

"Yes, I'm fine." I said sternly moving behind the door a bit more to keep him at bay. "I don't mean to intrude." He touched my face softly. I almost burst into tears.

My voice softened, "Thank you for your concern. I'll be fine … Really." I wanted to melt into his arms. I couldn't understand what came over me. I have never felt this way before.

Richard's deep brown eyes penetrated mine as though I didn't have the sunglasses on, right into my soul. I felt that flutter again but this time it was my heart. I thought I was going to swoon like in those romance novels.

I finally spoke, "Really, I'll be okay. Do you want me to tell Bill you're looking for him?"

"No!" He blurted out in anger. Realizing his tone, he answered a bit calmer, "I mean, no. I'll find him. Don't you worry yourself. I'll take care of this! Thanks ... and try to have a good day." He headed for his bike, just short of reaching it, he stopped spun around on his heel, "I don't mean to sound forward, but if you need anything ..." He cleared his throat, "I mean ... Please, call me if you do." His head dropped and he spoke harshly while his hands gripped the handle bars of the bike, "My secretary has my number."

Using the door to hold me up. I answered knowing he could not hear me, "Thank you. I will."

I watched as he drove away. I held onto the door with my life. Starring at this wonderment who just left my driveway. There was something about this man causing this stir inside. I felt some sort of strength fill my body while he was close. *What was this?* I pressed the door closed, turned, and leaned against the door as my knees began to give way again. I couldn't understand what I was feeling. It was as though I had no control over myself. I shook my head. *What are you thinking Kate? You look like hell! He felt sorry for you!* I looked at myself in the hall mirror and the reality from last night hit hard. *Yep, he felt sorry for you. Can you imagine swooning? Ha! Wouldn't that be a joke? He would have thought I was nuts! Kate, you better get it together!*

I nearly jumped out of my skin when the doorbell rang. *What now!* I opened the door slowly, finding Beth on the other side with a smile. It didn't last long, when she saw my face, it quickly turned into a frown.

"God damn! What in the hell ... I'll kill him!" Exploded Beth.

"Beth! Shhh! Get inside! I don't need the whole neighborhood knowing what is going on!" Jerking her into the house.

"Kate, I was off today and had this uncontrollable urge to get my butt over here. I am glad I finally listened to my intuition! Do we need to take you to the doctor?—Jesus!" Beth was trembling with anger.

"Please, settle down. I'm fine now. I just need some aspirin or something. My face is killing me." I took off my glasses and slumped into the couch as Beth ran into the kitchen to retrieve some aspirin, water and a bag of frozen peas.

When Beth returned from the kitchen, she stopped short and stared at me in horror, "Oh my God! What did he do to you? Kate, have you seen yourself in the mirror? I think we need to get you to the doctor!"

"Yep," I chuckled sarcastically, "I'm quite the sight, aren't I? I don't think I'll be running in the next beauty contest!" I laughed again, "Ouch! I can't be doing that!" I carefully placed the frozen peas on my eye and sank into the couch.

"Kate, this isn't the time for joking around! You need to do something! You can't let the bastard get away with this!" Beth was pacing the room in a fit. "I know! I'll find out if Pops has any of those friends left!" She took her finger and pressed her nose sideways so that I would get the point on "friends."

"No, that won't be necessary. Besides, I thought that only happened in the movies." I chuckled and flinched.

"Well, if you won't go to the doctor, I have the next best solution.—A hot bubble bath! You soak and I'll make you some hot tea. When you are finished, we'll sit down and talk rationally about what we need to do. Okay?"

"Fine with me." I needed to do something; my body was starting to ache. I guess it came from the position I was in while I was knocked out.

Beth called out from the bathroom; "Not to change the subject, but I almost ran over this dream of a guy on the way over here. He was on a motorcycle."

"Yeah. That was Richard. He was just here looking for Bill. Come to think of it ... Where is Bill? I mean, He didn't show up for work and it's not like him." I was curious.

"In Hell, I hope! I bet he got the hell out of here thinking you would call the police. Richard! Hmmm, that explains why he stopped and glared at me before I turned into your driveway. Man, was he mad!" Beth laughed, "No matter how mad he was, he has a set of the most beautiful brown eyes I've ever seen! Man! What do you know about him?"

Good ole' Beth, no matter what the crisis is, she could always find time to check out the beef. "Nothing. I don't know anything about him, only that he just started working at Cannon's and is the man of the hour."

I closed my eyes and rested as I soaked in the bubbles. My mind raced. *Strange that he just showed up at my door. What was this pull that I had towards him? I mean, this is crazy! I have never met this guy in my life and yet, I had this uncontrollable urge to just leap into his arms and let him carry me off into the sunset ... Man Kate, you've been hit one too many times in the head.—I don't understand, he looks like the guy in my dreams. I mean, I've had those dreams long before I met him. What about that?—And his eyes, those eyes were like mine. Could he be? I guess I'll never know ... I can't ... To know that he was out there, and I was tied to this hell ... What could I have ever done to deserve this?* I started crying. I slipped into the water and soaked my head. When I came up Beth was standing in the doorway with my tea.

"How are you doing sweetie? There, now you just lay back and sip on this."

Beth went over to the toilet, stared at the seat and laughed, "Can't men do anything right? What does it take to touch it like this—and see? Down it goes ... Was that so damn hard?" She dropped the lid and sat down. After a moment she took a deep breath and said, "Kate, you have to listen to me. You have to leave Bill ... Okay, now I want you to think very seriously about this. You know he isn't going to stop doing—*this* (she pointed to my face). You can stay at my place until we decide what to do."

"I can't," I sighed deeply, "I can't go right now."

"And why not? I don't understand you Kate. The man beat the hell out of you," said Beth, the confusion plain on her face.

"It's easier said than done. You've got it together Beth."

Beth laughed, "Okay, partially. But you must understand I didn't get this way over night. It's taken me years."

"Sure, Beth. You were able to let Anthony have it and walk away. I can't possibly see you being shy at any given time in your life."

"No, there hasn't. I never took shit from anyone. If I remember correctly, you were pretty feisty when you were young. You didn't let that guy bully you around. I asked you before, what happened?"

"Beat into submission. It was better to be quiet. You don't get hit so much when you do." I looked into the water wondering about my dilemma, but my mind kept wandering back to Richard. My stomach quaked every time I thought about it. *What am I going to do?* I started crying again. "Beth, I am so 'be–fused. I don't know what I'm going to do if I leave. If you remember, I was only a waitress when we first met. I can't do that anymore … Besides, Bill's a Catholic. He'll never let me go … All I know is, I can't leave now … I don't know why, I just can't. I knew it while I was in the hospital. Even though I fell down the stairs, the pain … I looked into his eyes,—I couldn't betray him. There has to be some reason why Bill and I are together.—I just can't explain it right now. It's why I can't leave no matter how hard I try. I know this doesn't make sense to you but that's all I know."

Beth patted my head and picked up my tea cup. "Look, let me warm this up, that will give me a minute to think on this while you get out of the tub. We need to get out of this place for a while. I'll be back in a few."

I smiled and laid back in the tub. With my toe, I pushed the pug to allow the tub to drain. I looked around the bathroom admiring it. I worked so hard to make it this way. No matter what has happened between Bill and I, this was my place of safety. This home and everything in it. Now everything's a mess.

Richard floated back into my thoughts. *What about him? Why is he really here? The friction between the them last night, one would think that he really could care less if Bill showed up or not. Hell, Bill not showing up would prove Don's point about needing Richard's help. Should I talk to Beth about this?* I didn't have to bring it up; Beth always had these six senses about everything.

"You know Kate, I hate to bring this up, but there was something strange about that guy—Richard? I mean, he left here *so* angry. I know he saw your face but—I don't know. There's something about him. I can't quite put my finger on it. Something so familiar."

"He looks like the man in my dream," I said softly.

Beth stared at me and shuddered hard. "Yes! That's it. I mean I know you told me about the dream, but I always blew it off as a dream and nothing more. But this ... This is too weird. This guy looks just like him! Man, those eyes." She shuddered from the revelation.

It was like she was hit by a bolt of lightning, "That's it! His eyes! They look so much like yours, Kate! This guy is like ... like he came right out of your dreams! What do you think this means?—Oh man, oh man ...!" Beth was walking around in circles as if she trying to figure out the answer of the ages.

I stood there, dripping wet, reaching for a towel, watching her in amazement, "Okay, Beth. Calm down. It was only a dream and I don't believe for one moment this guy just popped out of my dreams into reality. Okay? They'll put us away! Not that it isn't where I'd like to be right now, but let's face reality. This is only a coincidence, so let's get a grip."

One eyebrow raised and a gleam in her eyes, "Okay, I'll get a grip. But what if I had a way to find out? Would you want to?"

I didn't like the look on her face. "What are you talking about? I don't know if I want to know ... How?"

"I know this lady who is totally incredible. She can see things. You know the future." The excitement in her face was too much.

"Oh no, you are not taking me to some gypsy! This is just plain nuts Beth! It was only a dream for God's sake! No! Don't you look at me like that!" Madly towel drying my hair. I looked up and saw Beth staring at me with a firm look, a wise ass smirk upon her beautiful face and her hands on her hips, I weakened; knowing she had me, "Why do I let you talk me into these things?"

Beth's expression changed to a droll look, "Kate, there's nothing wrong with a good gypsy. She isn't like that. She calls herself a seer or something like that. No hocus-pocus. Just wait until you meet her. Besides, dreams do mean something and sometimes they have to be interpreted because someone is trying to tell you something Kate. You've got to admit this just is too coincidental. You even said so yourself!"

I didn't know what to think. I had to admit there were quite a few things happening to me right now that I didn't have the answers to. Maybe … It couldn't hurt.

I took a deep breath as the door opened. The woman on the other side of the door was tall and very blonde. Her smile was warm and delightful; her presence was very welcoming. A smile crossed my face as I looked into those sparkling blue eyes. No this was not the look of a carnival gypsy. I no longer felt afraid to be there.

"Hello, Anna," said Beth. "This is Kate. I am so glad you had time for us this morning. I really thought you would be out of town."

"Hi, Kate, nice to meet you," her voice sang. "If you had called me this afternoon, I would have been on my way to Arizona. I'm going to a vortex' with a friend … Please, come in."

"We don't need to keep you if you have something to do," I stammered. *Good! Now we can get out of here! And what the hell is a vortex? Dammit Beth, what did you get us into? My brains are still rattling from Bill's smack.*

Anna laughed, "Not a problem! The trip is just one of those last-minute things! I always have time for my clients."

She led us through her house to a small room painted in soft magenta. The room didn't have very much in it yet reflected her personality. In the corner was a small table holding a huge crystal with a light shining through it. There were a few shelves with a smattering of books and small figures of angels and fairies. In the center of the room was a table with three chairs. Anna took her place at the table and pointed to the chairs, "Kate, please sit here and I'll read for you first."

I obediently sat where I was told while Beth tossed her purse under the chair, plopped into the seat next to me. She leaned on the table promptly resting her elbows with palms under her chin giggling with uncontrollable excitement, saw the look of fear in my eyes her expression changed to one of soft concern. "Look, sweetie, you have to keep an open mind about this. If you don't, it won't be any fun. You want Anna to get a good feel from you, not all this fear you are harboring. Trust me, everything is going to be fine." She patted my hand reassuringly.

Anna laughed softly, "I won't bite, Kate … unless asked too …" She opened a blue lace bag, from within she retrieved a black scarf carefully wrapped around the tarot deck. "First I would like to explain what I do and what we are going to do. Okay?"

I nodded my head while forcing a tight smile across my face. Trying not to look nervous. *What the hell am I doing here?* My fingers naturally ran through my hair.

While shuffling the cards, Anne softly murmured, "Kate, there is no need to be nervous, love. This won't hurt a bit. No, I am not like the carnival gypsies. But we must remember everyone has their place in this world and I come from a long line of gypsies!" she winked and continued. "One must be careful, but then there are charlatans everywhere in every lifestyle. We just have to learn how to trust, in here, (she pointed to her heart) and know the Divine will guide us properly."

She stopped for a moment and touched my hand lightly knowing I was about to jump out of my seat for this mind reading act. "Don't run, Kate. I go through this all the time. It was one of the feelings I get when people come to me … Now we can get started." She looked at Beth and winked then began, "In a moment, I'm going to hand you this deck of cards. I want you to shuffle them until you feel you are finished. While doing this, think about what you would like answered. If you are not sure, all you need to do is take a deep breath and exhale slowly to release your frustration, then you will be ready to shuffle. Then I'll take them from you and do my thing. You may stop me during the reading and ask questions or wait until I am through. Do you have any questions?" She asked as she handed me the cards.

"Just one. How can you do this? I mean read into the future and all that." I nervously asked. I wasn't ready for anyone to look into my life.

"Everyone has the sight differently." Anne answered calmly. "My way was inherited from my mother. She was a nurse in a delivery room where she took care of newborns and while playing with their little hands saw that she could see what life they just arrived from in their little palms. I read palms just as easily. Later I developed into reading cards. I get different thoughts in my head. You may call them voices or other spirits. I call it the highest point of myself.—Or the *I Am*.

We can go into more detail about that later if you want. Please listen carefully Kate, whatever is read to you today is only what was, what is and what could be. The reason why I say what could be is; we all have the ability to change the future. It is not written in stone. We all have the capabilities to change. It is up to you to decide how you want to do it.—If you wish too."

You mean, I can change the future? I don't get it." I was confused.

"God gave all His children a gift, Free Will. There is only one catch, you have to realize it yourself and know you can do it *yourself*. I know this doesn't sound reasonable, believe me, at some time in the future, it will all make sense. Sometimes it is good to get information in little bites. It is easier for the mind to absorb and not become frightened or confused by the message. Confusion is good to a point. It is a signal to "listen" something needs to be learned and or cleared up." She softly chuckled, "Sometimes confusion is there for you to learn just to trust and know All will be taken care of.—Now, let's get started."

Anne handed me the cards and I shuffled them and handed them back to her. She meticulously placed them on the table, pausing and looking at each one as she placed them in a precise order. It seemed forever before she started to speak, touching each one and looking deeply into them, sitting back, then looking into them again. I was becoming quite anxious while Beth just intensely between Anne and the cards before us.

"I know, by just looking at you, what is wrong. This isn't the first time this has happened to you." She pointed to my bruised face.

I looked at Anne with a start look on my face, "Excuse me, but duh! It did not take a genius to figure that out!" I heard my own words and became embarrassed. Replied in a whisper, "No, it is not the first time."

Anne looked indifferent towards my reply while Beth's mouth hung open and eyes wide as saucers. Anne continued, "Your father was very strict with you and your sibling. I feel maybe a male?—Brother?" She looked for a response.

I nodded in silent approval.

Anne reflected over the cards once more, while pointing to a series of them she continued, "You spent most of your young life in fear. I can see within your heart, you harbor a large amount of hate within about this.—To the point that you have extended it into your adult life … Hmmm. Because you have past life matters to clear up with your present husband, he was the chosen candidate for this lesson."

I flew back into the chair, "What in the hell do you mean! Are you telling me that I asked for this?" I asked in shock.

"In a way yes," said Anna quietly. She continued to study the cards ignoring my concern.

"Let me get this straight." I leaned closer snapped my fingers in her face to gain her attention, "Wait one damned minute, stop right there! No more looking until you explain this to me. And I do not want this, you are going to have to wait and trust stuff. I want some answers lady." I saw Beth's face, I held up my hand, "No. Not a word from you. You brought me here to get answers and that is just what I am going to get … answers!" I returned my focus to Anne, "You're saying because of my hate for my father, I feel the need to continue being abused, so I married Bill to have this abuse continue?" I asked in a very curt tone.

Anne did not budge. The sparkle in her eyes became more vibrant as she replied, "In a word … Yes. See Kate, you must realize you are not here for the body. You are here for your Soul. Your Soul picked the situation 'It' needed to accomplish certain things in this life. Certain Karma that 'It' needed to correct in order to become enlightened. So, your Soul chose this set of circumstances and people, along with their approval, to accomplish this. Exposing you to what the Soul wants you to realize; forgive, learn and move on. It is all about forgiving."

I couldn't believe what I was hearing. "I am trying to understand this. Because I really do not. First, you want *me* to forgive my father and Bill for what they did *to me* and move on. All this because of some … Karma? What the hell is Karma?—And what the hell does it have to do with *me*?" I leaned back once again in the chair totally frustrated.

Beth chimed in softly, "Kate, Karma is neither good or bad and it is both. Remember the saying, *what you sow is what you reap*? That is Karma. Everything you do, everything has an equal reaction to it. For every good there is good and of course, for every bad … Do you understand? Sometimes you do not pay for something in this life, so it is picked up in another. The Soul knows "It" has to account for everything "It" has done. People do not understand that one is responsible for all actions, good or bad."

I sat quietly trying to take in all this new-found information. Trying to take it all in little bites, not believing that a small child could ask for such fear and pain. Tears began to fill my eyes as my body shook in anger.

"Kate, you may not believe this right now, but you allowed them to do this. I know it is difficult to believe a child asked for this, but if you could take in the grander picture, you would understand why all of this happened."

My voice trembled, afraid to find out what was next, "And that is?"

Anne nodded to Beth in agreement of her explanation and expanded a bit more, "That in some past life, you did it to them. That is the law of Karma. 'Do unto others' doesn't only reflect to this life. In turn, every good that you do in every life is also returned. It is not the "child" one needs to look at, but the Soul within. The child may appear young, small, delicate to us, however, when you look deep within the eyes of the child, you will see a very old Soul. Haven't you ever spoken to a child and got an answer that totally amazed you? Wondered where in the world did this tiny being got such knowledge for being so young? Until we as adults tell them they cannot have this knowledge, they remember a lot of things from previous lives. When you are able to see this clearly and fully understand what I am talking about, you will find it easier to forgive. It may be as simple as something that was started in one life and not yet completed."

After a moment of silence Anne said, "Kate, you don't have to stay in this situation. You have the capabilities to change all of this in your life. You have to realize you don't deserve this hell you have created. That is what it means to become awakened. To understand that you are deserving of all good and wonderful things."

"B-but you said that I did it to them in another life. So, don't they have to forgive me?" Tears were streaming down my flushed cheeks. Beth's hand on my back softly rubbing in circles like the nurturing mom instead of sister she had become in my life.

"No. That's the catch twenty-two. Every life we live is a drama of some sort and all you have to do is forgive *yourself* for what you have done, what you have allowed to happen to you, and know that this drama can come to an end. Others in the drama have to clear their own way and forgive for themselves. Sometimes it takes a little work. If your intentions are there—it will. A way will be provided. You may not think so because it may get worse before it gets better, but believe me it will get better … You have taken the first step. Your life is so precious. Your Soul wants to remember everything. The Soul knows that we are stuck in a heavy veil and wants you to remember that you are a Divine Being."

"Great. That's all I need—more problems! Well, is there any good in those cards?" I looked at them inquisitively. There had to be some good news in this mess. Mom-Beth handed me a tissue. "Um—what do you mean allowed? I did not allow Bill to smack me around."

"Allowed," nodded Anna, still studying the cards, "Yes, we attract what we feel about ourselves. If you feel that you are unworthy, you attract unworthy. Therefore, you have allowed this to happen to take you to another level of existence. Some people learn and move forward, some don't. You don't have to allow any of this. Once you realize that you are worthy of all good and wonderful. This will reboot your Spiritual software."

"Hmmm, there seems to be someone around you who has been with you before. He just walked into your life recently, though you have known about him for quite some time. I can't place where. … Maybe your heart? I can see this man is full of love. Hmmm. It also appears he has fought this battle with you before." She points to the "Lovers" card that laid with the "Six of Rods." Tapping the cards, "Old scenario for the two of you."

"What does he look like?" Interrupted a smiling Beth. "Sorry, I have to know."

Anna laughed, "I wondered when you were going to speak up. All I can see are his eyes. They are very much like yours, Kate. From what I can see, you are a part of each other."

"A part of each other. What do you mean?" I asked.

"The term is *twin flame*. There are times when a Soul wishes to divide so "The Soul" can continue with Its quest towards enlightenment, so it splits into two different aspects—male and female. He is the male …" She continued to chuckle. "And Kate is the female! Wow!" Said Beth under her breath.

"Why is he here now? Why didn't he come into my life sooner, so I didn't have to go through all of this?" I hit the table in frustration, "Why me?"

"Everything is in *Divine Order* Kate. You had things to do before you two can come together. Appears there is something all three of you have to clear up. That is why you are all here together now. He's here to assist you as you are here to assist him. He may appear to have it all together; yet … hmmm, he has his own challenges to deal with … You will be making some very difficult decisions in the very near future Kate. Please keep a cool head and you'll be fine. My dear, I know you have taken in a whole lot today, remember one thing, this is only a drama. Nothing more. I know it is very easy to get caught up in the drama of everyday life. Unfortunately, in order to clear things up we may need to stir in it for a bit while making decisions. However, in this drama, you have Free Will, the drama can go away if you want it. If you want major violence, which is exactly what you'll get. You may also choose to do it peacefully. Most just have the understanding that this is possible because they are stuck in the drama." She laughed softly to break the tension.

"How can we find out what happened in Kate's past life so she can clear it up?" Ask Beth.

"I don't do that kind of work, but I do have a friend who can help you. She lives in Arizona though. I don't know many people around here. Trust me, she is very good and worth the trip." I was relieved to see Anne gathering the cards, giving me the signal, the session was over.

"Thanks, I'll keep it in mind. I've had more than I can handle for now. I don't need anyone poking around the inside of my head, much less my heart ... Thanks, but no thanks." I realized exhaustion set in and wanted to get out of there. I paid her and thanked her again. I told Beth I would be waiting for her in the car.

Anna stopped me before I left; "I know this must be pretty frightening to you, Kate. You've been through a lot in the years you've been here on earth. Some of them not too much fun. It's difficult to believe deep down there is a reason for all of this madness. Time grows short for everyone; things have to be cleared up right away. We can't play around any longer. There is solace,—meditate for guidance. The Divine will give you the answers you need."

"I don't know how to meditate." I flatly replied, not wanting to open another complex issue of enlightenment. It was too much for one day. My faced ached terribly; I just wanted to curl up in a ball and cry myself to sleep.

"Then pray. You do it quite often. The Divine is listening although you don't believe it. It just takes time for the drama to unfurl so you may see and understand the answers." She smiled and pressed her fingertips lightly against my temple. "Know that you are loved dearly Kate. Go in Light."

I humbly said thank her and walked to Beth's car in a daze.

Anna watched in thought then turned to Beth, "I want you to know that you are here to assist Kate in this life, Beth. She is in a very destructive situation and will need your strength. Cleaning one's

Karma can be stressful. She has a lot more strength than she realizes. This is one of the lessons she is here to learn. Being by her side was your commitment to her. I know you will fulfill it Beth. Go in Light."

"I will take care of her … And thank you Anna." Beth whispered softly.

CHAPTER FIVE

Affairs of the Heart

I was pretty out of it for the next few days. Bill was mysteriously gone all the time. I was both very grateful—and curious. He slept in the guest room. He didn't call or come home for dinner.

Although I was relieved, I was spending way too much time pondering over what had happened the last few days. I listened to the recording of my reading repeatedly. I had to admit it made everything I've been through sound a lot more reasonable.

By the end of the week my thoughts returned to Bill. I was becoming concern about his behavior. I heard the car pull up late at night and leave early in the morning. I didn't have the nerve to confront him. I became angry with myself and decided to stay up that night and confront him. I was tired of this hide and seek.

I was working in my garden when the doorbell rang. I was met with a large bouquet of roses. The young man behind them could barely hold them up.

"Mrs. Sawyer?" Asked the young man hidden behind the massive bouquet.

"Yes, please set them on the table." I said in an aloof tone which took the young man by surprise.

"Man! Four dozen roses! Is it your anniversary or something? He sure does love you. Oh, I almost forgot, please sign here … The young man was taken back from the lack of expression on my face. I am sure he was expecting one of elation. He mumbled something to the fact as he left.

I stared at the roses in disbelief. The old pattern was about to reoccur. How could he do this! I walked over to them and retrieved the large card that protruded the flowers:

Katie,

I know an apology is the last thing you want to hear from me right now. I went to Father Flanders and his suggestion was much penance and to leave you alone for a while. I have finished my penance and have decided to check on the office in New York.

I'll be there for about three days. When I return, I would like to for us to see Father Flanders together. I believe there is nothing we can't fix as long as there is love.—And I do love you so very much Katie. I have faith you will forgive me in time. I know deep inside, you love me too. I'll call you later in the week.

Love, Bill

I started laughing hysterically. So, he did go to Father Flanders. I would have loved to have been a fly on that wall! I looked at the roses and decided to put them in water. It was a shame to throw them out, no matter how I felt about Bill. I began to wonder how the two of them figured out all I needed was three days to come to my senses and run back into his arms! I'm married to an ass that wanted me to forgive him! Anna said to forgive him?—Right! That lady was nuts and needed one hundred thirty-five dollars. There's is no way that Bill was ever going to let me go. How could I forgive him? I smiled as I placed the flowers in various areas of the house.

Bill knew exactly what to do to make things right. My heart sank at the thought of forgiving him. What happened? He was so wonderful in the beginning. We could do no wrong. I loved him so much. He was strong and handsome. I couldn't wait for him to come home, now I can't wait for him to leave. He wanted to conquer the world, now all he wants to do is conquer me.

I went into the kitchen and made a cup of rose tea. I looked out the window reflecting on my previous thoughts. From the corner of my eye, I caught a glint of bright light. Then came a deep roar came up the driveway. I froze, watching him dismount the bike and walk to the door.

My heart skipped a beat when the doorbell rang. I couldn't get my legs to work. To do the simple things they were supposed to do in aiding me to answer the door? I finally made it to the door by the third ring. I found it difficult to breath. My palms were soaked from sweat; I had to wipe them on my filthy jeans just so I could grab the doorknob.

He stood before me, with his windblown hair and deep brown eyes. "Good morning Kate! How are you doing today?" Said his deep rich voice as he leaned against the door frame.

"Good morning, Richard. I'm fine. Bill isn't here. I just found out myself he's left for New York this morning. You guys seem to keep missing each other. Maybe you need to get it together with your secretaries." *Come on legs. You can do it. Just hold me up.*

"I know Bill's in New York. I watched him leave," he said a deep quiet tone. His eyes linger into mine, I thought I was about to sink to the floor. I was grateful for the jam as I held onto it tightly.

Oh, you did. Hmmm. Now take a deep breath Kate ... "So, what can I do for you?" I asked in a steady voice. *Does he even know what he's doing to me?*

"I've got the bike and it's a beautiful day ... I thought you might like to go for a ride," He grinned and pointed to the bike. "I mean, if you don't want to, I'll understand but I thought it would be nice to get some fresh air. Scenery can look quite different from the back of one of these. What do you say? Shall we?—I promise I won't bite, nibble maybe." His eyes sparkled as he laughed.

I hesitated. *What am I thinking?* A part of me wants to jump on the back of that thing and ride into the sunset.—The other was still married to Bill. The fun part gave in to the pleading look in his eyes. "Sure, just give me minute to change. Come in, while I freshen up a bit."

I ran into the bedroom giddy with excitement. I frantically pulled on another pair of jeans and grabbed a sweater. I flinched as I looked in the mirror. *Not too bad.* The bruises were almost gone. I touched them up with a bit of makeup and pulled my hair back with a scarf. For a brief moment the feeling of guilt started to fill me, but I allowed the anger and pain take over,—and left.

Walking beside him along the driveway I noticed how immaculate he kept the bike. Richard patted the seat and said with pride, "I rebuilt her myself."

"It's beautiful." Not having a clue to what it took to rebuild one. "Aaahhh … It's a beautiful color of blue."

"Yes, it is," he said approvingly, looking at the bike as though it were a goddess. He stepped back, still admiring this thing of beauty.

"What kind of bike is it?" I didn't know one bike from another. If I didn't say something, I'd fall to the ground. It was though the sound of my voice kept me on my feet.

"She's a Norton Twin. It wasn't easy finding all the parts. Thought I'd never get her finished. I added more chrome.—Not like the Norton Commando. Her lines are more refined," passing his hand over the bike as if he were caressing it as he spoke. "Well, come on, let's get going."

He noticed my hesitation. "Never been on one before?" I shook my head no.

"Trust me. You'll be just fine. Just wait until I'm on and climb on behind me. That's all there is to it!" He patted his lady, urging me to hop on.

Trust him, I laughed to myself, *for some reason, I'd trust him to the ends of the earth.*

The ride was wonderful. It didn't take long for me to become accustomed to the way he drove the bike. I knew when to lean in certain moves and took advantage of the turns to move closer to him. He naturally picked upon my advances, adjusting himself to accommodate me getting closer. I rested my head against his shoulder. I haven't felt this safe in such a long time. I didn't want to remember the pain or Bill—or anything.

Leaning against him as we rode, the feeling of freedom was exhilarating. I don't know if it was the rush from the cars passing so close, or having him so near,—here with me. I found myself in a trance like state from the rhythm of the bike. It was as though the bike was making its own music along the highway. It wasn't long before I noticed I was getting a bit hungry. I was enjoying the scenery when the smell kept blowing towards us, we hadn't passed a restaurant in miles—so why was I smelling food cooking?

"Hey, why do I smell food? We haven't passed a restaurant in quite a while." I yelled over his shoulder.

"You'll find out soon enough," he yelled back. He geared down and turned onto a dirt road. Finally turning again into a small graveled driveway, past a huge willow tree; coasting to a stop by winding walkway to park the bike.

I got off the bike and looked around. There was a small abandoned church just ahead, with a small brook beside it. I ran my fingers through my hair taking out the tangles, then tied it back again with my scarf. I quietly watched Richard as he retrieved a small blanket from a saddle bag. He spread it on the ground and patted, "Come on over and have a sit. I want you to relax and I'll take over from here."

Richard returned to the bike, pulled out a small package that contained plates and glasses; then leaned over the bike opening the other saddle bag retrieving a bottle of wine. "I hope you don't mind the wine not being chilled correctly but I assure you, it's still great." He quietly poured me a glass, continued serving lunch. I sipped the wine while curiously watching him take off some foil from exhaust pipes. I tried to cover giggle as I watched Richard toss the hot foil wrappings from one hand to the other until he finally made it to the plates. With care Richard opened the foil wrappings and pouring the contents onto each plate.

"You'd think I'd learn by now to have the plates with me when I do this!" He laughed. "Well, I guess, if the truth be known, I usually eat right out of the foil!" Handing me the plate and watching as I stared inquisitively at the contents. "I hope you like it."

I took the plate and examined it carefully. *Hmmm, it smells pretty good.* "W-what is it?" I asked hesitantly.

Richard was busily working on his, looked up and replied, "Road Kill Stew. Go on—It won't kill you … Take a bite!" He laughed at the startled look on my face.

I shrugged my shoulders and took a bite, "Not bad … You'll make someone a good wife."

"Hey, one's got to survive. Sometimes there's not a place to eat and you get tired of eating at truck stops. At times, it's as close to a home cooked meal as I can get.—Better! You can toss the pots and pans in the recycle!"

I laughed, and began to relax, "So you've done a lot of traveling?"

"Most of my traveling was during the summer. I did a lot of odd jobs between school breaks."

"Must have been nice. The only traveling I've done was from Flint to Chicago. I don't believe running away counts as pleasure. Well, I guess I could count the few places Bill and I traveled to in the beginning …" I became silent. *(Good going, Kate … Why did you bring up Bill? Stupid! Just Stupid!)*

Richard chimed in to save the silence, "Well, most of what I've done doesn't really count as pleasure. Only the traveling to and from. Hiding from my parents was a full-time job."

"Is that how you ended up in Canada?" I asked in relief.

"Partially, Mom moved there after she and Dad divorced. Dad stayed in San Francisco with his latest, while Mom packed us up and headed North."

"I'm sorry."

"Don't be. It happens. My brother and I was a product of the sixties.

One day Mom and Dad found out material things were cool,—out went the beads and V.W. Bus—, and in came the diamonds and Porsche. The by-product was finding out you no longer had anything in common? Dad developed a taste for the ladies—and mom for money. It was very much a corporate type of decision. Very clean and very businesslike. Even the boys were handled in the contract negotiations. When I got old enough to say enough, I did it by working during the summers and whatever holidays I wanted; depending on who I was angry with at the time."

Richard saw that I was picking at the food. "It really isn't road kill, you know.—Grade A's finest."

"Oh, I know. I'm not really hungry, that's all." I couldn't eat. My stomach stayed pretty much in flutters. I rubbed my stomach as I put my plate on the blanket.

"Are you all right?"

"Hmmm, yep, I'm fine." I leaned against the willow, closed my eyes, and did my best to relax. A gentle breeze blew through the tree causing the willow's branches to rustle, and one softly tickling the side of my face.

Richard put his plate down and finished his wine. He sat next to me quietly until I opened my eyes. "Kate, we have to talk."

I became nervous, "About what?"

"Don't be nervous Kate, Remember, I won't bite. I'm sure you already know what we need to talk about. I am also sure that you have felt this uncontrollable pull between us." He hesitated, wiped his brow, "I know I feel it, I'm sure you do." He waited for my reply.

I did feel a pull, but I didn't want to admit it now. I looked into his eyes. I straightened up and hugged my knees knowing if I didn't hold on tight, I would leap into his arms. I had to be careful, though it took all my strength.

"Don't you feel the attraction between us?" He asked desperately.

"Y–yes, I do, but … "

Richard interrupted me by gently lifting my hands from my knees and holding them close to his face. "I'm probably going to sound nuts, but you've got to believe me when I say that I've been looking for you … Forever. Kate, it's as though we've always known each other. On the way to Don's party, I knew something was going to happen.—I just didn't know what. I knew you were there, I felt it … Then I saw you. You felt it, I know you did.—Didn't you?" He asked in despair. I could feel his fear of me rejecting all of this and declaring him mad.

I shook my hands free from his grasp. Unnerved, I quickly got up and brushed the leaves and dirt from my pants. Richard stood beside me looking rather helpless. I knew I had to say something. But what? I couldn't believe what he was saying. I picked up my wine and gulped it down. I nervously ran my fingers through my hair as I headed towards the brook.

Richard ran up behind me, "Kate, please answer me. Say something!"

I turned towards him and answered frantically, "What do you want me to say? Yes! Yes, I have felt that I've known you. I just don't understand all of this. How could you and I have these same feelings this strong and not have met. How is it, I can feel you before you even enter the room? This is too fast,—too soon." I turned away and looked into the brook. *This cannot be happening … This … This is nuts …*

"You're right. It *is* happening too fast … Damnit! That's the way I am. I needed to say something before I burst." Richard realized his shouting was frightening me. His chuckled calmly, "I guess my tactics are great in the board room. They need a bit more work with people I care about … Let's sit down and enjoy the brook. I think we need a breather from our—my little talk." He smiled. I nervously agreed. I needed a moment to gather my wits.

I kicked off my shoes and stepped into cool water. This allowed my mind to settle. My thoughts drifted back to my card reading. *Could all of this be true? I don't know … Anna said to keep my cool.* I watched Richard play with a small leaf in the water. His hands were smooth and strong. A shiver went through me as I remembered them caressing me ever so deliciously in my dreams. *How can this be? This man from within my very memory standing before my eyes?*

Clearing my thoughts, as well as my mind, "I want you to know, I really don't understand all of these feelings. I'm flattered you are attracted to me. I must have been crazy to jump on your bike and allow this ... I'm sorry, I–I just wanted a nice day. I haven't had one in so long. I don't mean to lead you on. I *am* so sorry." I looked into my fidgeting fingers. My heart was pounding wildly. *What am I going to do? Kate, you were crazy for doing this. Now look at what you've gotten yourself into!*

"Kate, please don't believe for one moment I thought otherwise," Richard replied quietly as he helped me up. "I'm sure it wasn't the other way around! I'm the one who is sorry to have moved so quickly. I didn't know how much time we had, and I felt it important you knew how I felt."

"Thanks, but we can't forget that I am married." *Real dumb Kate. He knew that.* "I can't just run off with someone just to forget my problems. Though that's not what you were saying ..." *No matter how good it all sounds.* "I mean, ... Oh, I don't know what I mean."

Richard lifted my chin and looked into my eyes, his words were in the gentlest tone, "Kate, when I saw what he had done to you, it was everything I could do to keep from hunting him down and beating the hell out of him. I was so angry, I almost ran over a friend of yours in the driveway!"

I laughed out loud, "That was Beth. She was pretty impressed by you—and your bike. And I am glad you didn't hunt Bill down.— But thanks for the thought. I've had pretty much the same, upon occasion."

"Why do you. I'm sorry, it's not my place to ask," he stared away from me lost in thought.

"Stay? I don't know. I've been told it's Karma—or something like that." "That makes sense, Karma has some very interesting drawbacks. I've felt the backlash from a few things myself. Some bad—and some good." His look returned to me lovingly. He looked down at the water and continued, "Karma does not mean that you are stuck in the situation. You can make the decision to do something."

I glared at him. Was he reading that card reader's mind? "Well, we better be going. It's getting late," I said. I knew we had to do something quick, before I lost what was left of my senses.

Richard went to the willow tree, gathered the plates, and started putting everything back where it belonged. I felt so bad. Here was the answer to all of my dreams and I'm crazy enough to let him go.—*Man, Beth isn't going to believe this.*

The gallant Richard had pulled out another jacket from a saddle bag, "It's going to get a little chilly on the way home. You'll need this." He placed the jacket around my shoulders pulling me close and kissed me softly. Before I could react, he was on the bike, gesturing for me to get on.

The journey home was ridden in silence. Upon arrival, Richard steadied the bike as I unmounted. I stood by the bike still very quiet; the moment was very awkward for the both of us.

Richard broke the silence; "I'll see you to the door."

I obediently nodded and walked by his side to the door without saying a word. My mind raced as we reached the door. There was so much I wanted to say to this dream come true. But what? What could I say? Please … tall dark and handsome, gather me into your arms and take me away from this? My heart pounded. I knew he could hear it, I could. Within my mind I screamed, *Stop this Kate! This is crazy!* The key had to find the lock on its own, for I surely do not know how it found it's mark. I hesitated as I unlocked the door the sob just on the edge of a choke, "Richard, I-I am sorry." My hand holding the key tightly; *That's it Kate, hold the key girl … just … just push the door open … You can do this. …* My face met his; I saw the pain within his eyes … Mine flooded with tears.

Leap into His arms Kate! Now! Do this you fool … I froze in my spot as he gently touched the tear that escaped my eye, "Everything is going to be fine, Kate." I stood there numbly as I watched the man of my dreams walk away, mount the bike and disappear.

Once inside, I leaned against the door with my eyes closed now allowing those tears to flow freely from my eyes. My shaking hand found my lips; the fingertips ever so gently circled them, desperately trying to recapture that feeling. "What have I done?" I muttered softly.

Heading for the kitchen, I jerked a few tissues from the box on the table, blowing my nose, taking a well needed deep breath as I opened the fridge. The cold air woke me from the trance I was in remembering why I was there in the first place and retrieved a soda.

The house was still dark, and I noticed the light on the answering machine blinking brightly. Numbly, I pressed the button and listened to the messages:

The first message was more chilling than the fridge. "Hi Katie ... It's me. I know it's late, but I wanted to see if you got the flowers ... No that's not it; I wanted to know how you were doing ... And to say I love you very much. Well, I guess I'll see you in a few days ... I love you, sweetie!"

I sunk into the nearby chair bursting into tears again as the next message answered. BEEP!

"Hey! Girlfriend! Where are you? Been looking for you ... Call me, bye!" BEEP!

"It's me again!—Yo! Call me! Thought you might want to go out and grab something to eat!" And again,

BEEP!

"Okay, girl. I'm starting to worry. It's not like you, not answer your messages ... Call me. Okay? Bye."

A small laugh escaped my lips as I erased the tape. "Wouldn't she like to know! I guess I'm not as predictable as everyone would like to believe." I took another sip of soda, locked the front door, and headed for the bedroom.

I mechanically undressed. I gazed in the mirror; something is different about me. A stirring inside. Why *do I feel so uneasy with myself? Why is this happening to me? Did I really ask for it? Was Anna, really right? Were we supposed to be together? She said I could change the future if I wanted. Was it that easy? No, nothing could possibly be that easy ... sighing ... My life sucks.*

So many secrets and so many lies. I never knew about Bill's drinking, well, I knew Bill drank, when we went out or during the games. I guess I thought of it as social drinking ... It just got worse in such a short period! The cocaine ... I don't even know when all this started ... And when I knew, I tried to deny it was happening. I guess I am as much to blame as he is. It was easier to ignore, than to face it. Now, it has gotten so out of hand! He has become so possessive!—So, controlling. He made me feel dirty. Just like Dad did to Mom. Now look at me, I live in constant fear, and have become more withdrawn than ever. What I tried so hard to avoid, I ran to with open arms.

I stood before the mirror, leaned close looking deep into my eyes and whispered, "Hey Soul, are you in there?—Or are you just as lost as I am? Do you hate me too? What's the deal? It seems to me; you and I have built one huge wall. A huge wall, deep, in my mind where you are safe within,—that's where you are. *Please* wake up and help me. Anna said you could guide me ... Assist me when I needed it ... All I had to do was ask or pray. Well, I'm asking ... Praying ... Guide me."

In my mind I was always safe. No one could hurt me, and I was strong. I sighed and pulled my hair away from my tear stained face. "Have you deserted me?" I sadly sighed and went to bed.

Jazz was waiting patiently in the bed, "Keeping my spot warm sweets?" I pushed him to the side and crawled between the warm sheets. As I turned off the light, I heard a soft voice from within, "No, Kate, I haven't deserted you."

At breakfast I was deliberating over my situation with Richard when the doorbell rang. My heart was racing as I opened the door.

"Hi sweetie! So, you're finally home! Where have you been? I was really starting to worry about you!" Beth stopped short and looked at the expression on my face. "Well, I'm glad to see you too! What gives? You look like you just lost your dog and I know you don't own one."

"Nothing. I'm sorry. Of course, I'm happy to see you. Beth, you read too much into things." I went back to the kitchen and set another place for Beth. "I'm having tea and toast. I know you hate tea, it won't take long to make coffee. Want some?" I asked absent mindedly.

"Yeah, sure," said Beth. She sat at the table watching me fumble around the kitchen. "Okay, I know something's up with you. I know you too well … You don't ever leave home and not check your calls, much less not return them. So,—spill."

I puttered around the kitchen making a lot of noise trying to ignore her constant prodding when the phone rang. Startled, I dropped the coffee container. "Let the answering machine get it. Damnit, I'll be right back." I went to the pantry and returned with the broom and dust pan to clean up the mess. *I hope the answering machine is low.*

Kate was staring at me from the doorway. "Hmmm, I don't believe I've ever seen you so nervous. Come on Kate, you can tell me." She looked like the cat that ate the canary. Seeing the expression on my face, Beth's eyes grew as big as saucers, "Oooh, was it something sinful? What did-you-do?"

I quietly finished cleaning the floor, brought in the toast and her cup of coffee. "Eat up," I replied curtly. Settled into the chair next to her, picked up my spoon, and continued in a somewhat cool voice, "I didn't do anything." I knew better than to look Beth in the eye. If I did, it was all over. It was impossible for me to hide anything from her.

"Look at me Kate. You've started to hide way too many things from me. I don't understand why. You've always shared with me. Come on now Kate, talk to me," she urged.

As she took a bite of her toast and gulped down the coffee, I finally gave in to her wishes and replied, "I was with Richard." The coughing and sputtering of toast and coffee was too much; I bite my lower lip to keep from giggling.

After regaining her composure, Beth shook her head and quietly said, "It's always the quiet ones. Damnit Kate, why haven't you told me? You know I wouldn't tell Bill."

"There wasn't anything to tell. We were only together yesterday."

"So ... What happened?"

"Like I told you, nothing." I said defiantly.

"Nothing happened? Nothing happened? You spent the day with a guy—which you are not married to.—Let us remember that you *are* still married and all you have to tell me is ... Nothing happened? Details, I want details!"

I couldn't stop the tears. Wiping my face, I said, "Beth, I am so confused. Do you really believe what Anna said was true? I mean about Richard and I being together before?"

"I don't know if you were together, but you can't deny there has been a strong attraction between you two ... And don't forget those eyes. Your eyes are a color I've never seen before and here he is ... Same color and pretty much the same shapes.—Go figure," replied Beth shrugging her shoulders.

"Well," I hesitated and took a deep breath; "We went for a ride on his motorcycle and had lunch. He told me how he felt, and I made him bring me home. At the door he kissed me and left. That's it, end of story."

Beth sat stunned. Clearing her throat, "You make it sound so—so bland. So indifferent. You are not fooling me in the least. I need another cup of coffee ... No, don't get up. I need to walk around and take this in."

I sat in my chair mulling over what I should tell her. *I must be crazy; I shouldn't have said anything.*

"Want anything?" Asked Beth returning from the kitchen. "Kate, I am glad you told me. I know there isn't anything I can do to help, but maybe it will do you some good to get it off your chest. You know, not carrying the weight of the world on your shoulders kind of thing." Beth returned from the kitchen with a fresh cup of coffee, sat down, and took a deep breath, "Whew!—Okay, let's take this one step at a time. There are some gray areas, Kate."

"I don't know what you mean." I replied indifferently.

"Well you've seemed to have left out some parts, like did he call or just show up at your door?" Beth smiled.

"Oh, I'm going to get the third degree."

"Well, yes. So, answer the question young lady," she said with that ear to ear grin of hers.

"If that's the only way I'm going to get you off my back," I said knowing I couldn't stall any longer.

It seemed forever as she dragged out all the details. As I relived the day before, I realized it was best I left when I did. Emotions I have never felt before seemed to rise through me. Not like the dream … That was purely sexual. These were feelings I have never felt for anyone, not even Bill. Something inside felt sad, lost in a way. I have always felt empty. I could never put my finger on it, you know? When Richard and I were together, it was right. It felt familiar,—Whole.

When Beth finished her grueling questions, I was outraged. "How could this happen to me? Why is he in my life now? Why did God allow me to marry Bill, when Richard was around the corner? This seemed like a very cruel joke to me. It seemed like God laughed in my face, allowing me to marry that-that- ass! Beth, you are into this, this New Age-life after death mumble jumbo, do you have any insight about this?"

Beth quietly watched my outrage. With one eyebrow raised, she just as quietly replied, "I have no response, Kate. I honestly don't know. Yet there are two things. One, from what you have told me about Richard, he is very understanding and enlightened Soul. And two, I'm glad I finally know about the both of you. Hell, I was going to hit on him myself," mused Beth.

"Come on Beth, this isn't funny … Stop laughing." It didn't take much to get us started. I began to giggle at the thought of Beth now dashed in the thought of not being able to hit on a perspective hunk of a man.

"Okay. Okay, now … Okay … I'll stop in a minute. I believe we need to refocus. Kate, what do you want to do now? I mean, right in front of you, is the most exciting man to have ever come along,—then? On the other, you're married to the biggest ass I've ever known. Man, Bill even beats Anthony in the asshole department." Beth, using her hands as a scale, weighed out the situation. "Nope, doesn't even look like a contest to me!"

"Now Beth, let's not get carried away. I've had some very good times with Bill. I mean, he's not all bad. He's trying, as you well know. I have to give him a chance." I sat deep in thought, *if Richard came to me, would I give in? Yes, yes, I would. It wouldn't be hard with these feelings inside. Is it loved? -—Or the thought of someone being kind to me.—Or it could be just a simple case of finding out if he were truly like the man in my dreams.* I leaned back in my chair facing the reality. *Maybe I do need to rethink my priorities.*

"To hell with Bill! You can leave him anytime. It wouldn't be too difficult.—Or has he finally beaten you into submission?" Asked Beth snapping me out of my train of thought, becoming just as angry. The smile had disappeared.

"I don't want to talk about this anymore! This is ludicrous. No one has beaten me into anything! I can do what I want when I want! Bill has no ties on me. Subject closed. Let's don't go there Beth. I don't need this right now, "my eyes hard and cold from the slap I had just received from my dearest friend. I cleared my throat," Besides, I better get dressed if we're going out."

Beth yelled into the bathroom as I washed my face, "Hey, why don't we go back to see Anna. Maybe she could shed some light on this. How does that sound?"

"No, I don't want to see her again. She knew way too much about me. It gave me the creeps. I don't understand why you want to see her again."

"I was thinking … "

"Well, *that* could be dangerous." I laughed.

"Very funny. Maybe she can give us a different perspective on the subject. It couldn't hurt. You've been through quite a bit in just a few days. I don't know what you are worried about. There isn't anything she could say that could hurt you.—If you don't want it to."

"—What? Truth hurt?—Yeah, right!" I commented rudely.

"Well, are you going to ring the doorbell or are you getting cold feet again?" Asked Beth pushing me towards the door.

"Okay! Okay, I'm ringing the damn bell! Now back off and quit being so pushy! I mean, how do I let you talk me into these things?" Taking a deep breath, I rang the bell. *What is there to be afraid of? Just some woman who knows me better than me, that's all.*

Anna answered the door and lead us back to the same room. "Well, I'm glad you called. It seems quite a lot has happened in the past few days, Kate."

"You can say that again. I thought you would be away on your trip?"

"It was suddenly canceled. Things happen for a reason. There are no mistakes, Kate. When it's time for one to awaken to who they are, it happens quickly. It's funny how the Divine intervenes when it becomes necessary."

"Now what do you mean awaken?" I was rubbing my forehead trying to fight back the headache all of this was giving me.

"To put it simply, the Soul has an alarm clock set within the body. When something of major importance is supposed to happen, it goes off? In this body there are certain agreements you made, before you came to earth, you have to keep. You cannot get out of these agreements. So, the Soul puts you in touch with those who are able to assist you when the time comes. Like Beth, she awakened first and was able to be there for you. If she hadn't, someone else would have been provided."

"And what is it I am supposed to do that is so damned important my Soul planted this alarm clock thing into my body?" I demanded.

"What you are supposed to do from the very beginning. Become enlightened. To work with the light that you hold within … Become lighter,—happier. Bottom line Kate, to love yourself."

I sat there speechless. I couldn't argue that point. I really didn't like myself very much.

I took a long look at this person sitting across from me, staring into those beautiful blue eyes that sparkled when she smiled. I felt good around her. How could I not trust her? I began to calm down. "Okay, what does it take to make this connection with my Soul? I thought with *It* just being there,—it was automatic."

"To a point, yes. But you must understand the Soul also understands the body can make its own decisions. If the body doesn't want to follow the Soul's path, the Soul will not interfere. It can get very complicated. You see the more enlightened you become, the more responsibilities you have. Some arrive here knowing what they are supposed to do. They come knowing they have great tasks. Like Buddha or Christ Jesus. The Mother Mary knew what her purpose was before she arrived and was reminded by Angels when the time came. We all have different ways we are awakened to what we are here for. It can be very difficult to sort out with all the "stuff" that is happening around us. Souls understand there will be a lot of conflict, now more than ever for us to dredge through in order to get back on the corrected path. The one thing we cannot forget, we put *all* the conflict here ourselves."

"So how do we get started with all of this?" I asked.

"I know this all sounds very complicated, so I will start you off by saying, begin with small meditations. You have to begin by making a connection within. Through meditation, you can accomplish this. Beth, you can show her how to do this ... "

Anne continued," You both, are about to embark into a wonderful journey, one the two of you agreed upon in the beginning. Before your births, each of you agreed to assist each other with certain tasks. From lifetime to lifetime one has been the carrier of this deed. However, in this one, it will take the both of you to assist each other. There is a lot of ground and clearing each of you has to do to get to a certain point spiritually in this life. Right now, Beth is here as your strength until you regain yours; in return Beth will gain spiritually. While on this journey, you must understand, everything, no matter what happens, is related to spiritual growth. *This* is the only reason why we are here."

"You keep talking about a journey, what does that really mean?

Are we going somewhere? What?" Now totally confused by all of this talking in circles.

"You have been on a journey since birth. Although not necessarily doing what you want, or where you want to,—you've still been on one. Right now, your Soul has said, 'Time to change course,'—and you are."

Angry by her comments about my past. Remembering the childhood pain. Knowing no one could have possibly asked for that my hand came down upon the table striking it hard as to give away my thoughts, "And how is that?" I asked.

"You *are* here, aren't you?" She smiled. "Not by choice." I answered glaring at Beth.

"It doesn't matter how you got here Kate, just that you did. People find enlightenment in the strangest ways. For instance, every day we see one who is in prison finding God—right? Everything we do leads us to a path that should be enlightenment. Not everyone chooses to go that route. Fear sets in and they have become comfortable in the lives they have created." Anne looked into my eyes, then into Beth's, "The two of you were sisters in many lives, are about to discover quite a bit about yourselves. Some you may like, and some you may not. Facing these things about yourselves will be the most difficult. Your friendship will be tested. In the end, you will understand what was being tested."

I was afraid to ask, "That will be?" "Your faith."

"My faith.—In what? Myself, others, what?" Now totally flustered. "Everything, especially, yourself Kate.—You too, Beth," pointing to Beth. "Me? I have a lot of faith in God and in everything around me!" Exclaimed Beth.

"You lack faith in yourself, Beth. You push men away from you. You really don't trust them. You use your intelligence to frighten them, making them believe you don't need anyone around to help you in anyway. There is one who would love to get closer but is afraid to." Anna looked deeply into your eyes yet in her calm soft voice.

"I'm not that way. I'm out going.—That's all. If this guy is that afraid of showing himself, that's his problem. I don't want anyone who is that afraid around me." Beth pouted. I knew she didn't like being cornered. I quietly sat back and listened, grateful that it was not me for a change.

"Beth, you are very much afraid for someone to see inside of you. Very deep inside you is this tiny little girl who wants to be loved. She wants to have someone who is her equal to show this side. You can be very loving and gentle, but you keep that part hidden to prevent anyone from breaking your little girl's heart. You have built a huge wall around her. This wall is your brashness and 'out going' you portray."

"Well, it's a tuff world out there you know. I don't have the time to weed out all the jerks," Beth answered wryly.

"Point taken. In return, I will state, what you put out there—you get in return. The men, who are attracted to you, are exactly what you reflect. If you want someone loving and understanding to come to you—my dear you will have to allow that to shine through. There are some men out there you have spent some wonderful lives with. They only understand 'loving' energy, not this brass one; so, they aren't searching." She shrugged and continued, "Except one. He sees through this and, until you are ready, he will not make his move."

"So that's why I've attracted Bill?" I interrupted, "Because I still have the "I hate me" feeling and since it is obvious Bill doesn't like himself, we became attracted to each other?"

"Yes, Kate! You understand! See these cards? Because you have some very important Karma to clear up, it is time for you to take your sword in hand Kate and banish it forever. She held the Queen of Swords between her fingers. As you can see, you will be triumphant."

"And the other card? The Nine of Swords that lies underneath?"

"It shows you still worry about everything, though you have the world," chuckled Anna. "There are some incredible things you are going to find out, just remember, they are all illusions.—Everything is. You will find a way to move in and out of them,—in the end you'll find yourself."

"Why can't you just tell us, so we get this over with? What are we supposed to do?" I asked in a tumultuous tone. I had enough of this going around in circles; I need the saving bullshit. I wanted answers. I looked at Beth who stared at Anna with the same question on her lips.

Beth finally spoke, "And who is this guy you keep talking about? Do I know him?"

"Yes, you do know him, he has been around you for some time. You only think of him as a friend. He has loved you from afar.—And to your question Kate, a teacher will be provided when you ask."

"You mean that lady in Arizona." I casually replied.

"Could be, there are many. It depends on what you want to do. I believe you and Beth have a lot of things to discuss at length, before you can decide what needs to be done.—Or, as it has happened to you recently, a way will be shown, one way or another. No pun intended," laughed Anna.

I sat in deep thought, I said under my breath, "I just wanted to know what most people wanted, how long will I be married? Any children in the future ... You know basic stuff. Not that my whole world was going to be turned into my own living nightmare."

"You've been living in a nightmare most of your 'lives,' now it is time to wake up and live in the glow of what life is truly supposed to be. I know this is great deal of information to take in. Just review the tape as you need it and take it in smaller amounts. Quite a few people are going through this right now.—You were not singled out ... It happened to me."

The ride back home was quiet. I know the same thing was going through Beth's mind that was going through mine. *What the hell just happened?*

"This person ... I've known for a long time, is Mike. Is it Mike, Kate? Asked Beth breaking the silence.

"Is what Mike? Oh, what the hell ... I can't keep anything from you. Yes Beth, it's Mike. He has loved you for a very long time and like Anna said, he has been afraid to say anything to you because of the way you treat him."

"How do I treat him? I'm always nice to Mike," defended Beth.

"You are ten years older than he is. You treat him like a little brother. He is concerned you will hold your age difference against him. You know Mike, he's shy." I said.

"Yeah, he is rather shy. Kind of odd for a hockey player isn't it?" Laughed Beth.

"You'd think so. You should see him on the court; he's in another world. It's as though nothing else exists."

"The age doesn't bother me so much. I've just never thought of Mike in that way. I really don't even know him. Whenever he's around, he doesn't say much … Hmmm …, Maybe I know why now, don't I?" Beth smiled and winked.

"Now that you know, what are you going to do?" I asked.

"I'm not sure. First things first. We need to get ourselves in order. Let's get you started with meditation," answered Beth.

"You know how to meditate? And you argue that I keep things from you. How long have you been doing it and how are you going to get me started?"

"Well, first we're going to a store I know, to get you a couple of books and a couple of tapes for your listening pleasure. oh … I've been doing it for about fifteen years. I did and tried everything. I believe I have finally settled into a way that suits me best."

It wasn't long before we pulled into an interesting little store. I remembered driving by this place before, but never took any notice. I guess if it didn't have a dress with sales sign on it, there wasn't a reason to.

I've never been in a store like this before, I mean, there were all kinds of books, cards and such but this had a feeling to it. Almost mystical with little gifts of angels and gnomes. There were statues everywhere, everything one could imagine. A scent of incense lingered in the air. It was a pleasant place and I really enjoyed being there. The young girl who worked there looked like a misplaced hippie and was very eager to help us.

"Look, I know that I've never told you about this, but you never showed any interest whenever I brought up the subject. You were beginning to have a lot of Bill's opinions about religion."

"You're right about that. He'd have a fit knowing I was in here. So, the hell with him!" I said as I picked up a stone and checked it out.

"Interesting you'd pick up that stone," chuckled Beth. "Why? I thought it was pretty, that's all."

"If you say so. Let's pick up a few books that will explain what just happened to you—and me."

Beth seemed to know the place pretty well and before long she had several books for me to read on meditation and prayer. She also had one about past life and noticed I still had the stone in my hand. "Still have that crystal, Kate?"

Startled, "Yeah, I really like holding it. It's weird, since I picked up this—crystal? I feel a bit better, more relaxed. I doubt it was this rock." "Whatever," said Beth with the look of amusement on her face. "Oh, stop it! Let's get out of here. I'm hungry.—Are you?"

The girl at the counter expressed her opinion about the things we bought. It wasn't too difficult to get caught up in her enthusiasm. She finished ringing my things up, "Is this yours too?" She held up the crystal.

"Yeah, I guess I'll get it since it's up here." I turned and looked at Beth, "What?"

"Did I say anything? But if you are going to take that crystal home, I'll loan you a book explaining some things about that stone."

"Okay, okay. Anything. Let's get out of here. Where do you want to go for lunch?" My stomach was growling.

"Let's go to the Grill around the corner. Their food is good and fast. A huge burger sounds good about now."

Beth and I both were consumed in the new books and tapes when the waitress arrived at our table. I thought the waitress was going to high tail it out of there when Beth came out of her chair.

Startled, the waitress replied, "I'm sorry, I just wanted to get your orders. I can come back."

"No, please. We're ready. I'll have the mega burger and fries." Beth said in a more placid voice. She looked up from her menu, "What sounds good to you, Kate?"

We sat quietly feeling rather awkward, Beth started to laugh, "Look at us! Don't we look silly! Hell, I almost scared that poor girl to death. So, let's talk more about it, Okay? I know you have a thousand questions."

"Well, yes. Look, I'll read these books, but I don't think I want to believe all this stuff. I mean, it sounds crazy. Bill will think I've gone completely out of my mind.—If he should ever find out."

"Kate, listen. I know all this looks weird to you right now, but you must understand there is something around taking care of us."

"I do believe in God, but what does he have to do with this?" I interrupted.

"Everything! When you've read the book about illusions, you'll understand a bit more. Remember what Anna said, when you need a teacher, one will be provided."

"Well … I didn't ask and it seems to me, one is being thrown at me. I don't understand why it is all happening now."

"In way, you did. Seeing Anna left you open to the possibilities of rethinking yourself.—Like the way you live, Richard–Bill,—that sort of thing. You've had guidance and teachers since birth. They may not have been great teachers, but you still had them."

"I don't believe seeing someone like Anna, opens the opportunity for someone to come in and change my life. I don't remember any teacher while I was growing up, except in school."

"That's right, they were all teachers of some sort. Believe it. Or not, your mom and dad were also teachers. You needed guidance after birth, how to talk, walk, and those sorts of things. Yes, I know they weren't great teachers, I am just trying to show you they are all around. We just have to look. In everything we do, there is something to learn. The answers could fall from the sky."

"Right, I'm gonna grow wings and become an angel." I replied sarcastically.

"Watch what you say … The guys upstairs love to prove you wrong.

Kind of like teens.—Ya know? You go around believing they are one way and right out of the blue—who knew?" Laughed Beth. "Well, enough of this. I know there is way too much stuff to consider at this point. The main thing is, take it in at an even pace. You have a lot to consider. What do you intend to do about 'ole' Richard? He's made his move."

"I don't know what I'm going to do about him. I'm totally confused about all of this—especially him. Out of the blue ... He just pops into my life. And turns everything upside down," I said as I stole one of Beth's fries. "I need to go home and check the answering machine. Maybe he's called. No, he probably hasn't. See?—See what I mean? I was never like this with Bill. With him I was always sure. I mean. I didn't worry about things. Now that I think of it. There wasn't the excitement with Bill as there is with Richard. Richard makes me feel *so alive* inside. I feel I can do anything when I'm with him.—I mean for the short period,—I've—Oh, you know! I feel this other person inside who wants to emerge. To come out and take over! It's exhilarating!—It's scary. With Bill, I was always, I don't know ... I'm this quiet. Mousy person. I feel like a puppy who wants to please its master! Now, I am so frightened of him. Oh Jesus! What am I saying? What is happening to me?"

"It's called Awakening. You are discovering the other side of Kate. One who's been locked up for a very long time? I guess we both have a few things to reflect.—Your brother."

"We've talked so much about Richard—I completely forgot! Mike has never been one to run out and speak his mind unless it's completely safe. I guess we both shy away from pain. I don't know what you feel, but please understand, Beth, he's a really great catch. He'll always be there for you. I can speak from my own experiences. I don't know what I would have ever done without him. The two of you seem to get along pretty well. Hell, you guys love ganging up on me!"

Beth laughed, "Can't help it if you're such an easy target! Hmmm? Well, I will *definitely* have to look at things in a much different light! He and I will have to talk before any leaping into arms happens here!—That seems to be your flare—not mine!" She winked and laughed again, "Enough already! Let's get out of this place! Have you got any plans this evening? Let's do something ... I mean, if you haven't got *that* certain message."

"Sure, I'll go to Cliff's with you." I was eager to get out of there. "I'll go crazy waiting around for him to call. You know?"

"Yeah, let's hit the road. Lunch is on me. You don't mind if I wear something of yours? That way we don't have to stop by my place. I'll call Lisa from your place and tell her what's up. Pops will feed her."

"Fine by me. I know you're dying to get into my closet."

While Beth showered, I listened to the answering machine hoping Richard called. Just Bill. He'll be home tomorrow night. I *can't* wait. I became flushed from anger as I remembered what Anna told us this afternoon. *Do I want to believe this Karma junk?* Too many things to keep up with ... Too much to soak in all at once ... The one and only thing I was sure of, I hated my life the way it is now. I dreaded Bill coming home and having to put up with his shit all over again. He'll never change.—That was another thing I was sure of.

Would I go with Richard if he asked me? Kate, listen to yourself! Your married! If you don't like it,—leave. Yeah, yeah, yeah, you've heard this song and dance before ... It's an old speech ... Instant replay.—Have I been beat into submission? Mother was, and now I can't even look her in the eye because of the guilt I carry from my own damn mess. How can I stay angry with her, when I can't even deal with my own situation?

I shook my head to clear the thoughts and went into the bedroom to find Beth admiring my red dress. "No, you can wear anything but that one."

Beth spun around and laughed, "No, silly. I wasn't going to wear this, I believe you should. I think this is the dress for you to be wearing tonight. Be daring!" Exclaimed Beth.

"I am not trying to pick up any one, you know. I only kept this dress because ... Well, I just couldn't get rid of it. I look great in it. No matter what Bill says about it ... It's funny; he really did like me to wear it when we were dating. Now, he doesn't let me out of the house in something like this." I commented.

"He's become quite the prude. Hasn't he?—Go on Kate, wear it. It's just for fun."

The cat is gone for the evening ... Let's play!"

I held up the dress admiring it in the mirror, "What the hell.—Let's do it!" I squeezed into the dress and noticed I may have put on a pound or two since I last wore it. *Man! I don't remember the dress being quite this short!—Or this tight!*

Beth saw the look on my face, "Not bad, dearie. You're going to knock them dead!—Whew! Heads will turn!"

"I don't need to be turning heads, Beth." I said bluntly.

"Oh, who cares,—lighten up. Tomorrow you can go back to be the stick in the mud when Bill gets home.—Tonight, we're having fun! I'll wear the green one. It's not as daring as yours—with my tits, I can make anything daring!"

"Beth, with your tits, you can stop a bus!—What am I saying, I've seen you stop one!"

Beth huffed on her fingernails and rubbed them on her shoulders quite proud of her accomplishment, "Oooh yeah, I'm hot!"

I soon remembered why I quit wearing spiked heels. I will never wear them again no matter how great they made my legs look. I grabbed the edge of the bar to steady myself, noticing the bartender was looking at me strangely.

"You okay lady?" He snickered from the sight.

"Oh yeah, I'm fine. Slipped outside and almost broke my neck. I got stuck on that damn grating thing. Beth, stop laughing!—And you with the smirk on your mouth, I'll have a Canadian Mist straight up with a Coke back."

"You'll have?" He asked while admiring Beth.

"I guess I'll have a Margarita, on the rocks, no salt.—First rounds on me."

We took our drinks to the table and watched the crowd for a while. "Well, what do you suppose we are to do? I sure can't pick up somebody—even if you do." My stomach started to feel like butterflies were dancing around in it. I tried to ignore them.

"You amaze me. For one thing, I guess *you* do have someone to meet here." She pointed across the room where Richard stood ... Staring at me.

Startled, "How did he know I was here? Did you know about this, Beth?"

"Hey, remember, I only found out about you two this morning. I need another drink. Wouldn't you know it? I came here to look for a guy ... And you ... you of all people have one ready and waiting. Go figure."

"I meant while I was in the shower, Beth.—Look, he's headed this way." I was in a panic; the butterflies in my stomach weren't helping the situation.

"Kate, what's wrong with you? Didn't you expect him to come this way when he saw you? I sure as hell did. Come back from wherever you are,—Earth to Kate ..."

That was the last thing I heard Beth say. My eyes were on *him*. The nervousness subsided as he got closer. My senses were on alert. I could smell his cologne. I got up from my seat and moved toward him. The pull was too great. It didn't matter to him, more than half the women in the bar had their eyes on him. I was his only focus.

"Red becomes you, Kate." His eyes moved over my body as He spoke.

"Thanks, you don't look too bad yourself." I looked into my drink. I couldn't look at him. "I thought you were angry with me."

"No. Why?"

"You didn't call today. I thought ..."

"No, it's nothing like that. I had to have some time to think. You aren't the only one that is going though stuff.—Looks like you need another drink. Bartender, another for the ladies.—Besides, I called you several times today, but you weren't home. I didn't think it was a wise idea to leave a message.—Remember Bill?"

My heart did a flip-flop at the thought of him trying to call. *Was*

I relieved to know this? Man, am I that crazy? What is this hold? I must be out of my mind to forget he couldn't leave a message. Wake up Kate. "You're right, thanks."

Before I could say another word, Beth chimed in, "Thanks for the drink. By the way, how did you know we were here?—And I'm Beth. You remember the person you almost ran over in Kate's driveway?—Hi."

"I didn't know. I remembered one of the guys at work mention this place was a regular hang out. So, I took a chance. I guess it was a good chance." He turned to Beth, "Hi Beth, I'm Richard. Yes, I do remember you. Sorry about that. It seems I was a bit distracted at the time. I hope you can forgive me."

"You can try to run over me any time. I mean … Well, you know … I think I'm starting to look like a fifth wheel, so I'll just mosey along and see what's out there." She disappeared into the crowd. It didn't take Beth too long before she snagged someone and was on the tiny dance floor. Nope, Beth wasn't the shy one. The guy didn't know what hit him.

We sat at the table feeling a bit uneasy when Richard finally spoke, "I know this is happening way too fast for you Kate. Believe it or not, it's a bit fast for me, too … I guess it's what I asked for."

"Wh-what do you mean, you asked for this?"

"Well maybe–not– well, Kate, it's not easy to explain."

"After what I have been though the last few months … No even days—try me." I sat back in the chair and prepared myself for what he was about to say.

"I guess the best place to start is the beginning; as long as I can remember, I've had these dreams …" He paused, looked into his drink, trying very hard to get the next words out. "They were always about a woman I made the most passionate love to." He cleared his throat and continued, "After having them for a while, a friend directed me to books about dreams and through them I learned how to work with these dreams." He stopped abruptly from the look on my face. "Kate, I know this sounds crazy, I hope you'll let me finish."

"No, it doesn't sound so crazy." I said as calmly as I could. A nervous breakdown would be apropos right about now.—*Right* in front of him.

Yep, I've gone crazy. Can this be possible? "Please, I'd really like to hear more."

With a sigh of relief, he continued, "I later advanced my learning to meditation and started talking to *you*, bringing *you* into a better view. About three years ago ... Yeah, about three years, that's when I saw your face. But you wouldn't give me your name. I guess I wasn't ready for that yet. So ... To make a long story short ... The next thing I knew, I ended up here working with Bill."

"It's strange how things work out, before I met you at the party, I really met you at the office. You must have stopped by to pick up Bill for lunch or something. I started to get this prickly feeling on the back of my neck, (As he rubbed the back of his neck) I turned around and there you were, talking with Bill. The feeling stayed with me until you left the building. I was grateful you left as soon as you did. I don't think I could have handled the feeling for too much longer ..." He cleared his throat, "Thinking back ... When Cannon approached me about the transfer, I got that feeling ..." He nervously downed his drink and with an indifferent tone, "I know when you are close, it is overwhelming ... I have been told when you meet your flame, there is no question about it. One may not be as aware, but when the two are together,—look out!" He chuckled as though this was something quite comical. Who in their right mind would ever believe this fabrication?

I gulped down my drink and ordered another. I could not believe what I was hearing. *He was having my dream.* This could very well explain why I felt so ill on my wedding day. I mean I never got ill after the dream ... Only on my wedding day. Could I have been forewarned?—*No, don't be silly* ... I couldn't look him in the eye. It was like getting caught. I had to look up. I had to do something ... "Wh-where is that bartender? They are never around when you need them." I softly chuckled.

"Did I say something wrong?" Richard ran his fingers through his hair, "What am I saying? I just told you—*and I* find it very difficult to believe! I'm sure you think I should be put away for even telling you this … Honest, Kate, you must understand, ever since I found out this wasn't just a dream, I have asked and prayed for this opportunity to be with you. It has been granted …" With a long pause … "And now I feel if I don't tell you everything—there won't be another chance. There were times I felt so desperate not knowing you personally. You were only a dream … I have compared others to you. What I feel for you may sound so utterly crazy; I couldn't and can't help it … I had to believe that maybe—just maybe I'll be with you … I hope I haven't upset you to much—you look rattled." He reached out and took hold of my shaking hand, lifted it to his lips … as he kissed it, I felt an electrical spark run through my fingers.

"Richard!" Clearing my own throat while jerking my hand from his grasp, "It's not you." I–I … "You see, I've had the same dream most of my *life*." Startled, it was now his turn to look at me in disbelief. "You're not the only one with dreams." I laughed softly, tears now filling my eyes … not knowing why; I shook my head hoping this would shake the tears back into my head, "I've had them for a very long time. Now that I remember, it was about three years ago when I first saw your face. Why do you suppose this happened? I mean, why then? Why not sooner? "Sadly, If I had only known …"

"Kate don't worry. Now that I know … No. I can't let anything happen to you. It drives me crazy to know Bill is such … If he ever touches you again …" His voice changed from loving to disgust.

Somewhat returning to my senses, "Richard, this is ridiculous! I'm married to the guy. We have to face facts. I don't understand this connection. Someone tried to explain it to me earlier today. Maybe these are the challenges or tricks explained to me. I don't know. Maybe it's over my head." I looked into his eyes. The dream flooded my mind, I knew I could get lost in those deep brown eyes. He moved closer to me … Almost … Then it happened, the awkwardness. "I jumped up from the table … The drinks rushed to my head causing me to stagger just a bit. I held onto the table to steady myself, I guess we better do something,—want to dance?"

"Sounds like a plan to me," he replied in a resigned whisper.

My head was reeling from the drinks. For the moment, I was grateful for the slow dance, I could lean against him and it wouldn't be so apparent how drunk I was. *Oh Kate, when will you learn to eat first!* Flushed from the hat of the room with the heat flowing through my body, I leaned closer. Maybe it was the drinks loosening my fear allowing me to accept the fact I was in love with Richard. I felt myself letting go, holding him tighter. His cologne filled my senses. My arms guided themselves slowly around his neck bringing my face closer to his neck. I instinctively began pressing my lips softly on the side of his neck. Richard's face dropped forward, just caressing the side of my face, a soft moan escaped from his lips as he responded with light nibbling on the lobe of my ear. *(God, how did he know?)* His hands moved slowly downward over my body pressing the thin material against me until his hands rested carefully upon my waist. Resting as though his hands were waiting for me to respond and I complied with a moan of my own. Damn the room. It no longer existed for me and my world. Richard was my world for this very moment, and I became lost in his touch. A touch so light and sensual, I shuddered as his hands moved back up to the nape of my neck, the touch so light, so caring … I moved away from his neck, looked into his eyes. I could feel his heat, his want, my heart was pounding so hard I thought it was going to pound right out of my chest. My hands in return pulled Richard closer … Our bodies moving still to the music, his carefully placed hands. Holding me like a tiny puppet, guiding me, knowing I would follow him anywhere … Each of his steps in rhythm, as I followed so naturally … His lips ever so softly brushed against mine. He looked deeply into my eyes … I was dissolving in his arms when we came to an abrupt stop. I was mesmerized in that spot, lost in his trance. I would not have been surprised if the room heard my heart, the sound was pounding in my ears; I wanted him so badly, it was all I could to keep my hands right where they were. *Oh yes … oh God … whirled through my mind. This is the way love feels? I don't ever want to lose it!*

"No, Kate," He said with tears in his eyes.

"Wh-why not? Isn't this what you wanted earlier?—At the brook?—

Well, now ... I want it! I want you. Can't you see that?" Disappointed and stunned by his reaction to the point of being angry, I struggled to get away knowing if he let go of me at this moment I would fall to the floor.

He did not let go. He pulled me back into his arms and in a rough choked whisper, "Yes, my love. I want you more than you'll ever know," his head dropped, "N-not like this. How can I explain this to you? It's not just sex. ... It's all of you ... I don't want it this way. Okay?" He whispered in my ear. "I know you don't either." His fingertip lightly caressed my face as he panned the room for Beth.

Good 'ole' psyche Beth. She stood standing at the edge of the dance floor wide eyed and flabbergasted. Holding me against Him with one arm ... Richard motioned her over.

"Man are you guys fucking nuts? Bill hangs around this place! Kate, look at you girlfriend, man *are you* drunk.—Why in the hell did you allow her to drink so much?—Damn you men!" Beth grabbed my arm placed it around her shoulder and leads me to the door.

With a mock giggle, "Hey Beth ... "Girlfriend! How's it going?" Pushing my finger into her chest. "Hey! Don't get mad ... It's not his fault. Don't blame him. It was all mine ... Yeah, stupid 'ole' me ..." I stumbled and caught the edge of a stool to stop my fall, "Hell, he turned me down. I guess this red dress has lost its magic.—Not to mention these damned red shoes!—Shit! What was I thinking?" I kicked them off so I could stagger a bit easier leaving them behind. No reason to keep those ole bait catchers. Richard ran up from behind catching me as Beth gathered my shoes.

Beth looked at Richard and softened, "Sorry, it's just that I can't seem to trust anyone anymore ... Especially around her. She is so damn trusting. Please, help me get her to the car."

"Oh, yes. Poor little me. Little Pollyanna, Kate ... Isn't that what Bill called me? Yeah, little Pollyanna, too stupid to understand what's going on in this world ... She wishes for her dream world and lives in her own hell." I spun around and flopped into the car. I looked Richard in the eyes; "Do you believe I'm that pure? That ignorant? Do you believe I couldn't handle this?"

Richard said, "I give you a whole lot of credit, Kate, more than you'll ever know ... Good night my sweet, I'll talk to you tomorrow. Okay? We'll work this out. He kissed me softly and tried to close the door.

Before he could close the door, I grabbed his shirt by the collar pulling him into the car. "Don't you want me?" I pleaded desperately.

"You know I do," he said softly. "I'll talk to you tomorrow. Beth, drive her home safely. You're carrying precious cargo there ... I love you Kate," he gently closed the door and I watched him until he was out of sight.

"Well, girlfriend, you sure have gone and done it! What were you thinking? Of all places to fall into someone else's arms. Half the people in that place know Bill." Beth stopped when she saw the look of pain in my eyes."

Beth, he's had my dream ... And ... And I love him. I can't help it." I cried into my hands, "What am going to do? I'm stuck. I'll never get out of this relationship with Bill ...

He'll never let me go. Oh God, please help me." All I could do was sob into my hands, feeling lost, truly lost for the first time in my life.

Beth patted my shoulder and said softly, "Lie back, sweetie and I'll get you home.

No need talking about it until morning."

I woke next morning with a slight headache. It could have been worse. Thank God for aspirins! Beth made me drink six ounces of water and two aspirins before I went to bed. One thing for sure, I'm a cheap drunk. I took a shower and wrapped myself in my robe. I decided to get dressed later. I had a few things to do before Bill got home. I found myself wishing for my period, so I had an excuse to push Bill away. He hated to come near me at that time ... Oh well, nothing I could do about it now. I went to the kitchen to fix a light breakfast when the doorbell rang.

"Damn that Beth! Why can't she leave me alone?" I swung open the door ready to yell at her and to my surprise there stood Richard.

"You have every right to close the door in my face. I–I thought I could do the right thing, Kate, I wanted to leave—or even try to stay away—I needed to see you."

I stood still. I couldn't verbally answer. We spoke with our eyes. I walked within his embrace. "Kate," he whispered, "I've been waiting so long …" His face caressed mine as he lifted me with ease and carried me to the bedroom.

My robe fell open as he bent over to lay me onto the bed … As I lay there one hand softly caressed my breast as he opened my robe allowing it to fall away. His eyes never wavered from mine. His warm wonderful body pressed close to mine, kissing me deeply. I caught up in his scent. My dreams became reality. His kisses were like fire on my skin.

Passion filled my body in response to his knowledge of what pleased me. I naturally responded to his touch knowing what he would enjoy. My mind and body were filled with him. His hands knew where and how to touch … I moaned deeply. His fingertips ran lightly over my body causing the tiny hairs to rise and fall with my breathing … He lovingly watched my body arch upwards towards his as he continued to play with me … His hand slid slowly over my body, my now flat tummy, making its way lightly to the top of my mons … I shuddered by his control over me. My body excited, welcoming this long-lost love. A love it had been craving for a very long time.

A soft long moan slipped through my lips, my eyes just barely closed, yet not completely; I did not want to miss a single move or gestured from his strong willing hands. Those skillful hands moved ever so gently over my mons, slightly spreading my very wet lips; smiling as though he approved of this. His finger slipped quickly into me as his lips lightly nibbled my deep caramel nipples. Pleasures that brought me day after day into the shower wanting more of him … Now finally, enjoying me as I surrendered myself to this man who was never a stranger to me.

I cried out in passion, my body lunging my breast into his mouth as his fingers devoured me … He looked up for a moment, smiled, and continued his sensual torture. My fingers ran through His hair finally pulling him toward me, needing him so badly. I thought I was going to go out of my mind with passion … Nothing. Nothing on this earth prepared me for this moment. Not even my dreams. For in my dreams the passion was a yearning. This I knew now. Because now he was here … real so real. The imagination could not feel this passion. This lost passion he and I have always had. I did not realize I was sobbing in his arms. Begging for him to allow me this ancient release.

Richard moved his face from my breast and his fingers from deep within me, pulling his body over mine. I could not feel his weight. My passion flooding my senses and overwhelmed by his devouring kisses seemed so natural at the time. My legs spread wide and lifted as his member embed deeply within me with a fast hard thrust. Richard arched upward with a deep gasping moan. The moan of pleasure so deep my legs responded the welcomed by wrapping over his hips. "Oh God. … Kate … You … are so … it was never like … Ooohhh …"

I knew, I knew his thoughts his feelings, my hands grasping about his hips pulling him deeper within my wet folds …" Yes Richard … oh please … I cannot … Oh God Please … "I cried in a deep guttural tone. My legs fell from his hips and firmly planted themselves upon the soaked sheets. Our bodies rocked in unison, the rhythm continued until our bodies quaked for the final moment we worked so passionately for. Yes, we were as one—now and forever. This was so different—so passionately gentle—so caring. This is what love was supposed to be, responsive to each other's needs and the want for more. The reward for our union, our insatiable spirit was swept into a climax encompassing each of our body's. It was as though the vital force was transferred directly from one body to the other. Grasping each other as the waves of orgasm flowed through us.

I reached out and touched his face, bringing his face to mine as he emptied deep within me. I softly chuckled as a splattered from a tiny bead of his sweat dripped into my eye … causing his to giggle and slip out of me. I groan from the feeling of him no longer within me. Richard slipped his arms around me and whispered, "I love you, Kate ... now and forever ... "

I lay beside him listening to his soft, rhythmic breathing as he kissed me tenderly on my head. "Kate, I love you so much," he again whispered.

"I know," pulling myself up from his chest so I could get a better look at his face. I placed my finger on his chin and looked deep into his eyes. It was so much like the dream; a shiver went down my spine.

He pulled me close, covering me with the sheet. "Cold, baby? I'll keep you warm," he teased. I laughed lightly and pushed away from him to get up. "Where do you think you're going? I'm not finished with you," he growled trying to wrestle me back into the bed.

"I'll be right back. I'm thirsty, want something?" I mused.

"No, don't leave me yet," playfully pulling me back into bed, rolling on top to pin me down. It was wonderful to react with delight to his touch. His scent was intoxicating. His taste was delicious.—More, please more, I never wanted this to end.

I played with his hair as I watched him sleep, studying his face still in disbelief of this reality. Soon I'll wake up and this would fade into the recesses of my mind waiting to haunt me another night. Were we so much alike? Yes, our eyes were so much alike, but is that where we stop? Our love making was so incredible, where I would stop, he would begin, and the connection was continual. I kissed him softly and got out of bed still looking at him in a dream state.

While putting on my robe, the phone rang. *Let the answering machine get it ...* —And as if a snake had come up from its coil within the pit of my stomach ... I stood frozen, clutching my stomach, listening to Bill's message. He was returning earlier than he previously thought. I turned on one foot hoping Richard had not heard, dismayed to see Richard standing in the doorway; and from the look on his face, I knew he heard it too. An old fear crept though my body and this reality came flooding back. Panic started to set in. Richard walked up from behind cradling me in his arms. He whispered in my ear,

"Kate, please, honey, you know you have to leave. Come with me, I'll take care of you."

He'll take care of me ... ripped through me like a knife. Bill said he'd take care of me ... Even made me quit my job. What is it, they believe only they can make my life better? Kate what is wrong with you? It was like my ego was fighting with me. My mind in a huge debate as the man I loved held me. A man I have been waiting for such a long time ... And I knew deep within my mind ... I knew ... I can't allow this to happen again, although I love this man more than life ...—I could not. I did not know why, but I knew I could not.

I pulled away from Richard, turned around and with the tiny bit of strength I could muster, "Richard ... "Taking a deep breath, "Listen to me. You know how I feel. I don't do this sort of thing,—You know—Jump into bed with every great looking guy that turns my world upside-down—isn't on my agenda. You have to understand I just can't run off with you no matter how bad it is here. If-If I don't start standing up for myself, what good am I to be for you?—Even me."

I gathered my hair pulling it away from my tear stained face looking defiant, "Beth asked if I had been beaten into submission. Well, maybe then ... But not now. Richard, I have to heal myself if we are going to be any good for each other ... No. You'll have to leave ... Without me."

"Kate! I can't just leave you here –with—this mad man! No! I won't do it!" Richard was beside himself with grief.

"Yes, you will! And *you will* understand I have to do this. Damn it, Richard, there may be someone else out there for you," I choke down the lie. "Please! You have to leave ... If I can do this ... You can ... Please ... Leave." *Before I return to my senses and run away with you. God, please make him listen! I can't bare this! Legs, hold me up!*

"Kate, please ... Listen to reason,—I love you. I–I don't want anyone else! You know damned well there is NO one else!" he pleaded in desperation.

"Now, please get dressed—and leave," I tried to keep my voice from faltering and from the depths from within found a cold cruel firm tone.

"We seemed to have forgotten—*I* am married." Somewhere my voice faltered and softened, "I don't know how long it is going to take for me to heal this mess. It's not fair for me to ask you to wait. I do know this much, if you hang around, Bill will find out and *God,* I don't even want to think about that. Please do this for me."

The look on his face was devastating. The pain in his eyes almost brought me to my knees. I couldn't look at him. *Please God, make him understand.* I prayed frantically, *please let him go.*

"Forgotten you're married? What do you think keeps me up nights? I'm livid at the thought you're with someone else.—And *this* is all I have?" He yelled aloud. "I almost lost it when I first saw you, a-and when my secretary informed me you were married!—*Do you* have any idea what I went through? I have searched for you for so long and,—and when I do find you,—you are beyond my reach ... To– to go to bed at night and know you are in someone else's arms?—Kate, please! For the love of God, please don't do this to me!" He looks whipped. I had delivered the final blow taking the wind from his heart.

My knees grew weak. Something inside held me there, immobile to do my heart's desire. I was mentally reminded I would still have to face all of this mess with Bill. *You can make it as difficult as you want,* kept running through my mind. I later remembered, I picked one hell of a time to stand for my convictions.

I watched painfully as he slowly he dressed. Before he left, he held me close and said, "Kate, I'll leave if that's what you want. Just please, don't make what we did dirty in your mind. Please. It wasn't. I will not stop loving you. I will not rest until you are where you belong,—By my side. I love you, Kate." He kissed me gently one last time. I clung for his scent one last time, breathing deeply as though my heart would stop if I couldn't feel or taste him. I reluctantly let go and he left.

I sank into my favorite chair and cried for hours. *Would I ever see him again? What have I done? What if I never hear from him again? Why did I let the only thing that would ever give me happiness go out the door? My body shuddered from the memory of his touch. Remember him? How will my body ever forget that tender touch? I* have never felt so alone.

Finally, I drug myself from the comfort of my chair and got ready for Bill's arrival. I knew I would never be the same again. The very fact of making love with my husband would become even shallower than ever.

CHAPTER SIX

It's Christmas!—Show's Over!

It was quite some time before I could get back into a routine and not have Richard constantly on my mind. Beth thought I was going to go mad. I even pretended to be ill on the day of the company picnic so he wouldn't confront me. I knew my awkwardness would tip Bill to something. Thank God for my migraines. Beth hung around like a good friend and stayed with me while I was "ill."

Enough time passed, it seemed like a dream … Like it never happened. I was curled up in my favorite chair with Jazz purring in my lap, warming my hands on my cup of rose tea while quietly watching the snow. I was startled from my thoughts when Beth barged in, "Hey, girlfriend, how's it going? Picked up your mail …" A sweet smirk crossed Beth's face. I could not help but smile. "Any more of that tea ready?—Hey! Don't get up, I know my way around," she chimed dropping the mail in my lap and disappeared into the kitchen.

After making all the noise she possibly could in the kitchen, she returned with a cup of tea and her usual side order of toast. "Hope you don't mind. I'm starved.—What's up, Kate, you look terrible!" She glanced from me to the letter I was holding in my hands. Her eyes turned from sparkles to a look of deep concern; "The news must be pretty bad. Talk to me, Kate."

"It's a letter from Richard," I muttered.

Stunned, Beth sat in the chair across from me. "Man, has he got balls or what? Bill could have seen that. What could the boy possibly be thinking?"

"No. The way he sent it was pretty cunning," I replied numbly. "It appears "the boy" was listening to me after all."

"Well … Are you going to sit there and stare at it or tell me just how damned smart this *boy* is," demanded Beth.

"It's not too difficult to understand." My fingers traced the return address as I spoke, "Richard was on his way back to Toronto and took a side trip to Flint. He stopped by Mom's to see Mike and while there, dropped me a line. Mike must have been aware of what he was doing because the envelope is in Mike's handwriting. They both knew Bill wouldn't take any interest in what Mike had to say, especially since they had words the last time, they were together. Richard felt safe knowing Bill would never question me about it."

"Cool! Got to give him credit. The boy knows how to use his head. So, *what* did he say?"

All I could do was hand her the letter.

> Kate,
>
> I haven't seen or heard from you since you asked me to leave. I have tried my best to let you go, but I found it totally impossible. You must understand, there is also my side to think about. I don't take love lightly. I didn't go to bed with you just to get laid. I know you know this in your heart. I had to say it … Kate, I-I am so lost …
>
> I've known about you for such a long time, even before we physically met. There were even times I could pick up your scent and now that I have found you, I'm pushed away.
>
> —Don't you realize, whatever you go through,—I know? Now more than ever since we have deeply made the connection, we are as one now and nothing can come between us. I am not telling you this just to drive you crazy, even though there are times I feel like walking into

your home and dragging you away from that ass. Yes, I do realize it would make matters much worse, making me no better than Bill.

I don't know how much longer I can maintain my cool not being able to touch you. I have asked for a transfer back to Toronto. I can't take it anymore. You can relax and not concern yourself about avoiding me. I realized this when you did not show at the Company picnic.

I do understand you are trying to put things in a proper perspective, it just isn't easy doing it knowing how I feel about you.

There is one more thing you need to know. I wanted to tell you before you found out some other way. Maggie is meeting me in Toronto. For some reason, Bill believes we are made for each other. It also appears she has more plans for me than I am willing to accept ... I have thought it though and realized this wasn't too bad of an idea to keep Bill from getting any other kind of ideas about us. I know this makes me sound as much of a cad as Bill, but I truly believe Maggie is doing this to see if she can conquer me as another one of her trophies. I had to do something fast, there was some talk about the incident at the bar that night. I told Bill you tried introducing me to Beth, but she already had her eyes on someone else.

I made sure you got home all right because Beth found her "date" for the night. He seemed satisfied with my explanation and proceeded to plant Maggie on me.

I really don't know what else to say to make things better. I love you Kate and will wait no matter how long it takes. Please be careful. No telling what Bill is capable of. I will kill him if he hurts you! I swear! Kate, darling please ... Please remember,

You my dear, are my love. I love you,

Richard

"Whew! Can the boy write a letter or what! I'm even in love with the guy!" Beth turned away to wipe her eyes. Then turned with a very dispassionate look, "Now, the million-dollar question is,—what are *you* going to do?"

I sat mesmerized in the chair. My fingers digging deeply into the arms. A low growl came up from the pit of my stomach and the glare in my eyes matched. "Damn that Bill! Why can't he mind his own *fucking* business?"

I hit the chair so hard causing Jazz to leap from my lap scratching me. "Shit!—Damn cat!" I began to cry as I inspected the tiny scratch.

"Wow! What a mouth! I don't believe I have ever heard those words come from your prim and proper mouth! Mine, yes,—but yours? By the way, the cat didn't hurt you that bad, so don't take it out on him …" Beth cooed at Jazz, "Come here puss …" Once Jazz was purring from Beth's loving attention, her attention sternly turned back to me, "Now, get a grip, Kate. This *is* what you wanted.—Isn't it?—Or are you facing the big denial once again? You told me things were going to change,— *But* all you've done is mourn for Richard since you threw him out. You act like he's dead or something. This isn't right, Kate and it definitely isn't healthy. How much longer are you going to keep up this charade with Bill? As far as he's concerned, you two are one big happy family! My God Kate, you are even going to counseling with him!"

I was crying uncontrollably. I didn't know what I was going to do. I hated myself so much at the moment, killing myself seemed like the only decent way out.

Reading my mind, Beth responded, "Killing yourself isn't the answer, Kate. You'll just have to come back and do it again. Maybe next time, it will be a *whole* lot worse. So come to your senses, and let's talk about it. There are other options."

I held my head up and asked with a spiteful tone, "And just what are these *"options"* I have? My life stinks. You know that."

"Well, the first thing you can do, is stop behaving like a damn baby and feeling sorry for yourself. Do something with this letter before Bill finds it or you won't have to worry about suicide,—Bill will kill you …

And second, go change so we can get you out of this house. You can't get it any cleaner, hell, the dust is afraid to enter!" Chuckled Beth.

"You're right as always … Maybe we got it figured out all wrong."
"Got what 'wrong'?" Mused Beth.

"*You* are my knight in shining armor,—not Richard." I softly chuckled getting up from the chair and heading down the hall.

"Well, my lady," Beth bowed deeply, "I seem to have the wrong equipment for any kind of knight, and I'm not fond of women. Not in *that* way. So, I guess we will have to settle for Richard. Besides, sisters are supposed to step in when needed and Kate, we've been sisters for a very long time. Now off with you and let's get the hell out of here."

I opened my closet and from deep within I pulled from my secret hiding place the box which held everything I kept away from Bill's eyes, including the tapes from Anna. Bill would never suspect a shoe box since it seems I have to have every shoe I find in the store. So, what's one more? I gently placed the letter on top of the books Beth picked out for me to read—still untouched along with the crystal stone.

Beth looked over my shoulder, "I knew you wouldn't read them. You weren't ready."

Bill walked in as we were about to leave, "Where are you two going? Oh, hi Beth."

"Hello, Billie–boy," said Beth smugly, "If you must know, I'm getting Kate out of the house and to a restaurant."

"That's nice," said Bill half listening to her, turning to me, "Kate, we've been invited to Don's annual Christmas party. I am giving you enough advance notice so you can plan your headache for another time."

"Bill, I didn't plan that damn headache! You know I get them, but I'll be sure to put it on my calendar so between my head and I—we can have one hell of one started." I snapped.

"What an ass," said Beth under her breath.

"*Excuse* me?" Questioned Bill giving Beth a look of distaste. "I said, I'll pass," giggled Beth.

I gave Beth a wild look to back off and said, "Now you've gone and done it, Beth. You're invited. You can keep me company while Bill brown nose's Don." Beth giggled, "No prob. I'll be there."

Bill hit the counter top with his fist. I jumped and backed away. He glared at Beth as he turned to leave the room smacking open the door, "Fine, damn it. Have a nice lunch."

"Whew!" Shaking her hand in the air in her Italian fashion, "Is he pissed!" Laughed Beth.

"Not half as pissed as he's going to be when he gets home later … Oh, the hell with him … Let's go." I replied in disgust.

We sat in our usual places drinking hot cider and having a good time. "Hmmm, this is nice, we need to do this more often." I purred.

"Well, we would, if Bill didn't cringe every time I came over. He doesn't give you grief when I leave, does he?"

I shook my head no and smiled, "I don't really care what he thinks. It's kind of sad I look forward to you being there, so I don't have to deal with him.—That didn't sound right, I'm so sorry."

"It's all right. I understand. Me coming over isn't going to help your situation. We've got to think of something. What do you think about what Anna said? You know, go to Arizona and see that friend of hers?"

"Oh yeah, I can see it now … Bill, I'm going to Arizona to find myself. You know damn well what his response will be … Smack!— Right across the head. Does that picture look familiar?"

"Very funny. You know that's not the way I meant it. Think about it, okay Kate? You have to do something. I know you don't want to be Bill's punching bag forever … I really don't know how long Richard will be able to keep Maggie at bay."

The day of Don's Christmas party arrived. I was deep in thought when Bill rolled over pulling me close. I tried to pretend I was still asleep and wanted to be left alone. All of my moaning and groaning was to no avail. Bill was in an unusually good mood. He whispered in my ear, "Good morning my love, how did you sleep?" nibbling on my ear.

"Hmmm, not now Bill, I'm still trying to sleep," I moaned."

"Come on baby, it's been a while. I need some lovin'." He started caressing my breasts. "I miss making love to you Katie. Since our mishap, I've tried giving you some space … But you must understand—I *need you*. Please baby," he begged.

It's been difficult since Richard and doesn't help that I detest Bill. I hated pretending I enjoy it. I knew deep down it would be easier if I gave in. I have to. He must never have any idea what happened. The consolation prize, he'll be in a wonderful mood for the rest of the day. I gave in and returned his kiss.

Bill slapped my bottom as I stepped out of the shower. "Ouch! Bill,—Don't start!" I giggled. It wasn't so bad being around him when he was in a good mood. In fact, I really enjoy it when he was.

"I'm glad my baby doesn't have one of those headaches." I felt the pulse of an erection build as leaned against me. "Bill," I giggled softly,

"I have a lot to do before this boring party. Okay?" I tried squirming from him in a playful manner. I wanted him to believe I really wanted to be with him. "Beth should be here any minute to take me to the mall." I ran my finger down his chest, pushing him away and dashed to the bedroom. *No reason to feel guilty Kate, you have to survive—don't you.*

"Damn that Beth," said Bill under his breath. Then loud enough for me to hear over the running water, "Katie, it's not going to be a dull party.—*Trust* me!"

"What do you mean? What's going to make this party so special?" I was curious now. It always meant trouble when Bill kept secrets. Someone was sure to get a knife in their back.

"Nope, ain't gonna tell you," he said smugly with that smile, the cat who just ate the mouse look on his face, "I'm sure you'll be with Beth all afternoon. Be sure to be back here by 6:30. I don't want to be late."

"Sure, no problem." My mind was elsewhere while I dressed in jeans and sloppy a sweat shirt. No sense in getting dressed up yet with all the running around I had to do. Little did Bill know my running around was pretty much going to be limited to Cliff's most of the day. The doorbell rang and I raced down the hall while braiding my hair, "I'll get it. It's probably Beth."

"Man, it's colder than a witch's tit out there! I need to get refueled before we head out. Got any Jasmine tea?" Beth dumped her coat on the hook by the door and went straight to the kitchen.

I was right behind her. Bill was rubbing Jazz under his chin while talking on the phone, "No, I'll be in shortly. I don't have any intentions of staying long today Martha. Just leave those contracts on my desk and go home. I'm sure you have some things to do. I still have a few things to do before tonight.—Yeah, Bye." He winked at me and hung up the phone. "See ya, baby. I've got to go in for a few—then have to get some things done for the party." He planted a very loving kiss, "I'll see *you* later," he growled softly, "Hi, Beth, see you later," and was out the door.

"Seems to me you finally gave in and put out," said Beth hiding the smile by looking into her cup.

"Yeah, well shit happens!" I returned sharply. "Cliff's?"

"Sounds good to me. But isn't there anything else you want to do? I mean, what are you going to wear tonight? I don't have a damn thing. I would have been just as happy sitting in my warm apartment than listening to the bullshit going on at this party. You told me yourself they were a drag."

"I–don't–know. Bill said something was supposed to happen at this one."

"You've peaked my interest—go on!" Beth was leaning over the counter with her hand propping up her chin.

"Don't know.—You know how Bill loves to keep secrets. Especially when he can use them as bullets. I guess you'll have to find out along with the rest of us. You warm enough now? Can we go?"

"Man, Cliff's is crowded. Are you sure you want to hang around here?" Asked Beth.

"It's warm—right? Look, there's our table. They knew we were coming." I tossed my coat over the chair and waved to the waitress. "Want to eat or start our drunk now."

"Let's eat. I would like to wait a bit before the drunk part starts. I don't want to pass out at the party and miss all the fun," said Beth sarcastically.

We placed our order and were settling in for the day when Beth said, "Ah … Kate, I think there's something you should know. Don't turn around …"

"I hate it when people say that! What *is* it?"

"Bill is here, and he is not alone.—He's with Maggie," whispered Beth calmly. "What? Do you believe? What is going …" I couldn't believe what I just saw, "So that's the big surprise. Richard can't be here, I would know." "How? You haven't seen him in more than six months."

"You don't lose that. I would always know when he's here.—Damn that Bill! He knew they were going to be in town and deliberately didn't tell me just to see the expression on my face. Let's get out of here before they see us!" We grabbed our coats and slipped out unnoticed.

"Man, that was close! What was Bill doing with her? They were awfully close for my taste," said Beth.

"I sure as hell don't know, but I do have my suspicions! Damn it … Damn it! Damn it all! I hate that man! You can't trust him! I have had enough of this. You know what this means?—Don't ask." I walked in circles venting my anger, "I'll tell you what this means. It means Richard is here or will be tonight. If I didn't see these two together,—both Richard and I would have played as fools tonight for their amusement.—Damnit! I didn't think little 'ole' Maggie had it in her ... Well, two can play that game! I going to look drop dead gorgeous tonight; everyone will have to take notice. Which means ... I'll have to spend money. You need anything while we're out? It's on Bill!" I slammed the door on the car so hard I thought the windows were going to shatter.

"Ah ... Kate, please don't hurt my car. It's not much, but she's all I got, okay?" Asked Beth calmly.

"Sorry, let's get to the mall, I've got some money to spend," I said sternly.

The rage of this afternoon was still simmering within as I dressed. *How dare that bastard and that simpleminded bitch do this to me? What have those half-wits got up their conniving sleeves?* My hands were shaking so violently I could barely put on my makeup. I stood in front of my full-length mirror and observed how I was stunning in my winter white wool dress. It clung to my small shapely body. It set off my auburn hair, and to touch it off, I wore the pearls Mother gave me. "Yep, I'm going to turn heads tonight," I said aloud.

"Yes, you are," said Bill standing in the doorway.

"How long have you been standing there?" I demanded.

"I just walked in to the find this beautiful being standing before me! Katie, you are positively radiant!" Bill slid his arms around my waist and softly kissed the base of my neck. I allowed him feeling triumphant.

This anger seems to have created a new sensation within me. I felt positively wicked. "Bill, let's not get anything started." I pulled away, "Did you get what you needed done today at the office? I hope you didn't have to stay too long."

"Yes, I did. I was able to leave early and grab a bite at Cliff's."

"Cliff's? What a shame I didn't know about it. Beth and I talked about going there for lunch. I'm sorry you had lunch alone, we could have eaten lunch with you. Oh well, we decided against it and ate at the mall." I said as sweetly as I could without throwing up. The look on his face told me all I needed to know. *Dumb ass. He should have known better than to take that bitch somewhere I might have shown up.*

He deserves to squirm! The rage was stirring up again. I tried my best to control it and was relieved the doorbell rang. "That's Beth." I said sharply, "I'll see you in a bit."

Beth had on a simple black sleeveless dress. "I thought you'd let me wear that brocade jacket you bought last year. I thought I had something to go with this. Thank Bill for the dress!—What's eating you now? You look madder than your red hair. Has the show started? What have I missed?"

"*No,* the show hasn't started. I'll tell you in a minute. The jacket is in the bedroom closet. I need to see what master Bill is up to," storming back to the bedroom.

I returned with the jacket and handed it to Beth, "The jerk's in the shower. He's probably washing the scum off. I'm going to get a soda, want one?" Beth shook her head no as I poured. "My objective has changed. I want to be completely sober tonight. I want to be aware of everything that happens. He's not going to pull a fast one on me … I asked him what he did today. He told me he went to Cliff's. The kicker was me telling him *we* almost showed up there for lunch. You should have seen his face. It was priceless."

"This is a side of you I thought I'd never see. The lion kingdom better watch out!" Exclaimed Beth. "The Bitch is hot tonight!"

"Damn right. The lioness is out, and her claws are ready for action. Watch out folks, the Bitch is back." I flung my braid back and stood regally, laughing out loud.

Bill came into the room, "Well, I'm the honored one tonight," he said smoothly, "I will be escorted by two of the most beautiful women there. Let me help you with your coat Katie."

Bill playfully spun me towards him as he helped me with my coat, "You are beautiful Katie," he said softly, "Ready?"

I surprised him by lightly licking his throat and with a soft growl, "I'm ready."

As usual the proper hostess, Marion met us at the door, "Nice to see you again Kate, Bill,—and this is?" She asked in her usual monotone voice. My heart went out to her. How could anyone blame her facade? No doubt I would be that way living with Don and her two squirrelly kids. I'm sure over the years she became numb about everything.

"This is my best friend, Beth. She's visiting us for Christmas."

Beth smiled at Marion, "Nice to meet you. I hope that I'm not intruding."

"No, you are not! We love to have you! As Don would say, the more, the merrier," Marion responded in her same blank tone.

"Appears Marion has been hitting the sauce early," commented Bill under his breath.

"How can you tell? Well, maybe she has a reason to drink. It must be unnerving to have these damn things and have something happen at every damn one. She has no control over those kids."

"They are hardly kids," said Bill.

"You could have fooled me." I spat back. *Stay in control, Kate, or you'll ruin everything!*

"What does that mean—no control? I thought you said these parties were boring," insinuated Beth.

"Yes, they are, until the entertainment arrives. Everyone here looks forward to the kids showing up. If they do,—well who knows? Give it an hour—or sooner, you'll see. Unless Daddy Don gave them the riot act before the party.—And sometimes that doesn't even work. All you can do is sit back and wait for the show." I handed Bill our coats and made our way into the living room.

The house was beautiful as ever. Marion took great pains to meet everyone needs or anticipations. She spared no expense on the Christmas decoration and decor. She made sure her tree was bigger and brighter than last year. If you looked hard enough, one would expect a choir to jump out singing Christmas carols, all dressed in Dickens outfits … Man, this lady had way too much time on her hands. Servants were everywhere with enough food to feed the city. I took my place in line with Beth. I didn't get to eat this afternoon. I was way too angry. Now

I was starved. Again, the food was served in buffet style with the usual servants to assist you.

"Man, what a spread," exclaimed Beth. "Only the best for Don and family." "Well, is *he* here?" Whispered Beth.

"I don't know, I don't—Yes, he's here." The hair stood up on end on my arms and yes, there was that undeniable feeling in the pit of my stomach. I took care to make sure no one would notice my heart was breaking at the thought of knowing he was in the same room. I gathered my strength as Bill walked up behind me.

"I thought you ate earlier?" Asked Bill.

Startled, I turned around with a quick reply, "Don't want all this food to go to waste. Besides, I want to get something in my stomach should I decide to have a drink. I don't want to end up with a headache and ruin the party for you." I gave him a peck on the cheek and continued to put food on my plate. *I hope that sounded like a good dutiful wife.*

"Good thinking, Katie," he patted my shoulder in approval, as he continued to check out the room. "Hmmm, I wonder where Don is? I haven't seen him all day. I'll be right back." Off he wandered to brown nose the boss.

"You handled that pretty quick on your feet Ka-*tie*," mimicked Beth. "Keep it up and they'll give you an Oscar."

"Look, smart-ass, sometimes you do what you got do. Ya know? See, it worked. Now I am the last thought on his mind."

"Looks like a bunch of penguins in this room. You were right about one thing; this is one boring party. I have never seen so many people in one room saying nothing in my whole life. The next time you ask me to one of these, just stick a needle in my eye, okay?"

"Give it thirty more minutes, I have a feeling all hell is about to break loose. I am positive Bill and Maggie is at the bottom of this program, and poor Richard is the attraction. *I'll* be Bill's personal dessert. This will set the stage for the rest of the evening. The party won't be dull for long. It will depend on how much Don or Maggie has been drinking. Relax Beth," I took a deep breath, "The show is about to begin." I pointed across the room where a crowd was beginning to form.

No sooner than I finished telling Beth who was who, the grand entrance filed into the living room. First was Don with Marion, followed by Jim and his latest date, not far behind was Maggie with her trophy, Richard. Of all the men in the room dressed in their finest tux, he stood out. All eyes were on him. My stomach sank. Richard didn't take his eyes off Maggie.

They gathered to the left of the buffet table where glasses were set along with several champagne bottles. Promptly waiters started to pass out the glasses and fill them. When they were finished, Don raised his hand to quiet the crowd.

Don cleared his throat and began, "I want to thank all of you for coming tonight. First, Marion and I would like to wish all of you a very Merry Christmas. Second, the company present to you, will be a larger bonus in your envelopes this year's thanks to several people in our firm. I would like to take a moment to thank them personally."

"We had these plaques made for them with an extra added bonus. For the highest in regional sales goes to Bill Sawyer. Where are you? Here, he comes." Don scanned the crowd looking for his prize salesman.

Bill ran from within the crowd directly to Don's side. Which made sense I guess from Bill's point of view, stealing all the lime light. "Sorry, I was on the phone.—Business."

Don beamed at this young salesman, "I guess you can all see why there's a hefty bonus in this year's envelopes. We are very pleased with the results due to his hard work. "He shook Bill's hand and slapped him on the back in approval. The crowd went wild. I wanted to throw up from this sham.

Again, Don raised his hands, waiting for the applause to fade. "In second place, we have something special, a trip to Hawaii. This goes to Richard Peterson. Richard, please stand by me for a moment … Don't run off. Maggie … My sweet, please come here beside me," He stretched out his hand and lead her to the opposite side sliding his arm around her waist in a very protected manner.

A huge smile broke across his face as he spoke, "Richard, we are very happy to have you with our company. To my relief, you are well worth what I paid for," he chuckled. "It seems you're the one with the extra bonus this year. Maggie has informed me, you two have become engaged ... Well, whatever makes my little girl happy makes me happy. I hope the two of you are as happy as Marion and I are." He allowed Maggie to return to Richard's side, waved Marion over and kissed her.

The cheers were overwhelming. Everyone toasted the happy couple. This was Richard's cue as the coming attraction to give Maggie a passionate kiss before all the approving crowd.

I could feel Bill's eyes on me as I gulped down my champagne. I was grateful for Beth's quick thinking to stand as close as possible to prevent me from falling to my knees. Then the worst possible thing happened, to rub salt in my wounds, Bill asked me to come to his side and share in this happiness. The crowd parted like the Red Sea, assisting me to my destination. All eyes were focused on me. I finally reached Bill and smiled brightly, "I am so proud of you." I joked, "So, this is why you've had so many late nights. I guess I'll have to believe you for now on."

Bill leveled me with a kiss. He wasn't about to be out done by Richard. "You know there could never be anyone else but you, Katie." He held up his glass to toast the happy couple, "To Maggie, may Richard be as good to you as my Katie is to me.—And Richard, may you receive all you deserve."

Richard was a bit taken back by Bill's toast and was about to reproach, when Maggie dashed past him and hugged Bill saying something about how sweet he was or whatever. I looked at Richard and like a wave it hit me. My heart sank so deeply my knees were about to give way and the room started to spin. As I started to fall, Don caught me.

"I'm sorry, it's a little warm in here. If I could step outside for a moment, I'll be fine," I stuttered.

"There, there, you little thing, let me help you," said Don guiding me outside to a bench near a large fountain.

Bill turned to Marion and clarified, "She'll be fine. She goes through this sometimes. I believe it's the crowds. It's getting more and more difficult to take her anywhere. She's so frail."

"Thank you for helping me Don. I'm fine now. I wouldn't be surprised if it was the champagne. Please, go back to the party. I am sure you're needed." I ran my hands through my hair and leaned back, taking a deep breath to clear my head. I closed my eyes, the breeze felt cool and misty against my face.

"Well, if you're positive everything is okay. I don't mind telling you little lady, you gave me quite a scare," he sounded relieved. He watched me for a few minutes and went back to the party.

It felt wonderful sitting in the breeze. The party continued in the background. The sensation overwhelmed me again. Grabbing my stomach, I opened my eyes to find Richard standing before me.

"I hope that's not because I repulse you," he nodded in the direction of my hand.

"Yeah,—and no. It's my signal informing me whenever you are around. See, you don't even have to call, I know when you're in town." I faked a small laugh and sighed. "Some news tonight, gone from madly in love with me to marrying Maggie.—Go figure." I shrugged my shoulders.

Richard dropped to his knees and held my hands in his, "I know this sounds crazy, but it's not what it looks like. It happened this afternoon ... Kate, if you would only leave Bill ... I'll take you where ever you want to go. I don't care." He looked so lost.

"You know that can't happen. Not now. I have things to do. I told you this before ... I know you can't wait forever. I don't expect you to. It's just,—so quick. Isn't it?—I'm so confused about everything." I pulled my hands free from his grasp and dropped my head within them. "Richard, do what you need to do.

I have no right to stop you. I'm sorry." I was crying. "You need to leave ... I don't want people to talk ..."

"Kate, please hear me," he said gently, "I said this happened today. Maggie went out to lunch and when she returned,—she was talking about marriage and had her grandmother's ring. Believe me, we are not going to get married. I figured, what the hell,—so well be engaged, that will make her happy for a while. What could it hurt? She changes her mind from second to second. Tomorrow, we may not even be together."

"That bastard! You didn't know Bill and Maggie had lunch together! They set us up! Beth and I saw them at Cliff's. Evidently, they were calculating something. Bill had his usual smirk and Maggie was all giggles." I was furious.

Richard was bedazzled. "Then it really isn't a great idea for me to be here. Not even if it were a friendly chat. Damn that Bill is one suspicious bastard. Man, I feel like a damn fool. I was played like a violin … I–I guess he didn't believe my story."

"No,—I didn't," said Bill stepping from behind the fountain. "It's not very polite for you to be hitting on another man's wife, much less trying to take her away." Bill moved in quickly, grabbing my wrist and jerk me away from Richard.

"You're hurting me!" I struggled to get away from his grip.

Richard kept his distance and demanded, "Where is Maggie? Isn't she in on this?" "No, Maggie isn't in on this. You know as well as I, Maggie is a flake. It didn't take much convincing to get her to fall for you." Bill was feeling quite proud of his achievement. "You're just her type,—Male! Yet, so much male, you also have my wife's feelings all wrapped up too. Things were just fine until you came into the picture … So, I used Maggie to get you out. Simple enough. It seems I have to work harder to get you totally out of the picture … You better listen up; *my* Katie isn't going anywhere.—Got it?"

"Hey! Don't *I* have a say in this?" I finally managed to pull away from his grip. "Damn you Bill! Why are you doing this? Nothing happened!—You always jump to conclusions! We were just talk—"

He grabbed me and started shaking me senseless, "You damn whore! Are you that stupid to believe I didn't know what happened between you two while I was away? How do you think I made it as number one in this company?" He venomously turned to Richard and spat, "I am really surprised at you, *Rich,* to believe this company would change their loyalty and fall at your knees! You really thought you could just waltz right in here and take my place?—Along with my wife? She's mine! I am not going to permit you to take what's mine!"

"Bill, stop this! Please, no one is taking me anywhere. Please don't make a scene!" I cried.

Bill was beyond listening. His eyes glistened red with rage. I tried once again to pull away from his grip and received a blow to the face. "I'll teach you to mess around on me!"

Before he could strike me again, Richard stuck him hard on the side of his face. He pulled me away from Bill's grasp, flinging him to the ground. I huddled by the fountain, to stay away from the confrontation. Beth came running to my side, followed by Don and half the party.

Richard had Bill pinned to the ground beating him relentlessly. Their faces met and Richard said in a rough whisper, "If I ever see you lay another hand on Kate,—you won't *live* to see another day. I'll see to it. You don't deserve her. For the life of me, I can't understand why she is staying with—you." He threw Bill back on the ground like a piece of garbage.

Don stepped forward demanding to know why his two top salesmen were in a heated argument.

Richard answered, "Too much to drink, and discussed the wrong politics. Kate tried to break it up before it got out of hand." He walked over and inspected my cheek. He said in a low voice, "Kate, I love you. Remember that." Then turned to Beth, "Please put some ice on her cheek so it won't bruise. Please take care of her, Beth. Call me if you ever need me for anything."

"You can count on it," she assured him.

Maggie ran up to her love, fussing over him like a child. She yelled at the both of them, "Men! Sometimes you make me sick! You can behave like children! Let's go Richard, I need to put some ice on that eye and clean you up. We are supposed to have family pictures—and now look!"

I dropped back onto the bench and sighed deeply. Beth sat next to me, "I'm sorry I couldn't find you, but this house … How ya doing, sweetie? I think it's time to go home,—don't you?"

I watched Bill half kneeling near the fountain splashing water on his face, then slumping to the ground exhausted.

I replied, "Yeah, let's go home … Show's over."

Bill drove in silence. It was all he could do to drop Beth at her door. She gave me a look of concern before he drove off. Bill seemed to relax a bit after she left. I tried not to look to relieve knowing what was about to happen when we got home. My mind was in turmoil trying to figure a way out of this mess. While staring out the window, my hands were as busy twisting my fate. *If I had only been smart enough to get out with Beth. I could have walked her to her door. I mean, I don't know what I mean, Damnit I can't take this anymore! I can't live in this fear!* I watched Bill from the corner of my eye rubbing his jaw the rest of the way home.

I couldn't believe my eyes; he went directly to the guest bedroom, slamming the door behind him. Mentally eased, I went to the bathroom and cleaned my face. *Not too much damage; I've had worse than this.* I took a deep breath, sighing deeply; relieved, knowing how much worse it could have been.

"I guess he won't bother me tonight," I said softly. I couldn't conceive how shaken I was until I settled into the bed and Jazz leaped next to me for his nightly rubs.

"You startled me puss! I bet your night wasn't as exciting as mine. Hmmm?" I rubbed his chin. He purred contentedly. I leaned against on my pillow, reflecting on the evening. *I'm sure the place was buzzing after we left. I wonder how Maggie handled Richard? I mean she had to have a thousand questions about why he was even out there with me in the first place. Maybe not. Maggie wasn't one to push things. Poor thing, she really believes she has a hold on Richard.—Or maybe she's just as whipped as I am but in a different way. She has Daddy to make sure everything is okay for his little darling.*

On some level somewhere this just didn't seem fair. *Why is he with her? Because stupid, you decided to stay with this idiot and make things right.* I sighed deeply. I knew deep in my heart I was crazy for staying here. *I mean why? What in the hell is even keeping me here? I can't possibly be that afraid of Bill. Maybe I do need to start reading those books Beth gave me. There may be answer somewhere. It couldn't hurt.* With another deep sigh and a final pat on Jazz's head, I turned off the light. "There, there little sweetie. I've never seen you so content. Are you happy because the ass isn't with us?" My answer was returned in the form of a purr.

I was awakened by the phone and looked at the clock. It was 10:15 am. "Hel–lo?" My mouth was dry.

"Hi sis, how's it going? Did I wake you?" Asked Mike.

"Uh –huh, hmmm, I needed to be up. Wait a minute Mike, I need to check on something, I'll be quick—okay?"

"Sure, I'll hang on."

I looked down the hall, confirming Bill had already gone. He must have left early without a sound. I didn't like the idea he hasn't had a response to what happened last night. A shiver went down my spine at the thought of him storing all that anger,—and knowing who was going to be the recipient of it. For now, I was safe and knew I had time to figure what to do before he returned home this evening.

"Hey, big brother, what can I do for you?" Trying to wake up.

"I'm not going to beat around the bush, Kate. I talked to Richard this morning and it's everything I can do to keep from killing Bill myself. I'm not going to lecture you.—I just want to know why."

"Well, good morning to you,—and as for Richard, I am stunned he would call you about this," I answered crossly.

"Richard is really concerned about you. It wasn't the right place to have this confrontation, but it happened. At least Richard had the good sense to call me about it. God only knows, you wouldn't have. You realize, both of you are in a bad situation … He loves you Kate. Why in the world are you pushing him into the arms of that air head?"

"Mike, I have no response. You and I had this conversation about

Bill on my wedding night and again while I was there for Dad's funeral. If I had the answer, I would gladly tell you.—And please, don't lay that wife abuse crap on me again. I can't handle it. Between you and Richard, I'll go mad … Don't get me wrong, I know deep in my heart both of you mean well.—Okay? I have to think this through carefully before I do anything. Bill has to be handled with care or we will all suffer the consequences. He knows about Richard and me that will make him all the more dangerous.—As for Richard, I told him I had to work things out. I am not going to run into his arms to save me. If there's going to be any saving, I'm going to do it.—Got it?"

"Chill little sister. I'm worried about you. I know you have ten times more sense than Maggie does. It's … Just that … Well, with the position you're in, you may not be thinking clearly. How do you know that ass whipping Bill got from Richard didn't make things a whole lot worse? *That*, my dear sister, is what I'm afraid of."

"Thanks for the concern, Mike, I'm fine. Besides, Beth keeps a close eye on me. In fact, I thought it was her calling … Last night Bill slept in the guest room and left without a sound this morning. He's probably in so much trouble with Don; embarrassed his little plan blew up in his face.

I don't believe I will be first thing on his mind today."

"If I were you, I'd take this time to decide what to do, and do it fast before he comes to whatever warped senses he has and turns on you. I don't like the idea he's storing this inside. I don't want you to be on the other end of the explosion.—You hear?" Said Mike with concern.

"I hear. I was thinking the very same thing before you called," I lied.

"Well, I'm glad you are at least thinking about it. If you want, I'll be on the next plane and get you the hell out of there … I know,—I know, you want to do it yourself … I'm here if you need me.—Call me. Damnit, Kate, I don't like the situation you are in. And if I know you, you're not listening to a word I'm saying, "he softened back to my old loving brother.

"I'm listening! You can bet your ass I will do the right thing. I don't know what it is yet. Please believe me when I say, I won't let him hurt me anymore,—that you can take to the bank. You'll be one of the first I call when I've come to a decision. I love you, too. I'll talk to you later, I promise. Bye." Jazz jumped on the bed as I hung up the phone, "Hi, kitty. You hungry? Come here." I picked him up and carried him into the bathroom, then set him neatly on the floor, "Run on, I'll feed you in a bit."

My face stung from the force of the shower. "Ouch!" I winced and quickly moved to the back of the shower. I stood quietly for quite some time pondering on what to do. M*ike was right, it won't be too long before Bill comes out of whatever daze he's in and I'm standing here like an idiot just waiting for it. Jesus, this is what Mom did.—Am I that crazy? Am I going to become like her and live in fear, backing away every time someone speaks their mind? Continue to live in denial to whatever happens to me?*

I slid to the corner of the shower, again in tears. *I can't go on crying all my life and I'll be damned if someone is going to make my life so damn miserable in the process! Damn it!* I slammed my arm on the side of the shower until I came to my senses from the pain. Everything seemed to be a blur. The only thing I knew, my body was reacting to what I needed to do.—Wake up.

I dried off and went to my closet and mechanically began pulling out clothes. I found my old tattered suitcase and filled it. Jazz must have sensed something wrong and was rubbing against my leg. "No, sweetie, Mommy will take you with her. She won't leave you with the bad man. I have to find your travel case … It should be in the garage."

My hair still wet, all my clothes packed and placed Jazz in his case, I sat at the kitchen table and wrote a note:

> *Bill,*
>
> *I have decided to visit Mom and Mike for a while. I need some time to think. I'm sorry about what happened last night, but you brought it on yourself. You wouldn't listen to me. You never do and I'm tired of it. I don't understand why you have to use drugs and alcohol to help you become a better person. I don't like this person. I miss*

the man I dated and first married. I really don't understand why you have decided to destroy yourself, everyone and everything around you. I guess it's easier to hit me, rather than deal with it yourself. Please don't call me. I won't come to the phone and I won't come home until I'm ready.

You need to get some help Bill, and I'm not talking about Father Flanders. You know as well as I, you are past that kind of help. I hope to talk to you soon.

Kate

p.s. I hate it when you call me Katie.
My name is <u>Kate.</u>

There. Let him chew on that. I called Beth, "Hi, it's me. Want to go to Arizona? I'll be over in a few, pack your things."

I took the keys to the Jeep, picked up Jazz and my suitcase; I glanced around my wonderful kitchen and sighed. Part of me wanted to turn back; I knew what waited here for me if I did. Anna said there were some decisions to be made. I made my first. My second, I went to the bank and cashed Bill's bonus check.

CHAPTER SEVEN

Awakening

We drove up a winding road that wrapped itself around a small hill. The top was flat with a few scattered trees and shrubs. The red clay was topped with a light cover of snow. In the center of the flattened area laid a series of stones that outlined a circle with a smattering of smaller stones in specific areas.

"Look how these stones are laid out." Said Beth inspecting them. "It feels strange here. I know this may sound weird to you, but it does. See, the hair on my arms are straight up." She walked around the encircled stones trying not to infringe on the way they lay.

I, on the other hand, was headed right for the center of the circle when Beth stopped me with a warning, "No, Kate, I wouldn't do that."

"I don't understand what the big deal is Beth—and what's more—*what* has come over you. I don't feel anything but cold." I replied irritably.

"Maybe Beth has a deeper understanding of what this place is. She feels or senses it," answered a female stranger. "It may be wise if you entered the Medicine Wheel from the opening at the South end." The small figure pointed to a small opening just opposite from where I stood.

"Ahh, that's okay, I didn't mean to upset anything." I nervously replied while wondering how long she had been watching us. I shuddered from goose bumps all over my forearms.

"I didn't say that you did, Kate," softly whispered the stranger. "I haven't been here too long.—Before I spook you any further, I'm Praise. I glad to see you found your way here easily. I might say, you sure did pick a cold time of the year to head this way. But then—our time *is* pre–chosen for us." As Praise spoke, Beth and I walked carefully towards her making sure we avoided the circle.

Praise wasn't very tall yet the confidence she carried made her appear taller than she was. Approaching her, I noticed a unique sparkle in her eyes that gave you a warm, safe feeling to be around her. Very much like Anna's. She extended her hands to me, I felt a flow of warmth extend from her hand into mine. I noticed Beth felt it, too.

"I appreciate you meeting me here. It is rather difficult to find my home and thought it would be easier to take you there. Why don't you follow me back to my place and I'll heat up some tea? You can spend the rest of the evening relaxing before we begin in the morning …" Praise looked to the sky as she answered, not missing a single step towards her car, "It's a shame it is so cold out here, it would have been wonderful sleeping under the stars. When you sleep within the Medicine Wheel, your dreams are truly incredible," she said with a smile. Before we could answer, she was already in her car and driving away.

"Well! I guess we'd better follow her to her place before we lose her!" Exclaimed Beth joyfully. "So, Kate, ready to begin our adventure? Let's get some food and warm up! Wow, I did not realize how cold I am!"

I was not so excited as Beth. A bit leery about what just happened and rather embarrassed at being caught at my blunder. I muttered under my breath, "Yeah, I guess I'm as ready as I'll ever be. But I don't think I'm ready to s*leep* under the stars. I've never been one to love camping of any sort."

We pulled onto another a winding driveway leading to a small house hidden behind tall cedar trees. At the end of the driveway a bronze statue of an oriental woman stood between the cedar trees on a small pillar. I remember seeing this statue on the cover of some books at the bookstore. The name did not come to me, however Beth knew and responded with reverence by bowing her head.

We entered the small home to find summer warmth from very welcomed fire in the huge fireplace and the whistle of tea already brewing. We were greeted happily by a tiny black cocker spaniel.

"As you can see, I've been expecting you." She said as she hung up her old wool carpet jacket, then placed her boots on a rack by the door. "Hi, Laran! See I told you I wouldn't be gone long! Don't mind her, she gets excited easily."

Praise's home was very simply done with bright vivid colors that added a wonderful feeling of welcome. "I love things comfortable. Please, just hang your coats on the rack and make yourselves at home. I'll only be a minute and I'll have something to warm you up."

Beth and I settled into a huge brightly colored couch, Praise walked in with a tray of assorted of teas, and goodies to go with it.

"I've taken the opportunity to add some sweets. I love 'em—have some? They're pumpkin bread muffins." She placed the tray on the coffee table, fixed her own tea and curled up in what seemed to be her favorite chair. The chair was as oversized as the couch and enveloped her small body. Without the floppy hat on you were able to see her deep brown hair cut short to lay around the nape of her neck with a long braid that draped over her shoulder and across the front of her shirt. On the end of her braid was a tiny silver crescent moon tied to it.

"I noticed as we came in, there was a lovely statue of an oriental woman. She's very beautiful," I commented.

"Thank you. That is a statue of Kwan Yin, The Ascended Mother of Mercy. Her origin in this world is Thailand, Chaing Mai, to be exact. It is said she is one of the Holy Mother's assisting Mother earth—Gaia, on her ascended path along with all of mankind … Right now, we all need some of her mercy—don't you think?" She smiled.

Praise placed her empty cup on the table and said, "I know you must be tired, so let me show you to your room. I hope you don't mind sharing a room, there are two beds. I keep this room ready for those who come to my classes."

She and Laran lead us down the hall that ran into three rooms. I realized the house was almost circular. "The rooms are larger than they appear from this tiny hallway. A friend of mine designed and built this place. He calls it an earth home. In the morning you can see from the outside how well it works with the environment. John is on a retreat for a couple of weeks. I'm sorry you'll miss him."

Our room was a simple as the rest of the house. Beth flopped upon the bed and moaned. "Well, what do you think?"

"About what?" I replied. "You know, about Praise."

"I don't know, I feel good around her. I guess I'm still a bit nervous about all of this. I really don't even know why I'm here … Mike seemed a bit upset we came though.—I wonder why?" I asked smugly. "Come to think of it girlie–girl, you haven't said a word about you and Mike since we left. Are you going to talk or am I going to have to *dra*g all the juicy info out of *you* the way you did me?"

"Ye-e-s-s. We talked. You knew that. I told him to give me some time. It's going to be difficult to have a relationship with him in Flint and me in Chicago, you know. There is also Lisa to think about and of course—your mother. I'm not too crazy about long distance relationships … Oh I don't know he's a really great guy. I am glad to see he was very understanding about my feelings. That's a first for me. I am use to the 'Hey Stel—la! Get over here and *Geet* my beer before I kick your fuc—*king* ass!' Type."

"I can see where he would promise to be a plus." I said sadly, "Yeah Beth, one thing you can definitely count on …"

"What's that sweetie?" "He'd never hit you."

"Hmmm! Is that pancakes I smell?" I asked. I rolled over, stretched then wiping the morning sleep from my eyes.

"It sure is! Sleepy head! I thought you were going to sleep the morning away. Praise and I have been up for a couple of hours now." Beth said delightfully. "It feels wonderful to be here!"

"Oh really? Why didn't you wake me up? You know I wouldn't have put up to much of a fight." I retorted.

"Why wake you up? You've been through some pretty rough stuff here lately. I thought you needed your rest." Beth shrugged. "Praise and I have had our morning tea. We had a wonderful discussion about our views on life, so on and so forth. We stopped so she could fix wheat pancakes. I wandered back here to see if you were ready to finally wake up."

The thought of breakfast sounded wonderful. We didn't eat anything last night except the muffins. I stumbled around the bedroom trying to gather all my things and get ready for my day. "I can't believe how disoriented I am this morning! You'd think I've never been anywhere before. I guess to make things easier, I'll just slip on my jeans and sweat shirt." I brushed through my mop of hair and tied it back. "So, what did you two discuss this morning?"

Beth laughed, "You do look a bit displaced! I was going to ask you last night if you were hungry but one minute you were talking about that picture of the bodhi tree on the wall—and the next … You were gone! Out like a light! I took off your shoes and pants. You didn't even move. I believe the stress has gotten the best of you Kate. Your body finally felt relaxed and did what it had to do in this safe environment—pass out."

"What do mean safe environment? I felt safe at moms."

"Really? I remember a few discussions between you and Mike about coming here.

Your mother wasn't very supportive either. She wanted you to turn around right then and head back to your husband."

My head fell in shame. Beth was right; I was constantly on my toes at mom's place. I thought we would stay at his place, but Mike had moved back in with mom. He didn't want to leave her alone. There were still a few unfinished feelings I haven't dealt with. The house felt strange. My body shuddered. "Can't we talk about this later? I'm hungry right now. I don't think facing your fears before breakfast is the best time."

"Good morning, Kate! How did you sleep? Are you ready for

breakfast? Tea is brewing and ready when you are!" Said Prai-se cheerfully.

I smiled and returned cheerfully, "Morning to you. I don't remember falling to sleep. From what Beth told me, I racked out. I can't remember sleeping that hard in quite some time. I think I needed it.—And yes, I am definitely ready for some breakfast! Man, I'm starved!" I went to the table and retrieved a cup; Praise met me half way with the pot of steaming water.

"Then have a seat. Feel free to stuff yourself. There's no need to face your fears on an empty stomach!" Prai-se smiled.

"Looks like this is going to be an interesting week!" I said with surprise.

I gave Beth an inquisitive look.

Beth shrugged her shoulders and asked, "So, what's on the agenda today?" "What do you want to do today? This is your time. What do you want to get done while you are here?"

"Spoken like a true psychiatrist." I smugly remarked.

"Let's get one thing straight, I am not a psychiatrist!" She responded sternly. "I am a facilitator."

"Excuse me, I don't mean to be rude, but what is that?" I asked shyly knowing my face had to be a deep shade of red. (Way *to go Kate! Insert foot!)*

"To put it simply, I assist you with your fears. With your permission; I take you back to a time you planted the fear and assist you in working through it."

"How do you do that?"

"I believe what you are going in circles to ask, is, what are my credentials and what makes me so special to do what I do? And the big question—am I the teacher?" Suggested Praise.

"No. I mean ... yes ... Well, I just don't understand all this stuff. I mean, how can you do in one week, what it takes doctors years to do." I flustered. *Well Kate, nice going ... Piss off the lady before you even get started.*

"First Kate, I never said you would be healed in one week. Everyone has to start somewhere. I don't have anything against doctors of any sort. Everyone is here on this earth for a reason. When the reason is no longer needed, then it is no longer here. We evolve, and as we do, new situations are created to assist. People want the quick fix to their problems ... Let me tell you right now—there are none! You can't snap your fingers and have it go away. No matter what you do and who you decide to see, you will have to do it a bit at a time in the only way your mind will be able to assimilate it. My credentials are very simple, I am a Minister of Light, a hypno-therapist, past life regressionist and third-degree Reiki student ...—And no," soft chuckle, "I am not pissed off."

Startled at her mind reading and deciding to use a tone of voice that appeared less threatening, "I-I'm just asking ... Exactly what denomination is a Minister of Light?"

"Good question. I have no denomination. I believe in only three things ... God, Myself,—and You. The only rules of order is to love yourself and harm none."

"And to love God.—Right?" I asked.

"When you learn to love yourself, Kate, loving God will come naturally. I know there a few people who say to love God first. Which is wonderful, if you look closer, they still don't love themselves. Why don't we go to my office and talk? Diana will be here soon to help me around here. That way we'll be out of her way while she does her thing."

Beth and I settled into large soft cushions on the floor. We sat in a triangle facing Praise. I was beginning to feel nervous. I began to wonder what I had gotten myself into.

"Before you jump up from your cushion Kate, and bolt for the door. Why don't we start by relaxing? We can take this any way you want ... We can jump right in—or we can talk for a while. It doesn't matter to me," offered Praise sincerely.

Beth also sensed my nervousness reached out and patted my arm with sweet assurance, "Why don't we talk for a while. Praise and I had a wonderful discussion this morning. Why don't we pick up where we left off? I asked you about people in general. Everyone seems to be searching for something. Everyone is trying so hard to find themselves. Why is this?"

Praise softly laughed, "Yes, everyone seems to be going through an identity crisis. Everyone wants to know who he or she is. For a while it was only a few rogues here and there.—Now they seem to be coming out of the woodwork. We all seem to have a sense of urgency. It is time for the Soul to take over the body …" Praise paused, gathered her thoughts and continued … "To make this a bit easy to understand, for some time now the Soul has come down attempting to follow the Divine plan. But once *It* entered into the body, The Soul 'forgot.' A cloak of forgetfulness clouded the mind and the Soul took a back seat to whatever the body did. This "cloud" was created by the ego. The non- importance of the self-became important rather than the fluid beauty of the One. The Soul knew this place of wonderment was created to learn and move forward once again."

"In order to move forward, there were rules implemented to aid the Soul. Free Will was one, and Karma was the other. This was planted as a seed within the heart of the Earth. And all that come here to play out their dramas had to follow those rules. The final win to the game is to remember who you are. Now is the time for the Body and the Soul to unite as one and finish the game. This is why everyone is deeply questioning and or fighting over what is right and what is wrong. They are all looking *outside* for the answer."

"What do you mean planted in the Earth? What does that have to do with me?—Or anyone for that matter? What did I forget and how? I'm afraid you are losing me," I leaned forward and asked.

Praise smiled knowing she had gained some of my confidence; her eyes sparkled as she answered my questions, "We are all part of this earth. Being in the body holds great responsibility. The body is tied to the Earth … Ashes to Ashes … Adam was made of earth …— Remember? We are here to remember the Truth. We are the Christ. We are all part of this Earth. She is our Mother. We are born from her and we go to her when we are done. She gives us life and death totally … Unconditionally as the Father does. The Breath of Life - The Vital Force within - The Soul, every Soul asks permission to enter this earth. Between the Father and Mother, we are granted so many breaths. When they are done … So is the body that returns to Mother. The Soul goes back to the Father and the cycle starts again. We need to keep it all together …—Body and Soul. Only once all negative Karma is cleansed, it will become easier for Body, Spirit and Soul to unite as one complete being …"

"We are the Christ?" I interrupted. My brain hurt.

Smiling, Praise answered, "Yes Kate, we are the Christ. When each are created the Christ is planted first. The Christ enters the body. You know this as your Soul. Your Soul *is* the Christ. We are here to remember this as well as to live this. To live in absolute unconditional love is to Live in Christ." Praise stopped and looked to see if I understood this, slightly blushing, I nodded with understanding.

Praise chuckled, "Kate, do not be embarrassed, you are here to learn, to remember. It is important to ask these questions in order for the flow of Light to flow and assist in you remembering." Her look to me at that very moment was so loving; my eyes were flooded with tears. Praise said nothing and continued on her train of thought as though I had never interrupted, "How we created the negative was very easy. It's called the 'Id' or the body self. This is what has kept the human body continuing separately for so long. The id became stronger by enveloping fear around us for survival until the 'it' had more control than the Soul. The 'id' believes when the Soul leaves the body, nothing else exists. What keeps the Soul and Body together is the Spirit or Holy Spirit."

"And so … What is this, Karma? I've heard it's all the bad we've ever done. So, if that's the case … It's gonna take me a very long time to clear it all." I sadly remarked.

"Karma doesn't mean good or bad. It just means action, or reaction, due to certain circumstances. Sometimes you have a few good lives with nothing to clear.—Right?" Asked Beth.

"Yes. Sometimes, it just isn't cleared. The body isn't aware enough to understand what it is supposed to do and keeps rerunning the same pattern over and over. Whatever had been the state of mind when you passed on in the last life, comes first. We keep returning in order to heal the problem and move on. This is why it is so important to have things in order when you leave, or the same state of mind will be carried into the next lifetime … This is why it is so important to move into the fears and understand them. See fear as it truly is and realize that fear is merely a waste of time for the mind. There is so much more to see and enjoy within the vast realms of the universe. And yes, one day we will remember everything, past, present and future."

"I thought future hasn't been written yet," said Beth. I thought that was the purpose of Free Will. We have the ability to change everything. So how can it be seen?"

"Once we remember the past without fear, the future will become natural. Everything that happens will be accepted for the way it is. We will be able to move from situation to situation free from fear. Without fear to cloud up the issues, it will be easy to see what is ahead/or now. Once the Soul has made the connection with the body, and one puts all trust in the Soul, all decisions will be correct. There is a saying that can be used in any given situation; Fear and the God presence cannot occupy the same space. God is here eternally. When we are in fear, we cannot feel the presence of God."

"What you are saying is, if I were to feel fear, and stay there, it is difficult for God, or the Soul, to intervene in assistance." I thoughtfully pointed out.

"That's it, Kate!" Exclaimed Praise.

"I guess it goes the same for hate." I added.

"Yes, hate is only an extension of fear. Should you find you hate something, look at it closely, you'll see it is something you fear greatly. It is probably something you hate or fear to look at about you. One valuable thing to remember, we are all connected! We are mirrors to each other. What I see that I love and or dislike about you, is what I love or dislike about myself."

"What do we do to clear all this up?" I asked. "You make it sound monumental." I looked down into my fidgeting hands; "The thought of Bill being the mirror of me is a bit much for me to handle."

"It not so monumental if you can see it from the grander picture. It's time to go within and look at all the *uglies* safely hidden behind locked doors. Everyone has them. If not, they have no prejudice, no judgments, and have Ascended or reached Enlightenment. Sometimes what we fear doesn't stem from childhood. This Karma may extend from another life. We believe it's been taken care of, then it crops up somewhere else in our lives. If we don't correct the problem, it will certainly take shape in other areas. Our children or other family members will have to deal with the problems as we pass them on."

"When you are able to look at the situation without fear, it is over. Your sixth sense—which is your direct voice from the Soul—will tell you it has been cleared." Praise answered. She noticed the sadden look on my face. "This is no reason to be upset, Kate. Let's make this a bit simpler."

I nodded.

"You are extremely afraid of Bill. I know there are times you hate him."

"Ha! Sorry … Well yes, I guess you may call it that. I know there are times I hate him, but something inside won't let me leave him. On the other hand, I feel very sorry for him … I can't quite explain it."

"That's my point. All levels of which you are want this cleared. In Bill, you see all things about you. You don't like you, Kate, and this have expanded externally thus you attract Bill. You emanated this energy to attract an alike to assist you in this lesson of self-hate. He is controlling and takes out all his aggressions at you, the poor little beat up puppy who truly believes she deserves this because you cannot control your own minds' thoughts and beliefs. Everything you believe your mind tells you, what you are—you believe. Therefore, Bill only reacts to those feelings … Now this doesn't mean you should fill yourself with guilt, Kate. On the contrary, you should rejoice in the fact you are now able to see the games your mind has been playing with you and learn how to control this." Praise stopped, looked at me, took my hand to comfort me as she continued, "Kate, you entered into this lifetime with a bucket full of life lessons about you that needed to be cleared up. Before you arrived, you made sure these conditions were set in place to allow you to have these experiences. All involved agreed to this beforehand because they too had their own scenarios to live through and learn from.

I was stunned. I wanted to throw up right there. Dearest Beth had a trash can right next to me, just in case. I shook my head no. I was about to feel flooded with guilt, I understood what she was saying and felt more at ease. It all made sense—somehow. I just knew that for the present I would trust this and *know* the answers would soon make themselves clear and this remarkable woman was going to show me the way.

"Correct me if I'm wrong ... From what I have been hearing, all the answers or guidance are coming from the Soul. Is this what you have been talking about?—People are looking outside for the answers ...—Not inside? It's hard to trust something in your head. Especially when you've not trusted yourself for a very long time. Not to mention people have a very poor view these days about those listening to "voices" in their heads," interjected Beth.

"You are correct, Beth. If God is the Father of the Soul and the Soul is within ... Where are the answers?—What you don't trust is the id. You can always trust the Soul. You have to learn how to discern them. It isn't that difficult. My next favorite Praise is ... Let go ... Let God ... When that happens, nothing goes wrong.—First you have to feel comfortable. You have to face your fears. Then, bit by bit, it is easier to let go. By walking into your fears, you will begin to see there is nothing to be afraid of. What we are mostly afraid of is the unknowns, the what ifs. Fear is the seed of many faces, hate, pain, and killing. They dissipate and you are able to move forward into the light. We have to unite the id, educate it and allow it to understand that it is part of the whole. The id needs to rethink react act to the Light. It is much easier than the muddled thoughts the id creates. Once you are in unison with the Light Voice, that is the only voice heard and that

Voice will speak with love and clarity. No questions would be asked about the "voices" one hears."

"I don't know if I can do this," I said softly. The thought of going inside and looking at something I've been avoiding most of my life was more than I could deal with at this moment.

"I hope you'll try Kate, it breaks my heart to see you like this," Beth said sadly. "I guess it's time for both of us to look into our closets."

"Well, we will make the first lesson very easy," said Praise in a whimsical tone, "I love doing this ... Beth, I would like you to *try* to pick up this pencil." She tossed a pencil on the floor. Beth, leaned over, picked it up and handed it back to Praise. "No, I asked you to *try* to pick up the pencil. You picked it up. Let's do it again."

This time Beth stared at the pencil for some time before she commented. "I don't understand what you mean."

"*Try* to pick up the pencil, Beth," insisted Praise.

I giggled. It was unusual for Beth to be put on the spot.

In frustration Beth snapped at me, "You think you're so smart, you try to pick the damned thing up!"

"Hey, I'm not getting into this one!" I laughed. I was very grateful not being on the spot for once.

"I'm not doing this to upset you, Beth. I am making a point. There is no way to *try* to pick up the pencil. You either can or can't.—You do or you don't ... Try is a word used for people who want to avoid doing something. Maybe to get someone off their backs.

You know, 'I'll *try* to get that to you in a few days ... The check is in the mail ... So, Kate will either do this,—or not."

"Oh. I never realized that. I guess I need a few minutes to decide if I want to do this. I know that I came here for a reason. I guess this is a bit more than I expected." I said in reflection of what just happened.

"God is patient ..." Praise smiled her wonderful smile. "Why don't we break here for now and come back to this later this afternoon. Go outside and get some fresh air. I need to get with Diana and prepare lunch."

I stretched and looked at my watch. The morning breezed by and

I was grateful for the break. There was so much information I needed to process and understand.

"Sounds like a plan to me! I could use a potty break!" Giggled Beth relieved to be out of the limelight.

I stretched again and yawned loudly. The sun felt warm against my skin even though it was cold. I snuggled deeper into my jacket to ward off the cool air. Beth was already ahead of me and in the back yard.

"Kate! Wait until you see this! It's beautiful!" Yelled Beth.

Outlining the yard were more cedar trees, to the back of the yard was a small pond with a fountain covered with fairies waiting patiently for the water to begin flowing. All around the yard were more tiny statues of fairies and angels standing watchful over the sleeping flowers. Beth stood in awe before a huge face, and only the face, of a most incredible statue protruding through the ground as though someone were trying to come out of the Earth. We leaned against the bench still in wonder of this magical scene.

"This is beautiful! Have you ever seen anything like this?" Beth asked breathlessly.

"It's like a fairy tale." I replied. This was wondrous compared to my small garden.

There were tiny lights twinkling from the trees and the small bushes surrounding her garden. "I am sure at night this is enchanting. You would expect those fairies to speak."

Beth settled comfortably on the bench and looked at me. "You look much better Kate. It is a nice change not seeing the stress all over your face. How are you doing? You brought up some pretty good questions to ponder over. I know she gave us a ton of new information. There was even a new perspective for me to look at."

"You've been looking into yourself a whole lot longer than I have. I don't know if I want to buy it all right now. I mean I never really went to church until Bill and I got married. Only then it was a crash course to get married. Bill puts on a good front for Father Flanders, but he sure as hell doesn't carry it home. It's like he does something wrong and runs to church, gets absolution and it starts all over again," shaking my head, "I don't know what to think. I mean if this Karma thing is correct, then it would explain why so many things go unanswered.—Or they seem to go unanswered."

"Kate, people have a misconception about the Catholic Church. Yes, you go to confession and ask for absolution, the trick is not to do it again. Unfortunately, it doesn't work that way. It got lost somewhere in the process. Every church has its problems, it's not the church that is the problem, and it's the people. If they don't like something, they change it to fit their needs and call it the truth of God. Even though I believe the way I do, I still go to church for the Sacrament. At first, I felt guilty and didn't go because I thought it wrong to go if I didn't believe in all of the doctrine. Then I realized I was following the doctrine of the church, if I truly follow my heart. I am going for my connection and me with the Father. When I go with love in my heart, receive the Sacrament, I feel God's presence flow through my body. This is why I do it. Praise feels differently. That is her choice. There is no wrong way.—Understand?"

"I guess, what you are saying is, I need to find my way. Doesn't it bother you the church doesn't recognize your divorce? I mean that's what I heard."

"Just take it easy Kate; I know you feel pressured about your situation. Let go and allow your inner self to guide you in the direction it needs to take you ... Maybe Praise will show you how to do that this afternoon ... As for my marriage ... At first, I was very confused. When I finally made my decision and realized a bolt of lightning. I started to take a second look at things. I regained control over the fact that no one has the right to deny me the Sacrament of God. I am the one who has to deal with my salvation." Beth giggled softly; "Father Flanders saw how stubborn I had become about this and went to Pops. They were in conference for hours! I was finally granted absolution because Anthony mysteriously showed up and confessed, he committed adultery. Of course, that made everything all right.—Divorce granted. Anthony had to do *quite* a bit a penance for his blasphemy.—Amazing how things get worked out!" Beth sighed deeply and said, "Enough of this! I don't know about you, but I'm cold and starved. As beautiful as this place is, I feel the need to feed!"

"Go ahead, I'll be in shortly. I think I'll start to—relax!"

CHAPTER EIGHT

Looking Within ...

Later that afternoon, we again settled in Praise's office. "I would like to explain a few more things before we begin this afternoon's session. I think we need to give our tummies time to digest a bit before we go on … Do you have any questions? Kate, you were quiet during lunch. I'm sure this is all rather confusing to you."

"Nothing like getting your foundation rattled. I mean I thought this was all about being abused. Now we're talking about God, religion, and past lives. Next you'll tell me there is no hell."

"Oh yes, my dear, there is a hell. You can create it anytime you want and live in it up to your eyeballs. In all things, there is good and evil. It just depends on where you want to be. Lord Buddha said something like this, 'The path to Enlightenment is the middle way; the opposite of both extremes.' You can go either way. The most difficult way is the middle path. People want to ignore the negative, the Hell and the chaos. They wish to only live in the happiness, refusing to see the hell. They don't understand it takes both sides to create the balance. The center of all chaos is perfection. What is even more difficult to understand, all of it is Divinely perfect. The positive as well as the negative."

"Of course, I want to ignore the hell! I don't want to be there anymore. How can there possibly be perfection in the middle of chaos.

I can't think when my life wasn't a mess, which, by the way, is most of the time lately … I find I want to hide in a hole when things get chaotic. It seems my life has been one continuous hell.—From my father to Bill. The only sane parts of my life are my friendship with Beth—and Richard.—*And* that one, I still can't explain."

Calmly Praise answered me; "You have to look into the "hell" Kate. It is part of the Whole. It is what we have created and have to take responsibility for. By ignoring it, that allows it to feed and grow within us. It becomes more important than anything else in our lives does. When we ignore the hell, the hate and cover our eyes to this part of who we are so many things develop, Lack becomes a big part as well as the in-considerations of who and what we are here for. It becomes difficult to concentrate on what we are here to do and to become. Hiding from this will not make it go away. When we recognize this and look into the hell, all of a sudden it becomes less important and it fades to its rightful place.—Within the Light.—Part of the Perfection of all things. Let's take this one step at a time. You can see the perfection when you learn how to find it; by paying attention to everything around you. Everything. You have to learn how to read the situation with displacement. I'll show you how in a moment. I know Anna explained to you about how you ask for all of this. That is a fact. You brought it with you. Kate, how would you know whether something was right or wrong if you didn't have something to go by?"

"You said the Soul would know." I answered.

"This is correct. So, tell me, how connected are you with *your* Soul right now? Would you know if It spoke to you?—Or would you think you're just making this up in your head?"

"Well …" I couldn't answer. I wouldn't know what my Soul looked like if It walked right up and bit me.

"See? So, we have to teach you how to listen correctly. Once you learn how to walk into fear, you will see the perfection. What we are trying to achieve through all of this is equanimity. Once you have moved through the fear and released it, you are able to begin living in peace and discern the difference between Soul and ego. Fear should never have been here. Fear was developed for control," said Praise.

"Until you see what you are so afraid of, acknowledge it, then there is room for God. If we are to go through this past life thing with Kate, it will be gone forever?" Asked Beth.

"Maybe, it depends on the person. I told you this wasn't an overnight thing. Some people go through their stuff with ease; they can shake it off and move on. Then there are those who have a great deal of pain and anguish to be rid of and feel every bit of it. The up side to it all, when you are finally ready to be rid of it, you can release it. What seems to be the most difficult part in all of this releasing is letting go and not hanging on to it once it surfaces. Some people find they want to pick through the garbage before it goes to the dump." Praise watched me closely as she spoke. I knew she could sense my fear.

"I–don't–know … There are some things I am afraid of, I don't think I want to run to just yet. I mean, I am having a difficult time with the connection of how all this past life stuff has to deal with my abusive marriage … I am sorry that I am being so thick headed about this. But it just—Well it just sounds like some weird back yard preacher chicanery to me. There! I said it." I spoke defiantly. No one was going to put one over on me. I have been through way too much here lately and I had had enough. I looked at Praise's serene face, as she paid no mind to what I had just said. She merely sat there watching waiting to see if I had finished my outburst. Beth's face, on the other hand, well it took Praise to silently raise her hand to stop Beth from smacking me into the next room for my rudeness.

Praise answered, "Your abuse came from many areas Kate. Your life as a child was a very abusive one." She softly smiled, "Now Kate, tell me, what child do you know deserves to be in that kind of hell?" Praise did not wait for an answer; she went on, "None that I personally know of. Childhood is a time of growth, Love, guidance and happiness. Isn't that what we are supposed to believe? So then, just where did this "hell" come from? It is that baggage we carry from lifetime to lifetime. By looking into the past, sometimes assists us in understanding why things are the way they are now. Why you are with the certain people you are with. Why you are attracted to some and distaste for others. There are many answers lying within. There are many ways to look at them or not look at them. This is a little more complicated. This is why I have chosen this method to assist people. We are visionaries and as the saying goes "seeing is believing". Praise watched me carefully as she softly spoke," You can start with something small and work your way up. Just taking the step is usually enough. Look, you took one already. You're here. You walked out of the mess to find the correction for the solution. That is a mighty big step."

I felt a knot in my throat. I knew what she said was right. I did walk away from Bill … Well maybe I ran I just knew I couldn't take it anymore. There was that connection at the hospital. After what he had done, I stayed. I did not know why, I knew I had to be with him for a while longer. Maybe this, this was the answer. Maybe not, but what the hell, I can't go back to that.—No, not any more. I have to put a stop to this madness.

Tears were flooding my eyes, I grabbed the pillow tightly, looked up and the question squeaked from somewhere within, "What do I do now?" I sighed deeply, to keep the tears from flowing.

"I want to explain, what I do isn't very special. I only assist you in seeing what has happened. This is only to aid you in understanding what is happening to you now so you can get a handle on your life,— not to cast blame. With that out of the way—let's get to work! I have to ask this of both you and Beth. Do I have permission to assist you in this endeavor?"

"Yes," said Beth. "Without question."

I shrugged my shoulders and thought for a moment, "Sure, why not. I need to do something.—Just what do you mean endeavor?"

Praise chuckled lightly, reached out for me and hugged me tightly, "Kate! Life is ONE huge endeavor! To walk forward and cast away the demons, that is righteousness! Blessed Be! Now my sweet Kate, lie down and welcome to your beginning! Shhhh eyes close and listen to my voice Kate. Hear the quiet of the room? I will first show you how to relax. Then I will give your subconscious some instructions on how I intend to do things. If your subconscious has objections, the process will stop. Understand Kate?" Praise noticed my nod as my eyes fell shut and my body began to feel the warmth of her persona flow through me. "Shhhhhh," I heard her soft cradling voice, "I would like Beth to be here while I'm with you and you here for Beth. I say this because there is a tie between the two of you and one will be able to lend the other strength while you are facing your stuff." Praise's hands moved lightly over my body. Her fingers did not touch me exactly; it was like a wave of tingly energy that flowed over me. "Sweet Kate, a slow deep inhale now."

Praise held my hand as I lay on a thin cot on the floor. I made myself comfortable, closed my eyes and started taking slow deep breaths as directed.

"I would first like to say a small prayer of protection before we begin. Is this fine with you Kate? This aids in relaxation when the ego feels protected. The mind needs these assurances."

I nodded, taking another slow deep breath. As I exhaled, the nervous energy left, and I started to relax. Each breath became easier and easier.

Praise commenced, "Our Father in Heaven, Our Mother on Earth. Thy Kingdom come, thy will be done, On Earth as it is in Heaven … In the name of the Father–Mother, Child and Spirit … Amen … Now, at this time I ask for Kate's Angels and Archangels to come forth to be present and assist … Her Masters and Ascended Masters … I now ask for the Highest I Am presence of Kate to fill her body and be present … Kate, I want you to take a very deep breath and let it go slowly. As you slowly release the breath, you will find yourself on the top of a flight of stairs … Do you see them Kate?"

I nodded.

"Good. That's wonderful … Take another deep breath and listen to my voice. You will step down as you release your breath. Each step you take, you will become more relaxed. On each exhale, you will go deeper within. (This continued until I was at the bottom of the stairs.) Now Kate, at the bottom of the stairs you will see a mirror. This isn't an ordinary mirror. Look closer, you are able to see *through* the mirror …" Said Praise.

I nodded.

"Very good Kate," said Praise with an even voice. "Now, listen very carefully. At this time, I wish to speak to your child within. Your ego. Listen carefully Little One, I want you to step aside and watch Kate go through the mirror. *You* may not go into the mirror. But you can watch. Kate will be fine. It is better for you to stay here for now."

I looked to the left and there stood a little girl staring up at me with large eyes of amazement. I could tell she was glad she didn't have to go through the mirror. As I looked into the mirror, there seemed to be something pulling me into it. Smiling at the little girl, I bravely assured her everything would be all right. Funny, with her standing alongside of me, I saw myself differently no longer afraid to walk through the mirror.

"Kate, I want you to walk through the mirror when you're ready." Praise's voice became very distant.

The little girl smiled as I stepped through the mirror. I was astonished from the breathtaking sight. As far as I could see was a field of grass laden with a smattering of flowers in various areas. In the background, I could still hear Praise's voice giving me instructions. She asked if I could see any object that I was being drawn too. I looked around until a large old oak tree appeared with its branches proudly stretched towards the sky. I felt I could almost talk to it. I strolled to the huge tree as instructed. I lifted my face to feel the sunlight warm me from above. What a wonderful safe place to be! I never knew this place existed.

My spirits began to lift. I felt happy. The feelings of joy were overwhelming. While basking in the sunlight, I caught a sparkle from across the field. I shaded my eyes to get a better view of the vibrant glow heading in my direction. As it got closer, I realized *the glow* was another version of me. *She* was much lighter, brighter. *Her* beauty was exalting. *She* held out her arms to embrace me. I couldn't resist *Her* embrace. I felt *Her* love flow through my entire body. I felt safe. I couldn't believe this person was me.

She laughed, "*We* all look like this Kate. I am the part you are afraid to bring to the surface." *Her* laughter rang through the air.

"I'm sorry." I replied sadly.

"Don't be,—I'm not. I knew that sooner or later we would be together again … Right now, I come forth in bits and pieces."

"What do you mean?"

"Your love for flowers and animals.—Not to mention for others. You're just stuck on other things. Soon we will be united together, always." My Higher replied lovingly.

"I sure hope you got time. From the way things look, it's gonna take some time to sort all of this out." I giggled.

"I,—have all the time in the world. See, for me there is no time as there is for you. Kate, it is time to begin. You are receiving a message to move on. I will show you the way … Take my hand. We are about to go back.—Now listen …"

"Kate, you are becoming lighter than air. You feel weightless,—floating … Ahead of you, there are a group of lines. These are the threads of your all your lives, past present and future. Your Highest will pick the one the beginning of *this* life's abuse. *She* will take you there. Don't be afraid. *She* won't let anything happen to you," echoed Praise.

My Higher Self took my hand and headed for the line pulsing brightly. As we hovered over the line, images began to form within my mind. "I want you *just* to observe, Kate. You may start to *feel* what is happening. You must keep yourself apart from those feelings and observe … Don't worry, I will help you," said My Presence.

The images became clearer in my mind. I was so caught up in this actuality, I wasn't aware I was explaining each detail to Praise and Beth. *She* and I hovered over an area watching the scene below. There I was! I mean it was me! I knew it! I didn't know how, I just did. I looked from the scene to My Presence astounded from the view. I was no taller than I am now. I had long black hair and after … Yes, deep brown eyes. That *was* me! I was standing on a shore looking into the sea. For some reason, I was so sad. I felt it. The emotion was overwhelming.

"You need to be objective, step away, Kate,—*observe*." My Presence stepped closer aiding the emotion to subside. *She* pointed to a tiny hut, after a moment I could see within ... I was sitting with two other women facing a small fire. They were in a heated discussion something about a trip. It appeared the younger of the two was to accompany me. As she leaned closer to the fire, I could see her face.—It was Beth! She was arguing with the older woman about me going on this trip. The younger girl jumped up and shouted irately, "No! It is not right for the daughter of the High Mother to go on this journey! I will go. Tanika's place is here, with you! I don't understand why you trust these people, Mother." She looked firmly at the older woman-standing firm in her convictions. *That Beth couldn't keep her mouth shut, from the beginning!*

The older woman stood up carefully. She leaned against her staff as to give her strength. Before our eyes she seemed to grow taller, brighter. "Do not argue with me, Asha! Do you question the word of the Great Mother? It is time for Tanika to move forward. I will not hear any more of this!" The old woman struck her staff hard on the ground and turned away. Tanika sat quietly looking into the fire.

I looked at My Presence for a moment, confused from the scene. When I turned back, the view had changed to some kind of marble building. I noticed my image as Tanika, was wearing a white tunic with a blue band neatly wrapped around the waist. Something was around her ankle ... A beautiful vibrant green ... It moved! I was startled to see a tiny snake wrapped comfortably around the young girl's ankle as a bracelet. Tanika held a tray and knelt before a tall elegant woman. As she took some items off the tray the tiny snake moved, startling the woman. She knocked the tray from Tanika's hands and beat the young girl. "How dare you bring that vulgar animal into my room! Eris! Come quickly!" Screamed the woman.

A huge guard entered running into the room, grabbing Tanika's arm, and shaking her violently. The fragile animal fell from her ankle; he promptly stomped on the little snake killing it.—*I could feel rage run through my body. Again, I was informed to only observe.*—Tanika retaliated by hitting the large man on the chest. Tanika looked up glaring at the huge guard, *I realized it was*—Bill. He was laughing hideously at her.

He jerked her from the woman's room, dragging her by the hair down a long corridor, finally ending up in a large similar room. He flung her on a bed and started tearing off her clothes. From the way she laid there, I knew this wasn't the first time he had done this. I watched as he brutally mounted the young girl. *The repulsion made me nauseous in the pit of my stomach.—I immediately stepped away from the feeling.*

Before I could respond to the scene, My Presence waved her hand and like ripples in a pool of water, another scene quickly appeared. Tanika was standing on the shore of another beach. She was watching for someone. Tanika smiled as a tall strong man came into view … *I knew this wasn't Bill. This feeling was excitement, love the same feelings I have when Richard was with me.—Richard!* I watched with joy as these two met and embraced.

"Nicolin!" She squealed in delight. The young girl leaped into his arms, I could feel the love as they kissed passionately. They fell to the sand with her still embraced in his arms. The love they made was the same as we did in this lifetime. It was incredible to know something like this could transcend time.

"That's because when something is 'right', it will never change, Kate. Love surpasses everything." Commented My Presence. I understood my thoughts were as words spoken.

I wanted to stay in this moment, but *She* once again, waved her hand over the scene and a new one appeared. Tanika was sitting in the room holding her swollen stomach in joy when Eris walked into the room. I notice the look on her face promptly change. *The child was Richard's! My Presence smiled at me and continued to watch the scene.* For some reason Eris became very violent, hitting her hard. Tanika ran to a corner trying to protect herself from any more abuse. *He knew!* He dragged her from the corner and threw her on the bed. I knew what was about to happen. I didn't want to watch. My Presence moved closer to me until I felt comfortable enough to view. I was amazed how *She* could look on with only one emotion—love. As the scene grew violent, My Presence became more radiant.—Protective of what was happening.

When Eris was done with Tanika, he tossed her across the room like a rag. She gathered her torn dress and slowly, painfully put it on. I watched her do the most inconceivable thing. As he lay there, half asleep, Tanika quietly crept to a small table where a leather object laid. She quickly unsheathed a long thin knife, slowly turned and looked towards the bed, watching Eris with hate. She seemed to gather strength for what she was about to do. Suddenly, she ran to the bed, pounced on Eris, stabbing him in the back. He leaped backwards with a scream, tossing her onto the floor. Tanika lay there, briefly holding her swollen belly from the pain, but only briefly. She moved quickly regardless. Eris managed to pull the knife from his shoulder, and it fell to the floor. Tanika clumsily retrieved the knife. It was as though the wound had no effect on Eris. He caught Tanika by the shoulders and slapped her. Tanika stood rigid, with a numb look in her eyes, she spat at Eris. In a blind fit of rage, Tanika lunged at Eris stabbing in the chest causing him to fall against the wall as he clutched bleeding the wound. With renewed strength and anger, Tanika stabbed him again.

His words of rage calling her whore, damning her for all eternity echoed through my mind. His next words were worse than the knife wounds I could feel his curse move through the fragile figure that stood frozen in the room move, directly into the pit of my stomach. With pain in his eyes, he cursed her.—*Us*. He vowed he and I would be forever tied. The brutality would continue forever. Tanika would suffer forever not finding happiness because he would not allow her to have it. She—*I* would never find happiness because he would never forgive her. The knife fell from her grasp as she watched him die. Her hand gently rubbed her swollen belly. The child within stirred, as this unborn being also understood the meaning of his violent affirmation.

My Presence waved her hand once again; we were again at the village. Tanika was screaming from the pains of labor. She was lying on a bed of straw surround by a circle of loving people. The entire tribe, men, women, and children gathered around her in support. Every pain she screamed, they felt in return as if to aid her in her time of need. To her avail, the child ripped from her body. It was too soon for the birth of her daughter. Nicolin was kneeling by her side in tears. He gently carried her to the small hut while the rest of the tribe took care of the tiny newcomer. As she lay in bed, she told him what had happened and about the curse. Through his tears, he vowed to always be there for her until they could break the curse ...

A gentle old woman placed the child in her arms and I tearfully watched this young woman die as she held her child in her arms.

I was paralyzed from the pitiful sight. I watched Nicolin cradle his beloved and his child in his arms sobbing. I turned away hoping this was all I needed see, My Presence pointed back into the room. I saw a faint image float from the broken bloody body of the young woman. She hovered above the room looking down at the haggard corpse. Quietly she turned, looked at me and smiled. She seemed untouched from the violent drama that was played below.

My Presence stepped towards the floating figure. Tanika's smile widened eager to be with this incredible Being. My Presence held up her hand to stop the small figure from moving closer and said, "Tanika, you have to clear some things." *She* looked sweetly at the tiny figure, "My dear, you need to look deep into Kate's heart and see what has happened to you today will transcend time. You must believe what happened to you this day were only words. They cannot hurt you in any way. You need not carry this from lifetime to lifetime. Only *you* can control what is—no one else. Believe this and this will stop here and now. As you heal, each lifetime will heal, continuing until it reaches Kate and beyond. Do you understand?" *She* lovingly explained.

The small figure nodded. She turned to me and finally spoke, "Kate, I am sorry I have done this to you. When we are in the body, it is easy to get caught up in the drama and lose touch with our Divine part. We forget that we cause these implications to ourselves and have to clean them up later. Do you forgive me?" She held out her arms for me to embrace her. How could I not forgive this wonderful Being?

"Of course, I do. As long as you can forgive yourself, how could I not? Aren't we one and the same?" I answered tearfully.

"Yes," she quickly hugged me then turned to My Presence and

said, May I?" My Presence opened Her arms; the small figure waved to me and stepped within Her Essence. I watched, as Her colors became brighter than ever. The light became blinding. I covered my eyes to shade the glow. When I dropped my hand, I found myself under the tree with My Presence sitting next to me.

"How are you doing?" My Presence asked.

Stunned, I answered, "I–I don't understand. If *You* could fix this, why didn't you?—Back then, when it all started?"

My Presence glowed ever brightly as *She* spoke, "Kate, please listen, I am here to experience the body. While here on Earth, I have to live by the rules.—Free Will and Karma. The end of the game is remembering who and what you are. Remembering the Soul isn't the only part of the Divine. The Body and Spirit are also part of the One. The Spirit works ever diligently to unite both of us. Only when the remembering begins can we heal everything in the past, present and future. We have to do it together."

"Well, I guess there is still some things to sort out … Is everything okay now? How do I know we 'fixed' the problem?"

She laughed, I can say trust me, *I* know that it did,—I'll quickly show you. It is almost time for Praise to start calling you back." She pointed to the ground and again the lines appeared.

"Are we going to fly again?" I asked.

"No, this time, I will bring the drama to you. Just look into the line."

One of the lines started pulsing. I was able to see into the line. Very soon the images began to form. This time my hair was a vibrant red and again I was pregnant. I was standing on a hillside. I could hear the ocean roaring in my ears from a short distance. My limited knowledge of history told me the clothes were from the mid–fourteenth century Ireland.

I wasn't alone on the hillside, Bill and Richard was arguing over me. The scenario was pretty much the same. The only twist was Bill shot Richard during the fight. I ran to Richard, placing his head gently on my lap. I was weeping uncontrollably for the loss of my love. Bill jerked me from Richard and tried to drag me away. I desperately fought his hold and managed to struggle free. Bill stood like a piece of granite laughing as I beat his chest. He grew weary of this, struck me with a hard blow sending me to the ground. I listened in horror as he told me the fate of my unborn child. The child would be left on the rocks to perish after its birth. He would not have any bastard in his household. It was his right as the slandered husband. I should be lucky not to be cast out in the cold. I sadly watched as this woman listened. She slowly dragged herself from the ground. At first, I thought she was going to him accepting her defeat, but she ran past him heading for the cliff. She stopped briefly, turned Bill, "I do not accept this fate. This life. I am no one's slave." She looked at her beloved on the ground, and without so much as a thought,—leaped to her death. I watched Bill scream in rage. I was no longer there for him to torture. He was alone, wallowing in his own hate.

A small wispy figure stood before me smiling. "Hello." I said as I watched her walk directly to My Presence.

She looked me in the eyes; her reply was simply, "Thank you." She stepped within My Presence's open arms and was gone.

I sat under the tree reflecting what I had just seen. My Presence sat quietly next to me. "I don't understand. I thought you said the healing would have continued on the line. She just jumped off that cliff. What am I not getting?"

"What you are not getting, my dear Kate, is *she*—*you* made the decision to jump. You lived before the healing. You stayed and accepted his abuse. You fueled his anger and deepened the commitment. You *took* control over the situation. What you don't understand is, every lifetime doesn't end in happily ever after. Every situation calls for a different ending to the story so we can view ourselves as part of the grander scheme."

"And that is?"

"As part of God. To know and understand how God can love so totally and absolutely unconditionally without judgment. We are the ones that created judgment. There is no need for the Divine to cast judgement, when we do it so well ourselves. Now it is your turn to look within and see yourself as you truly are." She said sweetly.

"How, how do I do that?" I asked nervously.

"Look at me Kate, I am *you* in the future. See how beautiful you are? You are going to make it. I have faith in you ... I always have."

Tears filled my eyes as I gazed upon the beauty of My Presence. This part of me filled with the Grace of God was truly a sight to behold. I held her tight and the words choked out, "Will I ever see you again? How will I find you?"

She whispered softly into my ear, "Of course you will. You've always known how to find me. You called out to me in the mirror—remember?"

I remembered staring into the mirror at my beaten face. "Yes, you did answer me ... I remember."

"It is time to go back now Kate. I'll be here when you need me."

I held on to her as tightly as I could until I realized I was standing under the tree by myself.—No longer feeling alone. I was dancing under the tree when I heard Praise's voice calling me back.

The mirror reappeared and I walked through it with confidence met by the little girl still patiently waiting on the other side. I picked her up and swung her around. "How are you doing? Still a bit confused?"

She nodded.

"I am too. But you know what? I believe we'll be just fine from now on. I don't know how or why,—we just will." I touched her nose and smiled, "We need to work on that fear thing. Okay?" I held out my arms and allowed her to run inside where she belonged.

I awoke to see Praise still holding my hand and Beth standing over me in tears. "How ya doin'?" Asked Praise.

"Like I've been to Oz—and back." "I'm sure you do," said Beth.

"How long—?"

"Almost an hour and a half. How do you feel?" Asked Praise.

"I don't know. I'm starting to feel kind of cold." I noticed an electric blanket was placed over me. Praise probably anticipated this. My teeth began to chatter.

"Why is she so cold?" Asked Beth nervously.

"This is one of the side effects of the regression. It doesn't happen to everyone. Each person processes differently …—Not to worry. She apparently went through a major releasing within and the residue is coming out. To explain a bit easier, if Kate were ill, the body might create a fever to rid itself of the unwanted bacteria, chills are a type of etheric fever. All I need to do is turn up this electric blanket a bit and let her get some rest," said Praise reassuringly. She patted my shoulder and said, "I know you feel a little scattered right now. Get some sleep and we'll talk when you are ready. Your dreams may be a bit strange. That's just part of the processing. Beth will sit with you until you're asleep … I'll see you later."

I barely heard her last words. Sleep came very easy. I found myself back under the tree. The sun felt wonderful against my skin. I looked up and realized it wasn't the sun. A bright light changing from white to purple to pink until My Presence appeared before me. "Hello again, Kate. I love dreams. It is the best time for us to talk. The mind isn't filled with conscious thoughts and clutter."

"How come I've never seen you in my dreams before this?" I asked.

"Simple. You weren't ready. I am here though. I usually have to disguise myself as someone or something else for you to partially listen. Now we have formally met, I can walk into your dreams and you will be able to acknowledge me without fear of going nuts or something.—Make sense?" *She* laughed.

"Yes, it does. I guess I'm pretty hard headed."

"I wouldn't call it being hard headed as much as carrying so much fear. I am the last person you want to face. The last person you want to see disappointment in. If you face yourself, the fear of facing the 'uglies' is part of the deal. Now that you are looking directly at me, do you see any?" Again, *She* smiled.

"No, I don't. Y–You are very beautiful. No. Magnificent is more the word. If you are so beautiful, then where are the uglies?" I questioned.

"That is the point, Kate. There is no such thing as 'uglies.' She explained, "Everything is perfect. You have placed those things in your mind. If you remember, in every transformation, you had a smile on your face. You lived your lives in perfection even though it didn't seem that way to you."

"How can all that violence seem like perfection. I felt it." I shuddered from the memory of the feelings.

"Yes, you would. Remember you were looking into each life—Like a TV." "Yes, but this was different."

"You were only looking at *you* in a different role. Now you are cast in a new role trying to fix the plot of the old role."

"If this is only role playing, then what am I doing all of this for?" "You! Or Me! We are one and the same." *She* answered clearly. "When I first saw you in this dream, you were different colors."

"As I come closer to you my vibration has to change until you can see me. Your highest form is white. Your vibration color while you are here is pink. When you saw the pink, you were able to see me. It will all make sense soon enough. You, see all levels of who we are, will be joined as one; then the most spectacular thing will happen." *She* said with illumination. Her hands gestured outward and upwards. *She* looked at me, reading the question of what was to happen, glowing ever brighter,—Enlightenment!" The feeling of exaltations filled from within.

I sat with this incredible presence trying to grasp what was just spoken and humbly asked, "Are you here to take me somewhere else?"

"No, I am here for you to meet someone you have had hidden away for quite some time." From behind her emerged a tiny little girl with a sad look on her face that almost brought me to tears. "It is time to get to know your child within, Kate. You have kept her locked up deep inside. It is time to heal her. You've been through a lot today. I only wanted you to meet, so you can do some future healing together."

"Who is she?" I stared at the tattered little thing. She didn't look at all like that this morning.

"Your smile." *She* coaxed the child from behind her skirts and pushed her towards me. We stared at one another. The little thing had an angry look on her face. "This morning, you were with your ego.

You have many children within. Each one will soon come forward and remind you who they are. Right now, 'your smile' needs the most work."

I forgot my thoughts were as spoken words. "Please don't hate me. I promise we will work together from now on. I am so sorry I have forgotten you." I pleaded to the tattered little girl.

"Oh, you didn't forget me totally," she squeaked.

"Really?" I was curious.

"You let me out on special occasions." She stubbed her toe in the ground and shyly counted on her fingers said, "Yeah, sometimes when you're with Mike. There were very few times with Bill. Beth has helped quite a bit. I don't know what we would have done without her." Her voice got softer, "The baby … Both of them …" Her face lit up, "The most smiles were with Richard!"

How sad, I thought, *this poor little thing could count my happiness on one hand.* I extended my hand to her. My Presence whispered something in her ear, and she crept towards me. She embraced me and I squeezed her as tightly as I could. "I won't ever put you back there again. I promise! I need you so much in my life. Will you help me?" I sobbed.

"Of course! All you had to do was ask!" She laughed out loud. I found myself uncontrollably laughing with her. We rolled in the grass and played as My Presence watched.

We rested under the tree. "If you come from my future, can you tell me what happens so I can be prepared for it?"

"No, I can't. It hasn't been written. You have to write it Kate. I can give you an idea, but you have the right to change. Besides, where is the adventure if I tell you?" *She* commented.

"What if I do something wrong and create more of a karmic problem?" I became worried. With my track record, no telling what I might screw up.

She laughed, "Kate, haven't you been listening? You can't do anything wrong! Look at me! Whatever you do will be absolute perfection! It can only get better from here. You have to remember one very important thing …" We leaned closer to her to hear … "I love you."

CHAPTER NINE

Righteous Anger

I tossed the blanket aside. My body was soaked from sweat. There was a towel hanging on the chair with a note attached.

> *Kate,*
> *Praise didn't want me to wake you. She left this towel in case you needed it. Should you wake in the middle of the night, there is food on the table for you. See you in the morning!*
>
> *Love you,*
> *Beth*

"Come to think of it, I am rather hungry. I think I'll grab a bite to eat before going *back* to sleep." I tiptoed to the kitchen and was met by Laran wagging her tail and leaping at the table.

"Are you hungry too? Sure, all puppies are naturally hungry when it comes to food. No matter what it is … Let's see what we have here. Looks pretty vegetarian … No meat for you … How 'bout a cracker?" I tossed her a cracker and helped myself to a few morsels. I looked around the room and wondered about Praise. Was this room done in her taste or John's? Her office was nothing like the rest of the house. It was done in very soft colors and had very little furniture. "What do you say, little girl? Which is Praise, the room or the house?" I asked the begging puppy.

"I would say,—both." Praise stood in the doorway watching her dog frantically beg for more food. "You'd think she was never fed."

I giggled and tossed Laran another cracker.

"I am happy to see you are doing okay. Beth was becoming concerned. It was all I could do to get her to go to sleep. I finally had to do a guided meditation to get her to relax."

"Yeah … Beth has always been very protective of me. I thought it was strange how she sort have attached herself to me after we first met." I commented.

"And now?" Asked Praise.

"I'm not so sure. I don't know … Yeah, I guess it does kind of make sense.—Man!" I leaned against the chair and fought the tears. "I don't understand what is happening to me. The last year has been one big disaster after another … Now I'm told that it's absolute perfection.—People have committed suicide for less! *But not me*, I hang on just to discover having the shit beat out of you is *perfection*! I caused it to happen—no less! You want to know what is even stranger?"

"What?" Asked Praise politely.

"For some strange reason, I believe it. I don't know why. If I were told this was going to happen a few years ago, I would have run in the opposite direction … But since Richard walked into my life … I don't know, I feel anything is possible," I answered.

"I understand.—Really. We can no longer hide behind the simple explanations of the church. People want something more. We *know* there is something more. This is why I love working with people and introducing them to their past selves. It opens up a well of knowledge they have been keeping secret for a very long time. It's not the complete answer of how to be rid of all these things. It's a start. Sometimes it helps them understand why they have these hidden secrets."

"Sounds like you enjoy your work."

"Yes, I do. You know Kate; this didn't just happen to me yesterday.

It has taken me years to come to this understanding. I had lots of challenges to overcome.—Lots and lots of anger. I drove away friends—and a few husbands." She laughed. "My personality changed like the wind. For a time there, I truly believed I was going to go mad. The more awakened I became, the more doubts I had ...—How 'bout some hot tea?"

"Love some ... Man, I sure do understand that going mad stuff. Thought I was going to end up in a nut house a time or two myself ... If the challenges keep getting more difficult, then why go on? How do you do it?"

"Faith," she said as she handed me the cup of tea. "How did you do it? Why didn't you end up in the nut house?" She watched as I carefully thought about my answer.

"I guess for me, it was just plain orneriness, I've got that Spanish/Irish hard head ... I don't know, I just knew. Somewhere deep ..." A light bulb went off inside.

Praise smiled. "This is why I love what I do. When you believe in past lives, you are able to 'see' everyone with a new and wonderful 'wonder.' You are able to understand why this person is the way they are. What it took them to achieve this lifetime ... If you were to look through the eyes of a child—Oh, the wonder of each new thing she sees!—The excitement and jubilation of achieving this wonder. This is how the Soul reacts to every situation in understanding what is the ultimate goal. The wonders of God, to see from every perspective—To see ultimately from the eyes of love. Doesn't this within itself means to rejoice?—The love of the self? We as humans believe we are not capable of the wonderment, yet we go from lifetime to lifetime from birth to death—again, and again until we reach that unreachable goal.—To see with the eyes of Divine Grace and finally understand what Jesus, meant, 'Unless you become a little child, you can no wise enter the Kingdom of Heaven!'" She caught her breath.

I sat spellbound, listening to her, when something deep, deep inside stirred. Then tickled ... A bubble seemed to float from the pit of my stomach to my lips. My lips quivered until I found myself sobbing.—

Not from sorrow.—From knowing. Within my mind I heard loud and clear—Yes! Someone does love me!—I do! I was able to pull myself from the chair and ran to the nearest mirror. I looked at my reflection, in return, this magnificent being looking back! Her eyes glowed! There was a sparkle in those eyes I have never seen before. Again, the voice echoed the same words I had heard a few months ago … "I haven't forgotten you!" I felt lovingness fill my body from my head to my toes. My eyes filled with tears and uncontrollable sobbing followed. This time, I understood the tears. I was relieved.

Praise guided me to her large chair and held me like a small child allowing me to cry these emotions through. "Welcome back little sister," she said softly. There was nothing but the gentle sobbing flowing through me as the woman held me in her arms and cradled me lovingly. More lovingly than my own mother had ever had. And in this moment, I was able to forgive her, and understood, she could not do this because she was caught up in her own fears. I let go of all of this emotion and my body went limp into Praise's arms and allow this pain to flow free.

I was startled by another sniffle. I looked up to find Beth standing in the doorway crying. I wiped my eyes and asked, "How long have you been standing there?"

"Long enough to see you liberated." She rushed to the chair holding both Praise and I.—Crying and laughing … It became one big emotional scene.

We found ourselves laughing hysterically. I don't know how we ended up on the floor. My sides were aching from the laughter. "How did we end up from crying like fools to laughing like this? I was feeling as though I was going to explode one minute and—then it was gone!—Whew! I feel wonderful!" I exclaimed.

"Well … Wait a minute, let me catch my breath before I answer that. Hmmm. This is what is so wonderful about healing. When it's gone, you have to fill with something. I am grateful it was happiness. Let's try and keep it that way—okay?" Laughed Praise.

"What else could have replaced it?" I asked.

"A number of things," said Beth. "Sometimes, we let go of one thing, and we don't embrace our child with love and understanding, it is filled with another emotion. You wouldn't believe how much room lack fills. You should feel wonderful and know you deserve it. Happiness makes it impossible for lack to fill that space. Until you are used to dealing with the removal of these emotions, it is best do it with someone with you. This way you will have someone to support you during and after the emotion is released. You cannot depend on your ego. 'it' wants the old program, not the new and improved."

"There has to be an easier way to fight this invisible emotion that seems to fill us with such ease." I said halfhearted.

"If there were, I'd turn it into a pill and bottle it. Boy, the money I'd make on Instant Karma removal! Kate, there is no easy way to clear Karma. The only way *not* to face it in this life, is to wait for the next. There is only one problem, we're running out of time! All Karmic dues are to be paid in full—no exceptions … Since we are all up, why don't I fill the car with some wood and a pot of coffee. We can go to one of the vortexes. The sunrise there is exceptional," said Praise regaining her wits.

It wasn't long before we were climbing out of the car and setting up a small fire. I was shivering to the bone. I watched Praise build the fire with ease. She seemed oblivious to the cold. Beth and I sat on a large rock gazing at this marvel.

Praise walked over with two tins of coffee, "Here, wrap your hands around this, you'll be warm in a few." She smiled and threw a small blanket on the ground and sat down. "I love it here." She sipped on her coffee and sat quietly.

I was afraid to interrupt her. She seemed to be in a trance. "Praise … I …" Beth poked me in the side to be quiet. I couldn't be quiet, I was freezing to death. "How come you're so warm and Beth and I are sitting here with our teeth chattering? I mean, we're from Chicago, I should be used to this, but man, it's damned cold!—No, don't answer that …

You're gonna tell us that you have some kind of control or something like that—right?"

Praise laughed. "Yeah … Something like that. Kate, I'm not some kind of guru. It has taken me years to finally have control over certain things in my life. Thousands of steps, a few forward … and a great deal of them back. So many damned decisions, it would make your head spin. I drove everyone I knew crazy trying find the answers. I lost quite a few friends in the process.—But I made great many more."

"So, what's the answer?" Asked Beth wrapping herself deeper into her coat. "Let go." Praise took a sip of her coffee and looked at the sky.

I watched her silently waiting for her to finish. After a moment, I looked at Beth puzzled. Beth was also stumped. She shrugged her shoulders and continued to drink her coffee. "That's it? That's the answer? Let go? That's the answer of the ages? Let go of what? I don't understand! I didn't expect to come here, for some kind of –of—damned quest! I don't feel like one of those books I saw in that–that bookstore … Of people who are trying to find themselves—or whatever." I felt rather foolish realizing I was shouting from the top of my lungs at two people who were only trying to help me. I plopped back on the rock and dug my hands deeper into my pockets. "I–I'm sorry. I don't know what got into me. This has been too much …"

Beth stared at me wide eyed and stunned. Praise looked indifferent. "Are you warm now?" Beth asked.

"Well, yes. I'm quite warm now. Foolish and warm." I replied sheepishly.

"Why do you feel foolish, Kate? Why should you feel foolish for expressing your feelings?" Questioned Praise.

"I shouldn't have yelled at you. You haven't done anything wrong."

"I didn't feel like you were directing your anger towards me.— Or Beth. You were 'letting go' of some stuff.—Fear. You feel foolish because your ego believes we will judge you for questioning all of this. You've taken a major step in your life. That's more than most. So, why shouldn't you question it?" She responded.

"Oh, Kate asks a lot of questions, sometimes she questions things to death," implied Beth.

"That may be true, Beth. Sometimes asking questions is the only way to look at fears." Said Praise.

"So … Praise tell me how to let go. I really want to understand … You make it sound so easy." I commanded.

Praise stood up and was looking around for something. She came back with a large stick. "Stand up Kate and hold out your hands."

I stood in front of her and did as I was told. She handed me the stick. "Turn around and walk." I walked into the dark and heard, "Stop! Now, let go of the stick." I did. "Very good. See, that wasn't so hard, now was it?" "No."

"You have just *let go* of your first thing, it's that easy," she said aloud.

My mouth fell open. I couldn't believe what she just said. I didn't know how to respond. I stood in the dark alone and listening to this crazy woman! I have placed myself in the hands of a mad woman! She had to be crazy! I became enraged. "If you think for one minute, I can just go back to Chicago and *let go* of that bastard up there, even after what I saw in my mind today … You are a bigger nut than I could have ever thought!" I shrieked.

Praise walked over to me with Beth right behind her, "Kate, you have to listen to me! You walked into this darkness by yourself. Sure, you did as I asked, but you, and *only you* had the option to do or not do as I asked. Then you and *only you* let go of that stick. Not me or Beth—but you!"

I could barely hear her. I was sobbing, "He'll never let me go! I'm stuck in that hell …"

Praise grabbed me by the shoulders and started shaking me, "Look at me … Look me in the eyes!" Again, I did as she asked. "Now, take a slow deep breath; through your nose and into your stomach. Now exhale through your mouth. Slowly … Now, again … That's good. Feeling a bit more centered?"

I nodded my head. "And warmer."

"Ye-a-ah. I feel warmer, too. This is neat!" Blurted Beth.

"Kate, I want you to tell me something ... Can you, right now, see what Bill is doing?" Asked Praise.

"That's dumb ... How can I possibly know what Bill is doing?" I retorted.

"You didn't answer me. Can you see what Bill is doing right now?" She asked sternly.

"No, no of course not." I was exasperated.

"Can you make any decisions about what he is doing right now?" "No!" I had just about enough of this questioning.

"Now, can Bill see what you are doing right now?" She firmly continued. I rocked from one foot to the other. My patience was wearing thin. "No." "Can he make any decisions about what you are doing right now?"

"No!"

"Did he tell you to walk into the darkness and drop that stick?"

"No! What are *you* getting at?—Damnit, you're making me nuts!"

"Kate, if you don't have any control over what Bill does in a day, how can he possibly have any control over what you do? You've just proven to me that you and *only you* dropped that stick! Bill's control is only mental. He cannot have any control over you physically. Therefore, Praise tapped her head, "His mental control is in *your* head and only you can decide whether or not *you* want him to have it. Abuse is an addiction, and all addictions control the mental. The ego needs to *feed*; therefore, the use of addiction becomes important. Once *you're* in control of the mind, *you* are in control of the addiction ... Kate, you're the only one who can—"

"Jesus ..." I gasped, "I'm the only one who can let go."

Praise looked over my shoulder and said, "Will, you look at that ..."

I turned and witnessed one of the most beautiful sunrises' I had ever seen.

Beth and Praise returned to their spots and began to meditate. Since I didn't have a clue as to what to do, I watched them for a while and decided to walk around a bit. I quietly walked down a small path. Everything was beautiful covered with morning dew. I never realized how active the morning was. All around me were sounds of different wildlife making ready for a busy day ahead. I found a small clearing, not too far from our site and sat to watch. I sat with my arms curled around my knees, propped my chin, and continued to watch the sun rise in the sky.

A small dot appeared in the sky that seemed to float effortlessly in the air. It wasn't long before realizing it was a small hawk enjoying the morning. As it floated, it appeared to be looking for currents in the sky catching a ride gliding within them. I closed my eyes and took a long deep breath. In my mind, I could still see the bird floating in circles. I still saw the clouds float by, one by one. I felt warm all over as I controlled my breathing and continued to listen to my breath inhale—exhale. My body relaxed as the rhythm of my breathing slowed steadily.

After a moment I thought I was staring into the sun. It had to be I had so shield my eyes from the blinding light in front of me. As I cupped my eyes trying hard to see within this radiant light, I happily thought once again, my Highest Self had returned for a visit. I patiently waited for her to appear. Instead, a tall man walked towards me. From the skipped beat in my heart I knew it was Richard. I was disheartened by the frantic look within his eyes. It appeared he had been desperately looking for me. I heard his soft deep voice, "Kate, I miss you so much. No one will tell me where you are. I want to help you any way I can … Allow our love to free us from our hidden ghosts … We have paid the price here on earth in so many lifetimes. It is time to heal. See me in your heart beside you. I will send you my love. I–I need you by my side … I *will not* betray you.—Trust what you feel. We have been parted before—never again … We are forever connected … We will find a way." He smiled and reached out for me. I smiled in return, nodding my head in agreement.

I looked into his eyes remembering the few lives I viewed with this man. I wanted him to hold me. As I walked towards the glow, he was gone. Yet, I was filled with his presence, his scent. A shiver trickled down my spine from the memory of our last encounter. Could this be a mental trick? Do I want to be with him so much, I concocted this dream? No. This can't be another dream. It doesn't feel like one. I could feel him. I know he was here ... *I guess I'll just have to trust ... I softly laughed, trust—me trust, well that is a new one for the books. It has been a very long time since that I have been able to look at that word much less place faith in it. Taking a deep breath, Well Kate, it has to begin somewhere. Your foundation has been rattled to the core. You know that in your heart you cannot continue living in this constant state of fear. In this state one day I will not be able to come out ... And what then? Have Bill finally beat me to death? Have him come home in one of his drug influenced drunken stupor and one blow in the right place—this girl has another lifetime to clean up. No, I cannot—Not any more.* I felt the rage and anger of all the dramas I have lived over and over flood through me until I tasted the hard-salty tears within my mouth. My body shook as I sat there in my trance state breathing in the world around me thinking I would never be lost like this again. No one was going to control me like this—not ever. This is not a "need" I require to survive. I want to be happy and in love. I want to be with the person who helps me move forward with him.

I was jolted out of my meditative state from the sound of shrieking birds. I opened my eyes to view several hawks now flying in a low circle above my head. They seemed to be performing an aerial dance, just for me. I watched them as I headed back to Beth and Praise.

"Looks like you are being honored." Said Praise.

"Yeah ... I guess so ... Whatever that means. Aren't they beautiful? I've always loved hawks." I shaded my eyes as I watched these magnificent birds in their aerial dance.

"Well, they seem to love you, too. You must have gone through something wonderful!" Said Beth. "The circle seems to be getting larger."

"Hawks are messengers. All animals have meaning. You have opened quite a few doors Kate, and on a higher level they can see this and honor you. This is a wonderful sign. The birds seemed to be pleased enough to leave you a gift." She walked ahead, picking up a feather and handed it to me. "They don't let go of these lightly. Keep it. It is their gift to you," she whispered as though speaking out loud would ruin the moment.

"Thank you." I was speechless. I sat on the blanket and studied the feather. "You know, Praise, with everything that has happened to me, you haven't asked me what's gone on. What I've seen or anything!"

"You spoke a great deal while you were in regression, whether you know it or not. When it comes to talking about it, that's only your decision, Kate. As I told you before, you are in control of you. You've had so much thrown at you, I knew you needed time to absorb all the little things and sort them out before you decided to say anything. The most important decision was, whether you believed it or not. That's when you begin to understand you are not crazy and *it* did happen … We haven't begun to understand the mind,—it's true purpose. Who's to say what is, or is not real? You have to connect within yourself and trust the answers. When this occurs, there will be a calmness you've never felt … Everything will feel right, almost fluid. You will be able to face any situation without fear. That's when you will truly believe what you went through this week was real … I am not here to judge you for what you've done in this life or any life.—Remember that."

"Thank you, I needed that … You're right, I was feeling a ti–*ny* bit crazy." I replied in relief. "I do want to ask you one question. While I was sitting on the cold ground watching the sunrise, I found it very easy to go in some sort of meditative state.—I guess that's what you'd call it, what the hell do I know? Anyway, I saw this bright light right in front of me. At first, I thought it was my Presence,—or Higher Self, but it turned out to be Richard. It was like he was trying to send me a message … I mean, I could *feel* him. I–I don't know, this is too weird …—Was *he* trying to send me a message?"

"First, I want to congratulate you on meditating on your own. See it doesn't take much and it is very easy. It is all in how you breathe and *not* focus.—As for Richard, well … He may be trying to send you a message. I mean the way you have explained him to me, he knew about you before you guys met. You two have even had the same dream. It seems to me, for twin Souls, you two have a very tight connection. So …

That would make it very easy for the two of you to communicate via meditation. I've heard of people connecting in dreams. I've done it ... You've had an incredible experience Kate."

"Boy, leave it to Kate. When she takes off, she doesn't mess around!" Responded Beth with astonishment. "So, can you tell us who communicated with you in your dream, Praise?"

Praise laughed, "Aren't we inquisitive? I met my twin flame through a dream." "Is it John?" Asked Beth.

I scolded Beth, "Be quiet! Man, you can be nosey! I think she told us enough!"

"Well, she opened the door! Now I'm delving deeper.—That's all. I mean, if you don't want to tell ... Well ..." Beth replied cautiously.

"No, it *isn't* John. There isn't much to tell. He just came to me in a dream and told me who he was. It was time for me to know. I thanked him and he left. That's all there been to it. Sorry if it's boring. Not everything is lights and action, Beth. Besides, John is my Soul Mate. I like having him like that." Praise chuckled.

"Aren't you curious about meeting this person?" I asked.

"Yes, when the time is right. I did have an opportunity to meet him, but I chickened out.—I wasn't ready," justified Praise.

"Aren't you afraid that you'll never meet? Does, everyone have a twin? They seem to be coming out of the woodwork," rattled Beth.

"No, but there is someone for everyone. If they choose to have a companion. Many within any lifetime choose to walk alone. We have many Soul mates, and in different lifetimes have made more and more connections. —And I am not afraid I'll never meet him. I once had someone tell me I had to meet him by a certain time, or I would never meet him. I laughed and promptly told her I had more power than that. When *I* decide it's time for us to meet ...—Providing he is also ready—The time will be arranged for when and where.—If we didn't, there would be a time in the future. You cannot keep twin Souls or soul mates apart forever. They will sooner or later make the connection. It's inevitable ... I react this way whenever anyone gives me limitations. It becomes my gauntlet." Praise slapped her thighs stood up and began gathering the coffee cups and cleaning the area indicating this was the end of this subject.

I took this as a cue to change the subject, "When are you going to work with Beth? I seem to have taken up most of your time. I'm sure she has things to clear up." I looked at Beth; "I want to thank you for being here for me. I know that I take you for granted sometimes. I've seen you take the gauntlet in hand and run. You have been a rock. I tend to forget that maybe you have problems that need working out."

Beth laughed, "Thanks, sweetie. Nice to see you back. Praise and I talked about it and I believe the only reason I am here is to be your strength. I'll be fine. Don't forget I've been doing this for some time. Don't get me wrong, Praise has helped me a get deal with some things I needed help with."

"Oh? Care to share?" I winked at Praise.

"Oh, I get it. Now it's my turn ... If you must know ... I've decided to have a very long talk with Mike. I don't know how we are going to do it, but I won't know unless we can at least first talk about it and maybe give it a try. I mean whirl—right?" Gloated Beth.

"Sounds good to me. I'm sure Mike won't object." I laughed.

"Not to change the subject," interrupted Beth, (Beth could talk about everyone else, never about herself.) "But the day is definitely here, and you haven't been to bed. What do you say we rest today and go into town later to do some Christmas shopping? I have to get some things for Lisa or I'll be hung if there isn't anything under the tree! She's funny like that."

Christmas! I almost forgot. What am I going to do? "Sure, it's sounds fine with me.

I guess I could get a few things. I don't believe he's frozen the credit cards yet." I giggled. *I should call Mike and find out what's going on. Has Bill called to find me? I didn't want to think about it.* Right now, sleep did sound good.

I closed my eyes as my thoughts drifted to Bill and my present situation. So much has happened to me in last the few days. *How can I go back? What am I going back to?* I haven't thought about Bill's reaction when I return. He was enraged before I left … He has had time to do two things. Let the anger sputter out—or make plans to kill me upon my return.

Before I left, his control over me was pretty tight. To be honest, I'm really surprised I did leave. This small freedom I've had these past few weeks has been wonderful, even with all the bizarre things I have just faced. It's strange to say this, but it's true. I like this freedom. I like having control over my life. Have I really let go of a lot of this pain? Is this why I feel this way? Now I have the opportunity to look at things from an entirely different perspective. To think, words spoken so long ago affect my life now. I mean, this would certainly explain why I just couldn't leave before.

"Hard to believe isn't it?"

I looked to my left and smiling at me was My Presence. "I didn't realize I've gone into a meditative state."

She shrugged her shoulders; "It's really easy once you get the hang of it."

"It's nice to see you. I know it was only a few hours ago when I last saw you. I mean, I understand that you are part of me,—this is all strange."

She laughed, "No stranger than having to go through life and death believing this is all there is. No stranger than believing all God has time for is deciding whom gets the wonderful life and who gets all the hell.—Like all God and Company has to do is wait until we die and go to Heaven. Most of the things that happen are pre-decided if certain things don't take place. After you are able to see the vastness of what is happening, you will understand God doesn't pick on little children."

"Like what?" I was lost as to the little children comment and what brought that up.

A soft airy chuckle escaped my Presence's lips, "Kate, haven't you been listening to Praise? To look within and face yourself. If you don't face it someone else will make you face it by allowing it to happen to him or her. Then you will have to see it.—Or it will occur over and over until you do. In each lifetime, we take the last one with us. Whatever garbage we created is brought along with us—if we haven't gotten rid of it. Once it's gone, it's gone. –Unless you decide to hash it back up. Why bother? Move forward and enjoy all there is out here! As far as the little children comment, it is simple. There are really no little children. Only the child within. This is how we return to One. These tiny bodies merely house the Soul within. If you look at it, some of these tiny bodies running around here are the homes of some VERY old Souls with VERY old dramas to clear up."

"That doesn't seem fair. From what I have just learned, we forget. Sounds like a disadvantage to me."

"Who said anything about what is fair? Disadvantage? Remember Kate, we did this ourselves. We have the capabilities to remember all the way down the line, back to the beginning. Things have to be done. Time is short, so God and Company do what they have to do to help you along."

"Who is this Company you keep talking about?"

"Me, your guides, angels, whatever you want to call them. We are all here to help me connect better with you. So, you and I can finally become One."

"Oh. I know you are my Highest form. I mean that's what Praise and Beth say. I guess you are my—Soul? Who are you really and why are we separated?"

"I am the Highest form, the Soul. I *Am* what *My* Christ Brother became so angry about when He entered the Temple and saw how abused it had become … I *Am* your Temple of God … The *IS* … We became separated when the Body and Mind began to believe in the doubts and fears rather than in Me."

"I am sorry I ever doubted you. It boggles the mind, seeing you here and believing I could ever doubt this incredible Presence."

"Kate, it didn't happen overnight. Well, maybe in the fact for me, it was a wink of an eye, but for you,—lifetimes. Everything happens within Divine Grace. One day we will be as One, and you will remember everything."

"So, what does God and Company do if we carry all this stuff from lifetime to lifetime?" I asked.

"Everything and everyone is one. We are part of God and God is part of us. As we grow, believe it or not—They grow. Every single thing you experience, love, hate, happiness, drama is experienced through God and Company. All the way down to the diminutive quarks in our bodies. We are *all* connected. If someone enters the room with hate heavily on their minds, don't you sense it? How do you know what hate is supposed to feel like, if you haven't felt it before? If we weren't all part of each other, all thoughts each person felt would only be theirs. You wouldn't be able to *feel* hate much less happiness," *She* answered with a smile.

"Could you answer one more question? I–I have had some good lives,—haven't I?" I asked meekly.

"Of course! We only looked at those that needed attention. You have been here many, many times! Would you like to see a happy one?"

"Please!" I said excitedly.

My Presence sat quietly for a moment and finally said, "Praise is now here with you. We can begin ... Let me see ..." *She* looked down and again the lines appeared before us.

"Why is Praise here ... How—?"

"I sent for her. She will help with her energy to guide us. You're very tired Kate, you have been quite a bit in just a few days. So, we will make this short ... You ready? Now look ..." She pointed to the line.

I looked into the pulsing line; an image began to form. I could see a young woman giving birth. Was this me?—No. I looked around the room until my eyes fell upon a tall fair man pacing the floor in the adjacent room. He flinched each time he heard the cries from the young woman. Another, older, man was sitting in a chair laughing at the young man. The older man walked over to the young man and said, "Calm down son, my Julia is well. Do not fret, she is strong and healthy. Your child will arrive soon. Come Edward, sit, with me and leave the worry to the women folk."

I recognized the man sitting was my father—and he was full of joy! Edward flinched as he heard another cry. I saw in his eyes how he shared in this pain. It is me! I was the father of the child being born! Edward spoke in anguish, "Please sir, excuse me. It–it's just … Damn-it all! I cannot bare this any longer! How can she stand this?"

Suddenly, the door opened, he rushed to Julia's side. He looked into her eyes with pride. Julia could not return the look. She turned away and sadly told him she birthed a daughter. Edward quickly dispelled her of any doubts, "How could you possibly believe I could love a daughter less than a son? Julia, God has sent us this child for us to love. P–Please, my love, do not despair." His love for the young woman was deep. I could feel it deep within my core. In my heart I knew the woman was Richard. It was uncanny how I grasped this.

My Presence waved her hand changing the scene. The future was wonderful for these two. They had everything one could ever ask for. My family was happy. Love was rich and full in my life. We had five happy and healthy children. I watched them grow old together. In the end, the young man freely left his body and stood before me. I could feel the happiness that filled his presence. "See, things aren't always bad," he said as he hugged me. Once again, I watched him walk within My Presence and disappear.

"It was a wonderful feeling to see I had a wonderful life. It was also amazing to see my father so happy. In this life he was filled with so much hate and grief. I still cannot decide how to cry for him. My feelings are so confused."

"Let go of the hate, Kate. It won't do you any good. Festering is the only thing that comes from hate. It doesn't affect your father now. It only affects you. Hate will grow into terrible things. It will only attract terrible things to you. It also prevents you from seeing things clearly. It makes it impossible for love to do its job within the heart. We don't want it to grow into a cancer. You and I have so much to do, let us move into a better direction. As you can see my dear, you are capable of happiness. I assure you, it will happen to you again."

"I see you before me and wonder if Richard sees a whole Soul. I mean are you split between the two of us?"

My Presence laughed, "Our Soul decided it was time to grow further.

The way was chosen to divide. At first, each only had a female energy or male. As time went by, each of us grew; we are now individual Souls with all aspects of each … Because we derived from the same Soul, we will always have that connection. We have gone through many lives apart. In this life, his Soul and I decided it was time to clear up loose ends, as it were. This would be the perfect time for us to unite so we may move into the future more fully integrated."

"Does this mean we are supposed to be together?" I asked.

"Only to clear up the Karma. Once this is done, you may decide if you still wish to continue this life with or without him. Should you decide to have children, the road will be much clearer for them. Our children come here with the vision we refuse to see within ourselves. They have chosen to step forward to live and sacrifice so we may move closer to the light. They will be born with eyes open. They are able to see our fears and act them out. It makes it a rather heavy load for them to carry having to clear their Karma along with yours. It pleases *Me* to see you and Richard have chosen to step forward on your own."

"I can't possibly see the future without him … I feel complete when he is with me …" I thought for a moment, "I agree, I am grateful I won't pass this pain to our children."

"Good, but you must remember you *are* complete without him as he is complete within himself.—And know that your child has his or her mission here also." She touched the side of my face and once again turned into a beautiful pink light … My eyes filled with tears. I was elated to know such happiness did exist and to understand that I was worthy of this happiness.

"How ya doin?" Whispered Praise.

I rubbed my eyes and stretched. "Wonderful."

Praise tucked the blanket around me and softly said, "Why don't you try to get some rest? I'll tell Beth to go on ahead into town. We'll talk more later."

It was several hours later before I got out of bed. I knew Beth wouldn't return until she touched and felt everything Flagstaff had to offer. I yawned deeply and was aware of the growling in my stomach. I remembered seeing the bowl of fresh fruit on the kitchen table, "Hmmm, that sounds good! But first I need to make a pit stop!" I went into the bathroom to clean up a bit. I was startled when I looked in the mirror and saw a ragged mess looking back. "Man, Kate, you could scare the dead! Me thinks I better shower before everyone gets home.—But first, those grapes await!"

After inspecting the grapes, I opened a can of club soda and settled in the living room to feast. I was engrossed with this morning's events with Richard when I heard a door close down the hall. As I nervously rose from my chair, I heard Praise's voice, "It's only me." She sat in her favorite chair and Laran parked herself in her usual spot. "Didn't mean to give you such a start, Kate. I've been in my office meditating and having my period of silence," she giggled. "Once you catch your breath,—finish eating … Beth has been worried about your lack of food intake since you've been here. I told her it wasn't unusual, but I would see to it that you ate when you woke up. She went into Flagstaff to do some shopping and see the sights. I thought this would give us some time to talk—if you wanted."

I was munching on the grapes, not quite minding my manners. "I'm sorry, but it's strange, one minute, I couldn't eat anything—I mean, the thought of food was revolting," I choked out between gulps, "—the next, it's like I've been starving for a month!—And the food … It's delicious! I mean, I know it's only grapes, but—but,—man! Are they good!"

Praise laughed loudly, "That's what happens when your senses are heightened as yours are. It's as if your palette has been wiped clean and you're tasting everything for the first time. Wonderful—isn't it?"

All I could do was nod. She waited patiently for me to finish. I felt rather awkward behaving as I was. When I caught my breath I asked, "You know … I am dying—*how* did you know!"

"Yeah, I thought you might ask. When I have someone I am working with, I pay extra attention to everything around. I get messages up here." She pointed to her head. "I have learned how to trust within and know when I am needed."

"So, you heard me calling you? I mean my Higher self." I asked curiously.

"Yes. Of course! I was there—wasn't I? From the look of things, everything went well. You seem to be moving and listening very well by yourself, Kate. I've seen very few who naturally respond this quickly when they are awakened."

"I need to ask about this *awakening* thing. What's the deal? What am I awakening to? I mean, is it like a call to God? Do I have to become a nun or something?" I asked feeling rather foolish about the question.

Praise laughed out loud, "You are a breath of fresh air! Forgive me, sweetie, I'm not laughing *at* you. But to answer your question, yes,—something to that effect. It means different things to different people. To some, an understanding of things has to change. They cannot keep going like they are. To others, it's a call to wake up; you have things to do! You cannot sit on your laurels any longer. It is *all* a call to God. It doesn't matter how you arrive to the call," she shrugged, "You just do … Sometimes it takes many, many lifetimes.—And no, you don't have to become a nun. They get a call too, they know in their hearts this is what they are supposed to do.—Is this what you are hearing?"

I lowered my head, "No, that's not what I'm hearing … I'm just new to all of this. If I had heard these voices in my head six months ago, I would have had myself committed. Does it pretty much happen the way to others? I mean, is there so much havoc in their lives?"

"No, some go through with ease and some need the rafters shaken a bit. Apparently, you needed *your* rafters shaken up,—hmmm? You've been listening to those voices for some time, you call it your sixth sense, or Guardian Angels." Praise answered.

"Looks that way. I've had my rafters shaken as far back as I can remember." I sighed with a sullen look.

"Kate, it isn't that bad. It doesn't matter where you begin. Some people are a bit farther along while others take it slow. Where you are right now is perfect. The subconscious knows this. All we need to do is get the body and mind to accept it. Don't be so hard on yourself. It will happen," she comforted.

"I just ... I just don't know how I'm going to forgive Bill or even Dad, for all the shit I've been through. I know, you're going to tell me I asked for it, or it is a byproduct of a past life nevertheless, it still happened and I'm finding it very difficult to find it in my heart to forgive."

"Sounds to me, like your heart is a very crowded place." She leaned closer, "Kate, it all starts here." She pointed to my heart. "What is keeping you from forgiving them, is not forgiving yourself. You have seen only a few lifetimes. I know you're Highest Self explained that within each life you viewed, how things changed once the act was forgiven. What you must not have realized, you were forgiving yourself. *She* saw everything in perfection. You will become strong from this challenge and be able to move on. You have to allow yourself to absorb the experience; know that *was* and *is* perfect. The knowledge will find its way and heal. Only you can rewrite your story. I will always be here—if you need me."

"I know that you and Beth are leaving tomorrow. I've been working with Beth's meditation. I asked her to show you. Meditation is very important. I don't like telling anyone they have to do it. It seems then it becomes a chore then they don't receive the wondrous benefits from it. She was concerned about falling asleep when she first meditated. I explained that it's the body catching up on what it needed. If you should fall asleep during meditation, you can't have a better sleep. To prevent falling asleep, sit up somewhere that makes it impossible to lie down.—Okay?"

"You said something about a period of silence. What's that? Is it another form of meditating?"

"Sort of, it's really where I would like you to start. When I first learned to meditate,—it was difficult! Man! Do you know how much noise your brain makes when you try to settle down? There is constant chatter! It's kind of hard to meditate when you brain is going a hundred miles an hour. It gets distracting! I discussed this with one of my teachers; he suggested periods of silence. All you have to do to start is take about ten minutes and sit quietly with your eyes closed. I know it won't be easy, but do it," she said with a gentle sternness.

"Can I do busy work?"

"No. This will only create more chatter for the brain to work on. I would like you to sit somewhere and just sit quietly for ten minutes. Next, focus on your breath. Feel everything there is to feel about your breath. How it goes in and out. Do you breathe soft or heavy? How it brushes against your upper lip. During this time, you will begin to hear all the noise in your head; what you did that day, is Beth coming over—you know everyday stuff. Every time a thought comes up observe it, breathe deeply, exhaling through the nose, and let the thought go. If you dwell on it, you are not sitting silently. Focus on them like clouds. You know how clouds float by? That's the way thoughts are to be treated. Soon you will be able to treat your thoughts as clouds. That's when I want you to move your silent time up ten more minutes. When you get to thirty minutes, get with Beth and have her show you how to meditate."

"So, what will I get out of just sitting there silent?" I asked.

"Being silent will put you in touch with yourself on a level you can't even imagine. It will enable you to regain control of your mind, instead of the mind in control of you. That's why I do them both. I do my periods of silence or quiet anywhere in my office or even in my garden. That way I can connect with the earth. You will become more centered and decisions will come easier. The big plus Kate, when you make the connection, you will find it easier to see the perfection and understand the healing or forgiveness. When you do that, forgiving Bill and your father will painlessly come in time."

"If you say so … I have decided what I am going to do tomorrow. I hope Beth will understand."

"What will Beth need to understand?" Inquired Beth with a smirk upon her lips while standing in the doorway with arms loaded with packages.

Startled, "Did you leave anything in Flagstaff?" I laughed.

"Only a little. There were so many neat things! Lisa is going to love the vest I bought her. I bought Pops one of those turquoise wrist bracelets. I know he won't wear it.—Who knows? You are going to *love* what I bought you." Beth took a breath and continued, "So, what is Beth not going to understand?"

"Let me help you with those packages. Which one did you say mine was in?" I teased.

"This one. You might as well have it since I won't see you for Christmas. But be careful, I have Mike's gift in there with it. I'll wrap it so you can give it to him," Beth said in a nonchalant way.

"Leave it to Beth. She always knows what I'm going to do even before I do. Yes, I'm going to stay with mom and Mike for a while … I can't go home yet. If I do, no telling what's going to happen. I haven't talked to Bill since I've been here. Well, that is what the plan was—right?" I became nervous, "I believe I'll call him from Mike's."

"Breathe, Kate. Bill has no control over you. You haven't walked out the door—and there you go! Whenever you get excited, I want you to yell 'Stop!' within your mind. This will help you to focus. It will also give you a moment to clear the nervous reaction from the fear." Responded Praise.

I sat down and breathed deeply. I couldn't believe that all I had to do was even think about Bill and I would react this way. *I needed a bag to keep from hyperventilating! Sheesh! Was I ever going to break free from this fear? I can't allow this! He has no control over me!—No! I'm going to go to moms for a while and get my act together.* "I have control over what I do. Bill doesn't anymore! I tried. I lost everything, my home, my baby and almost my mind. No! I'm going to take care of me! From this day forward, I am released from whatever ties I have had with Bill.—No more. Ka–*tie*, is a thing of the past. He no longer has a power over me. I take it back. It belongs to me!" I said aloud with all the confidence I could muster.

Beth ran to the couch and held me in her arms. "Thank you, Beth. Thank you so much for being here for me. I know we haven't spoken to each other a whole lot since we came, but I want you to know that you are very special to me. I don't know what I've would have done without you. I guess Anna was right. I have come a long way. To a point, yes, our friendship was tested. I believe we've passed." I smiled.

"Yes, we have sweetie, I knew you were going through some pretty heavy stuff. I discussed it with Praise and stayed out of your way. Sometimes a friend can get in the way too much ... Look at me, I'm a bundle of tears! You haven't opened your gift ... Go ahead. I believe you'll love it." She said as she wiped her eyes.

I slowly opened the tissue and revealed an intricately beaded leather pouch. Inside was another smaller one. "They are beautiful!"

"I thought you needed something to hold your feather and small crystal." She said smugly.

"My crystal! It's still in the box ... No, Bill will never find it. When I decide to get my things, I'll get it then. It's amazing how I had to keep things secret. It all seems rather silly now. Well, no more. No more fear ... No more secrets." I whispered.

I hugged Praise tightly. I didn't want to leave. I wanted to stay in my new, safe place. I cried on her shoulder, "I don't know how to thank you. I still don't know if I believe everything that happened, but I do know I am a very different person thanks to you. I will never look at anything the same again."

"Thank you, Kate, you did most of it yourself. Remember that you saw it, I didn't. You're going to be just fine. I will be there if you need me." She wiped the tears from my chin and smiled. That sparkle was still there in her eyes.

I watched her as we pulled out of the driveway. An incredible glow appeared around the edges of her body. I shook my head and tears filled my eyes.

"Are you okay sweetie?" Asked Beth as she patted my knee.

"Yeah ... Everything's fine ..."

—Or is it? What am I going home to? I can't go back to Bill. Deep in my heart I wanted to call Richard. To have him in my arms again ... *No, I can't run away from this.*

—No more running. It's time to get it together. I can do this ... I cleared my throat. *Can I do this?—Control Kate, control ...*

CHAPTER TEN

New Realities

I stayed with Mom and Mike through Christmas. I didn't know which was worse, Mother's lack of understanding or Mike's over protectiveness. Whenever I brought up the subject about Bill's abuse, Mom changed the subject. Mike's constant repetitive argument on *how* I should have thrown Bill in the slammer grew weary on my nerves. I gave up, resigned myself to my room and diligently worked on my silent periods. Praise was right; it wasn't difficult to get caught up in memories. Thoughts of Richard would float in and out. I found myself wanting to stay within those feelings. When my thoughts strayed to Bill, I noticed they became less and less frightening. I was beginning to become a bit more in control of my emotions.

    I talked Mom into planting a few flower bulbs. That's when I began to feel better. It was a wonderful to put my hand in the earth once more, even though I was only setting flower bulbs into pots. I enjoyed explaining to her where they needed to go in her little garden this Spring. I even drew a diagram where they needed to be placed. This was a great diversion for the both of us. It kept her from lecturing me about Bill and kept Mike at bay. Mom couldn't understand the basis of Mike's anger. His arguments about Bill's abuse were never in front of her. Deep inside I was grateful Mike and Richard kept everything a secret.

Mike reluctantly went to Chicago for New Year's wearing his gift from Beth.

I guess the merchant in Flagstaff ran some sort of sale on bracelets. It took both Beth and I to reassure him I was a big girl now, so he could leave me alone for the weekend.

I was just returning from the airport when I heard the phone ring. I felt ill within the pit of my stomach. Bill, I knew it was Bill. Mother called me to the phone confirming my ill feelings; "It's Bill. He wants to talk to you."

"I told you I didn't want to talk to him! Tell him I'm out!—Gone! Or even better—Dead!" I snapped. *I don't want to talk to him! I can't!* Another wave of ill feeling wretched through my stomach. I wanted to crumple to the floor and melt away under something. The fear was overwhelming. *Kate, get hold of yourself. Remember it's only a mental fear, he can't hurt you! Breathe!*

"No! Kathleen Sawyer, I will not lie for you," she firmly snapped. "Mike may have done this for you, but it was with my disapproval! Now, young lady, you will get on this phone and speak to your husband!" She shoved the phone receiver into my hands and stormed out of the room.

"Hello? Baby ... Katie, I mean Kate, are you there?" Asked Billed in a sugary sweet desperate tone.

"Ye–s. Yes, I'm here." I stammered as a sullen child. My body began to tremor violently with fear as my eyes filled with tears.

"I thought they were never going to let me talk to you! Baby, when are you coming home? I miss you terribly. Everything's fine here ... Well, I say that, but I don't know where your cat ran off too. He's been gone for some time. I'll get you another," Bill stammered nervously.

"No, you don't have to get me another cat, Bill. I left Jazz with Beth. He's fine." I replied flatly. I began to notice a new feeling starting to take over my body. Anger and rage began to replace the violent fear.

"Oh," Bill cleared his throat and changed the subject; "I couldn't handle you being away for Christmas. I bought you some wonderful things. I can't wait for you to open them. Whe–When are you coming home?"

"Bill, you shouldn't have bought me anything. I–I don't know when I'll be home. I need time." I answered with impatience. I leaned against the table holding the phone, rocking from one foot to the other. The rage was overwhelming; it took everything I had to keep from hanging up on him. I knew deep inside I had to maintain my cool ... Just *a few more minutes ...*

"Need time for what? It was only a spat for God's sake. Katie, if you stay there, how can we work things out? I want you home to me! This is where you belong!—Not there! Please, let me come get you!" He pleaded desperately.

Panic began to replace the rage. Fear once again was finding its way into my throat, squeezing it tight. My throat ached, I couldn't talk. *Can't breathe ...* Within my mind I screamed—*Stop!* and gasped a deep breath. *Good girl! Take another!* I heard from within. I slowly breathed in deeply. As the breath entered my nose, passing through with ardor, my throat eased—relaxed a bit. I became placid. I was so caught up in this, I forgot Bill was on the phone.

"Katie, –er –a Kate! Are you still there?—Baby, please let me come get you." His continued pleading brought me back to the conversation at hand.

"No!" I straightened up and persisted in a somewhat calm voice, "No, Bill, please stay there. I can't come back yet. I can't go back to the way things were, "I took another deep breath, "You need help, Bill. I tried it your way, seeing Father Flanders,—it didn't work."

"Father Flanders said the same thing! He gave me a name of someone to see. I'll see him,—I promise! I'll do anything to get you back. Baby, I swear! Katie—er Kate," he stammered, "I haven't had a drop to drink since you left. I don't need the coke; I'll go to the meetings! I'll do anything for you. I love you! I need you! I can't do this without you," he became silent. After a moment of silence, I could hear him softly crying, "I love you sweetheart, please, come home to me."

I thought I was going to go insane. Listening to him cry made me weaken once again. I felt as though I was on a roller coaster of emotions, "Bill, P-please stop." I began to cry. *God, I can't think. He can't hurt me anymore. I can't let him. Please God, please give me strength!* Within moments I felt a warm glow flow through my body, I was able to gather myself up and continue, "You can't see someone for me. It has to be done because it's what you want to do. You have to do it for *you*. I can't come back.—Not now."

"Yeah, yeah … I'll do it for what*ever*. Please come home!" He sounded strained.

"I have to go now." I said softly. My body was drained from the mixture of emotions. I didn't know how much longer I could keep this up.

"No—no—wait! Kate, please don't hang up! Damnit Katie!" His sobbing turned quickly into rage. "No! You can't do this to me! I'll show you—you Bitch! You belong to me! You're mine, Katie! You hear me!—Mine! Katie, are you there?—Don't hang up … Katie …"

I could still hear his yelling as I dropped the phone onto the receiver. Mother came back into the room. I knew she had been listening from the kitchen. "From the look on your face, Kathleen, you didn't work anything out! What am I going to do with you?" She asked in frustration.

"Mother, please shut up! This wouldn't have happened if you had only told him I wasn't here. But no! You had to do what was right! You've always been that way!" My anger got the best of me; "You are no different now than you were when I was a child! You told Dad everything to keep the heat off you! Nine times out of ten, it didn't work! He'd beat the hell out of you anyway!—*Don't* you see? I've followed the same road! I am not going to live my life scared to death of my own shadow! I am going to be happy! I deserve to be happy!" I was screaming from the top of my lungs, totally out of control.

"Kathleen! Don't you talk to me in that tone! I did what I had to do,—you know that!" She was floored. She staggered back to the couch and sat down in disbelief from my accusations.

"No. I don't know that! I was a little girl, Mother. What in the hell was I supposed to know? How was I to even protect myself from Dad? How was Mike?" I waned from the look of shock on her face.

"Mother," I softened my tone, "I don't blame you ... I really don't. I love you. Right now, I am scared to death! Now, please, let's sit down. I have to think."

Mother obediently sat as I paced the room. "Kathleen ... I am so sorry. I didn't know ... No, I didn't want to face the thought this was happening to you. I didn't realize ..." She looked so pitiful. Again, I felt an inner strength fill me. I was able to see this woman with love. I loved her with all my heart. At once I realized it wasn't hate I felt towards this woman all these years, it was pain from the lack of love I received as a child. This feeling no longer existed. I knew she really wasn't to blame. She played victim and it caught up with her. I threw my arms around her and held her tightly. "Hush. It's okay. I'll work things out—somehow. God, I love you Mom."

I went to the phone and started dialing. Mom asked, "Kate honey, what are you going to do?"

"I'm calling Mike. I know he's at Beth's right now. I hope I can catch them before they leave for the evening. I want you to go upstairs and pack a few things. You need to go to Aunt Ruth's. I don't want you here."

"But what will you do?" Her face became stern. "I never liked your father's sister," she said pouting as a small child would in distaste.

"Like it or not, that's where you are going! Bill doesn't know where she lives ..." I held my finger to my lips to silence her, "Hold on the phone's ringing ... Beth. Hi. It's Kate ... I'm fine ... I need to talk to Mike, is he there? No, Beth everything is fine now. I'll talk to you about this later, right now; I need to talk to that big lug of a brother. Mike, Bill just called."

"Damnit! I knew I shouldn't have left you alone there with Mom. Is everything all right? Should I come home?—Damnit!" Cursed Mike. I could feel his anger through the phone, as well as his panic.

"Yeah and no. Don't get your feathers flustered Mike. Mom made me talk to him ..." *Damnit, I don't need this! Chill Kate, regain control. You can do this.*

"What—?"

"Don't worry, it's okay. Bill is a bit hysterical. I don't know if he will try to come here to get me, so I'm sending Mom to Aunt Ruth's and I'm getting the hell out of here." I replied a bit more composed. *Good Girl! You got it!*

"Man, Mom hates Aunt Ruth. Well, do what you have to do. I'll be on the next plane out. Are you going to stay with them?" He asked.

"No. You stay there. I'm taking the next flight out back to Chicago. I need you guys to pick me up at the airport. I figure, if he's on his way here, we won't meet on the same plane. I'll fly via Praise's name. I'll be paying in cash, so they won't be asking for any I.D. I also want you to get me a room at your hotel. He'll suspect Beth's place right off. I don't want him giving her any more grief. I'll see you guy's in a few … I'm sorry to screw up your New Years'."

"Don't think that." He answered a bit more collected; "You're my sister. I'm here for you. Let me talk to mom. I want to make sure she stays at Aunt Ruth's until I get home. I don't want her thinking everything's fine, go home and meet that bastard. I'll see you in a few hours. I know there's a nine o'clock flight. I'll pick you up around then.

Don't worry about the room, you can have mine. I'm staying with Beth."

"Say what? My, my, my. I let my brother go to the big city alone and look what happens!" I mused. "Here's Mom … Love ya—Bye!" *Yes!* Feeling proud of my actions.

I handed Mom the phone and ran up the stairs to my room. I quickly found my small ragged suitcase and started refilling it. As I picked up my clothes, the pouch Beth gave me fell to the floor. I picked it up, sat on the bed holding it gently, lightly running my fingers over the bead work, remembering my stay with Praise.

Could a few days make this much difference in my life? Maybe, maybe not, all I know is, I can't go on living the way I was. I will not live as my mother did. Nor will I allow things to continue with Bill no matter if there was a lifetime before. I had to stop this now … God I wish I were safely back in Flagstaff!—No, there is no safe place for me until I resolve this mess … I took a long deep breath, gently placed the leather pouch in the suitcase ... *Praise, I need your strength more now than ever ... Soul, don't fail me now!*

"Well, we got you to the hotel room, what's next?" Asked Mike. "Don't get me wrong, Kate, I appreciate the fact you thought fast on your feet and you got Mom out of the house. But where do you go from here? Are you going to keep running?—What?" I looked at my brother as he spoke. A soft smile crossed my face as I thought of all the years and times, he has been there for me, for mom. I could see as well as feel the genuine concern he was going through at this moment. Mike the rescuer. Yes, my knight in shining armor towered over me, ready to protect his little sister once again. I shook my head. Time for him to begin taking care of another. Time for me to let go and move forward.

Beth sat on the edge of the bed watching us. "You know what? I don't know. I am taking this one step at a time. I don't need your big–brother routine right now.—You know? I do believe one of us should call Mom and tell her I'm here and fine." I replied sternly. I tossed my battered suitcase on the bed and myself after it. I was determined to stand my ground and not allow him to bully me into fear once again.

"I don't think we should tell her where you are. I don't want her to accidentally tell Bill," said Mike in an agitated tone. He hated it when I pointed out his over protectiveness. I realize I haven't made too many great decisions, but he must begin to see they were *my* mistakes and I need to be the one handling them.

"Oh, it's fine to tell her. I don't want to keep any more secrets from her ... Don't worry, she won't tell Bill.—Trust me." I said with exasperation. "Give it a rest, Mike. Everything is fine for now.—The mission is almost complete—sir!" I dramatically saluted him while rolling my eyes. Beth burst into laughter.

"Fine! I'll call her then," he held back a grin, "Jes–! The things I gotta put up with!" With continued big brother firmness, "I'm sure you want to talk to Beth." He winked in Beth's direction.

I looked at Beth. She was blushing! "Sooo? Are you going to tell me?—Or am I going to have to drag it from you?" I was relieved for a lighter moment.

"We had a very long talk. A-a-a-nd, I think we're going to give it a try … You know what I mean! Man, I've got to get that word out of my vocabulary!—Anyway … We've decided to meet on weekends. Kind of switching. Lisa thinks he's great—so why not? Kate, I'm tired of being alone. Lisa is practically grown. Hell, she's more grown up than I was at her age. Mike said he'd work things out with your mom … I don't know. Kate, what do you think? How will your mother handle this?" She asked.

"I don't think anything. You once told me I was crazy to give up a wonderful guy for an ass. I didn't listen, so who am I to give advice? I will ask one thing,—Are you happy? I mean, I know he's my brother, but that doesn't mean a damn thing when it comes to being happy. If you both are happy, then that's all that counts. I'm sure Mother will approve of this. I understand now, she really wants us to be happy." Remembering our last encounter.

"For the short period of time we've been together, yes … Not to change the subject, but what are you going to do about *that* wonderful guy? I'm sure he'd be here in a second if he knew what was happening. Mike could call him." She patted my hand.

"I don't want to think about him. I don't believe having him here right now is the answer. I'm finally working on the problem, one step at a time. If he were here, I couldn't think straight. You know what he does to me. "No, I shook my head, "I need a clear head. The next few days are going to be tough enough as it is. I have to know what Bill is up to. I have enough money for a while. If I withdrew some, he'd know—that fast!" I snapped my fingers. "Which only leaves me with a few days to decide what to do and how to do it." I said half in thought—half aloud.

Beth and I jumped when the doorbell rang. "Relax, I ordered some

Champagne. It's almost midnight! I thought we'd toast the New Year!" Said Mike, "Man, we're all so damn skittish!" He shuttered comically.

"Good thinking, sweetie!" Said Beth in a lighter tone. "I sure could use a drink right about now. I know Kate could use one, too!"

I laughed. *It was good to see these two so happy. God only knows, someone around here deserves it.*

"You'll be just as happy soon enough," replied Beth.

"Stop reading my mind! Pour us a drink and let's toast! I'll go first." Mike handed us our glasses and we all held them high, "To Mike and Beth, may they find true happiness with as little Karma as possible!"

"Karma?" Asked Mike looking at Beth curiously.

"I'll explain later, drink, it's a good toast," said Beth. "Me next. To Kate, may this year prove to be the start of many wonderful experiences! May you find your answers, and may they be in your highest interest.—And Mike, thank you for coming into my life," she leaned against my brother and smiled into his eyes.

Mike was caught up in the moment of Beth leaning against him. Just as He was about to kiss her, I softly coughed. Mike's face turned a deep crimson as he smiled cleared his throat and spoke out loud, "Now, it's my turn … Kate, little sister, may all good things come to you because I know you are so deserving of them." He looked into Beth's eyes, "To you, my sweet Beth, thank *you* for coming into my life.—And wait—To me, for being the luckiest guy in the world to have two incredible women with him tonight of all nights!"

Beth placed her arms around his neck and whispered, "Yeah, but you're getting lucky with only one tonight!" Kissing him sensuously. Mike reeled back as though he was hit by a rocket.

Feeling rather awkward, "Well, why don't you give me a quick kiss and get the hell out of here! It's past midnight and from the look of things, you two have other things to do tonight!" Leading them towards door. I knew they wanted to be alone and so did I.

"I'll be here in the morning. Well, not to early." Mike smiled. "I don't want you going anywhere unless I know what's going on—hear me? Even if Bill were to check this hotel, he'd think you were with me.

I know you'll be fine." He kissed me on the forehead and touched my chin, "Happy New Year, sis."

"Happy New Year," said Beth while hugging me, "We'll be here first thing in the morning.—I promise." Holding up her palm and crossing her heart.

"Well, don't make it too early. I may want to sleep in! So, Happy New Year, now get out of here and stop worrying about me!"

I was greatly relieved they left. I slipped into my old tee shirt and picked up my glass, "Well, here's to you thinking on your feet, Kate!" I toasted myself in the mirror. "Now, all I have to do is think very hard about what I am going to do next … Yep, it would be easier to just call Richard and have him come in and save the day just as he's done many times before … Oh Richard, I wish I could do that." I paced the room talking to the air. No. It wasn't air. I knew he was here. He's always with me. He knows and feels everything I feel. "How do you feel now, my love? Is your heart breaking? Are you going mad at the very thought that you can pick up my scent, feel my touch, wake up to find I'm not there? You know, I deeply regret sending you away …"

My braid had become unraveled; I paused and ran my fingers through my hair causing it to cascade along my shoulders. "Why didn't you just gather me up in your arms and just take me with you?" I sobbed, "No, he couldn't do it that way. He knew I would hate him if I were forced …"

I ran back to the mirror and looked deeply into my eyes, past the tears, "Is it true? Did you really come to me in Arizona? If I only knew … Is our love impossible? Is it wrong for me to love you so much? It was so hard to give you up. I should have known …" Did I really? I closed my eyes and brought back our love making again. My body ached for him. I shuddered from the memory of our love. My heart … My heart is breaking. Tears escaped my closed eyes.

I poured the last glass of Champagne. *Have I waited too long? Does Maggie have a hold on you? What right do I have to split them up?* "I knew about him long before you did Miss Maggie!" I said a loud. "No, I can't do that … Maybe someday fate will bring you back to me." Once again, I held up my glass, "To you my love, I wish you all the happiness in the world ... And to me, may I have the strength of ten to face this greatest fear and move forward!"

Deep from within I heard, "Bravo!"

I was up bright and early the next morning. I had a light breakfast and was sitting quietly on the balcony when the answer came to me. Excited and impatient, I decide to go for a walk. Beth and a very upset Mike met me in the lobby.

"I thought I asked you to stay here until we arrived? Damnit Kate, why don't you listen?" Stormed Mike.

"Mike, please settle down. If you thought I was going to the house,—you're wrong. I was only going to the park for a walk this fine beautiful morning! I'm excited! Have you guys had breakfast? It's on me!—I can't wait to tell you," I saw the glow in Beth's eyes, "Beth! Hmmm, looks like you had a great evening. I'm really surprised to see you here at all!"

"Well, some of us are concerned about your welfare," muttered Mike.

"Mike, settle down. She's fine. Kate, tell us your idea." She gave Mike a kiss to appease him.

"I'm going to call Mrs. Logan for an apartment. This Spring, I'll go back to school and finish up my major in Arts. For the time being, I'll see if I can get a job at the museum. I know it won't pay much, but it's a start. I know Mrs. Logan will help me out ... And finally," I took a deep breath, "I'm going to tell Bill, I want a divorce."

"Well, why don't we just tie that up in a pretty bow. It sounds so perfect," said Mike smugly.

"Mike! That's horrible! I cannot believe what you just said." Scolded Beth staring in disbelief. In a natural reflex, she hit him on the arm.

"Damnit, she doesn't have enough money to live on," grabbing his arm and rubbing it, doing his best to look pitiful. "Bill will have an all-points bulletin out on her when he finds out that she's no longer in Flint. She'll barely have enough to live on at the museum.—I can just see Bill giving her a divorce. I can't leave her alone to fend for herself with that nut running loose!" Mike slammed his fist on the table.—No! It's out of the question!"

I blew up; "Listen to me you horse's ass! I'm a big girl. I'm going to Father Flanders and ask for the divorce. The church will surely grant it after they find out what I have been through.—If they won't—What do I care. I have to get away from him no matter what's at stake. As for the money, I was going to ask for a loan until Dad's insurance pays off. I'll be fine. I can't walk around in constant fear. If he bothers me, I'll have him arrested. An attorney should know how to handle that."

"Kate, this sounds well and good. Why don't you stay with me until you get things straight? That way you can save the money you need to get back to school. We can work things out … There's no reason for the two of you to fight. Right now, we all have to work together. If you continue to fight, Bill will have won the battle … I hate to ask, what about Richard?" Asked Beth.

"What about him? He's with Maggie." I retorted.

"*And just what* about Maggie? You know he doesn't love her, Kate." Pushed Beth. "Well, I really don't know. Besides, I don't want him around while I'm trying to get all this straightened out. If he were to show up now, there will be no reasoning with Bill. I've explained this before. I don't know why you have to keep bringing him into this. Please, let's keep Richard out of this.—Promise!" I pleaded.

Mike looked at Beth and smiled, "Well if you were stay with Beth, Kate, it would make things a lot easier. I can get back to Flint and work things out with Mom. I would feel a whole lot better knowing you are not alone and vulnerable to Bill."

I looked at my brother and read the fear in his eyes. I am trying to move forward here. Maybe I should do it in little steps for now, just stay a bit constant in what I am doing. Still there was a part of me that felt a little let down about my idea not going totally over. "Ok Mike, I will stay with Beth."

I softly chuckled within, *but not before I check to see if there is a room available with Mrs. Logan!*

Mike brightly smiled and patted my hand, "Thank you sweet sister.

This means a lot to me. And I am sure you will see it was for the best just after you go look and make sure Mrs. Logan has nothing available!"

Beth and I burst out laughing … God did he know me or what?

Mike's prayers were practically answered. Mrs. Logan didn't have anything available. She promised to put me first on the list, so I moved in with Beth. Mike seemed to be happier knowing I was with Beth. Pops threatened to kill Bill on sight if he were to come near the apartment. This in itself made Mike a great deal happier. Lisa was all for the move in, she got to stay in the extra room with her grandfather which quickly turned into misery when she found he had a keyed dead bolt put on the outside door next to her room. Of course, Pops had the key.

Good old faithful Bill found out where I was and called the apartment a few times. Which promptly stopped after Beth explained that should he call again, she would cut off his nuts and feed them to the cat. I heard her tell him and I believed it!

I was able to get a job working in the museum. It turned out one of the coordinators, a friend of Pops, grew up on his diner food. In the meantime, I contacted an attorney and was waiting to have Bill served. My attorney explained he couldn't have Bill served because he was out of town. I called Bill's secretary to confirm this. This also explained why the phone calls really stopped. Naturally, I thought this would be a good time to go to the house and retrieve some of my things.

Tears filled my eyes as I pulled in the driveway. I really missed the house. I stopped short of the front door, caught my breath and nervously tried to put the key in the lock.—*Stop this! Bill is out of town. There is no reason to be nervous.* I took a deep breath and opened the door. *Good 'ole' Bill. Didn't change the locks. Why should he? His wife is scared to death of him!*

The nervous feeling was still in the pit of my stomach. Once inside the dark house I relaxed a little. *See? The place is empty … Nothing to be afraid of…* The house felt strange, it smelled awful, as though the garbage had not been thrown out in sometime. *Just like Bill not to get rid of the trash before he went out of town. He must have thrown something out and it went off.—More like died from the smell.*

I went straight to the bedroom to retrieve my things. I tripped over some small bottles by the bed and decided it was best I turn on the lights. The place was trashed. My stomach went into instant turmoil. I quickly scanned the room in disbelief to see everything was in disarray. Everything I owned was strewn about. I don't believe a single drawer was shut. "What is the deal?" I said aloud. The closet door was slightly ajar. I tossed my purse and keys onto the bed. My knees started to tremble. I leaned against the bed for support and pulled myself together. With hands tightened into tight fights, I slowly crept towards the closet, peeking in to discover all my things were scattered all over the floor. I knelt to pick up my secret box, finding all the contents inside were missing. My favorite red dress laid crumpled beside the box was torn to shreds. Panic set in; I tried to breathe, finding it impossible. My chest seized tight. *Damnit! What a fool I've been!*

"Looking for these?" Asked Bill sarcastically just a few steps away from the closet door holding my tapes and crystal in his hand.

"Jesus!—Where did you come from?" I screamed spinning around, losing my balance and dropped to the floor. Bill stood by the bed looking smug. He looked haggard and unshaven. It appeared he hadn't cleaned up for some time. I noticed the same glare in his eyes from our last major encounter. I slowly stood up trying to maintain my composure. "I–I thought you were out of town."

"Yeah, I'm supposed to be. Made it up. I figured you'd fall for that." He sauntered closer to me, and rudely snickered, "Your damned attorney sure did."

Stepping away, "I had to get a few of my things. I see you've arranged for them "not" to be needed,—so I'll be leaving." I flung my braid back and straightened my dress.

"I—don't think so, *Kate*," making sure I noticed the correction, "We are going to talk. You love to talk … That's the way it sounds on these tapes. Did you enjoy your trip to Arizona? Oh yeah, I found out about that little trip, too … Did you *find* yourself?" He leaned in closer. Fear prevented me from slapping that smug look on his face.

"Doesn't look as though we'll get much accomplished like this. Bill; let's talk later.—Okay?" I faltered.

"No. I want to talk *now* … Better yet, I want to *do it* right now. Let's see whom you'll enjoy more,—Me or 'ole' Rich baby. Yea, I knew it.—Bitch! I knew you screwed around on me!" In furious rage, he lunged for me. Quick thinking, I slammed the closet door into him causing him to fall backwards.

Using this moment, thinking he was far enough away, I bolted for the bathroom believing I could climb out the window. As I reached the door, Bill had my braid in his hand. He violently jerked me back then slid his arm around my waist and began kissing me along my neck. I kicked and screamed, "Please, Bill. Please let me go!" I began to cry. All the old tapes of fear and panic set in. Everything I learned in Arizona fell into the deepest parts of my mind to be forever lost. I must be the biggest fool to think I could change. That I, Kate, could win this battle of fear. There was nothing I could do. The fear of him killing me was over whelming. He pulled me close and began rubbing his groin against me. I froze allowing him to violate me as my body reacted in disgust.

"Oooh, but I love you,—Ka–*tie*," Bill mocked as he continued to awkwardly grope my shaking body. I became nauseous from the smell of stale beer. "I'll show you just how much." He dragged me to the bed, threw me down pinning me to the bed with the weight of his body. His hands immediately went to my breasts squeezing them painfully hard. "Oh yes my sweet Ka-*tie*, you are gonna love this." Bill's mouth covered mine as he slammed his tongue deeply causing me to gag against the beer stench of his breath. I pushed his face away. He laughed. My pleading for him to stop only added to his delight. He slid his hands down my dress, ripping it out of his way. With one hand, almost one motion, he tore off my underwear, slid his fingers deeply within me and began to violate me. Bill had no care about the pain he was creating within me. I lay there crying from behind that wall I thought was lost, the memory of this scenario being replayed sent me into a panic. *It was going to happen again! No! I can't let this happen again! Someone please help me!* I stared at the wild rage in Bill's eyes. The memory of my past life filled me to the core as I felt the sensation of indignation. *This is wrong! I screamed within. Kate, you can't allow this! You have to get yourself away from this crazy man!* I struggled harder to get away.

Bill mistook my reaction as one of lust. He laughed, "See, you love it! You're going to love it more in a minute." He moved his wet hands to my face pressing me against the bed, kissing me, and forcing his tongue in my mouth once again. He worked his way back to my breasts biting them hard. Breathing hard he whispered, "Oh yes, whores love to be treated this way. Is this the way 'ole Richard used you? He just took what he wanted?" Bill's laugh shot through me.

While fumbling to pull off his sweat pants, and maintain his hold on me, I noticed my keys on the edge of the bed. I quickly decided to use Bill's reaction to benefit my situation. I quickly changed my mood to catch him off guard. I stopped hitting him with my free arm; began caressing his chest and returning his kisses. I moaned softly, "There is no need to be too rough. Come here, let me help you with that." I slid my free hand to the top of his sweats and untied the knot allowing them to fall.

Bill's reaction was startling. He stopped and smiled hideously, "Oohh, so you like it rough. Sorry I didn't know before. It would have saved us a lot of trouble." He relaxed a bit and said, "Maybe this is what I needed to do a long time ago. Show you who's boss, hmm?"

I helped him with his pants. When they were around his knees, he leaned back to kick them off. I lunged for my keys and sprayed mace in his face. He jerked away before I could get him directly in the eyes, but it was enough to distract him, aiding in my getaway. "I can't believe you fell for that! You idiot! You'll never touch me again, ass hole!—Man, you are so stupid!" I quickly straightened what was left of my dress. Sobbing with disgust, "You could never compete with Richard. You'll never understand!—He loved me. You don't know the meaning of love.—Boss this, jerk!" I picked up a vase and threw it at him. He ducked and it shattered against the wall. It was time for me to get out of there.

I could hear him curse me as I ran down the hall. I became excited believing I could get away. When I got to the living room, the furniture was so disarrayed; I stumbled over the ottoman falling to the floor. Bill leaped over the couch and slammed into the front door to prevent me from heading in that direction. I quickly jumped up and headed for the kitchen. I knew I could get out through the garage.—I had to.—I made it! I had the knob in my hand and turned it ... To my disbelief, I watched it drop slowly into my hand. *Oh my God! It fell into my hand!* I clutched the only means of my escape in my hand as I listened to Bill's demented laughter from behind, ringing in my ears. It was maddening. *Oh, dear God, please help me.* I prayed. *Please don't let this happen again.*

Bill slowly strolled to the door taking the knob out of my hand in triumph. In slow motion, I watched his hand raise and fall on my face. I went flying into the cabinets and heard something crack. I fell crumbling to the floor. Bill leisurely walked over picking me up by the throat. My hands were blindly grasping for something on the counter as he squeezed. My search was not in vain, for patiently waiting was the butcher knife. It was as though destiny carefully placed it safely there so this drama would finally come to completion. I held the knife firmly in my grasp and flung my arm back to strike ...

I shook my head to clear the strange sensation that flowed through me. My tear-filled eyes looked Bill squarely within his glazed eyes. This wasn't the man I knew. It didn't even look like Bill. This stranger's mouth fell open when he saw the knife in my hands. He had not anticipated this. There was nothing he could do. One swift movement and the strike would be a deadly one. The rage tried to overflow the strange glowing sensation. Something ... Someone was reaching out ... Not to Bill but to me. I felt triumphant. *Yes, you bastard, what are you going to do now?* He could see it in my eyes. He couldn't stop me ... His look of aghast turned to sincere surprise as he watched my expression change as I willingly let go of the knife and dropped my arm. The words fell from my lips as though I had no control, "Please, kill me. I can't take this anymore … It ends here." I closed my eyes waiting for the inevitable. Beaten, battered and bruised, death was a welcome … It didn't come. I felt my body being gently placed on the floor.

I opened my eyes to see his teared-filled ones in return. The glazed look was gone, and Bill had returned. Bill then went to the phone, and I heard echoing within my throbbing head, "Please send an ambulance. She needs an ambulance." He dropped the phone and walked out the door.

CHAPTER ELEVEN

Moving Forward

I awoke to a gentle hand brushing the hair away from my hurting face. "Hello, sweetie. I didn't think you were ever going to wake up," choked Beth.

"What's the damage." I roughly whispered. "Three broken ribs, a swollen lip and a black eye." "Could have been worse." I said weakly.

"How much worse did you need it to be? You look like hell, Kate. He beat the shit out of you." She flamed. Beth held my tattered dress to her face and cried. "The doctor said he didn't rape you. From the looks of this dress, and your body, it was a major thought on his mind."

I laughed very softly and flinched, "Well, I guess Bill would have said I used a whore's technique for survival. Speaking of survival, I'm cutting off this damn braid if it's the last thing I do. I'm tired of it being used against me every time I get into a mess. It seems, this is one of Bill's favorite items to grab every time I try to get away!" I laughed lightly while grabbing my ribs from the pain. "—Hey, girlfriend," I squeaked, "Lighten up, it could have been worse ... I could have been dead ... and. Thanks for not saying it." I said in between breaths. It was difficult to breathe.

"Saying what?" Beth chuckled as she wiped her tear stained face with my dress. "Reaming me after I was told not to go over there."

"No, I thought I'd save that for Mike. He should be here tonight—

with Richard." Beth flinched as she spoke. Thinking of angering me at this moment was not the thing to do, but best to tell me before Richard arrived.

"I know, you told me not to call Richard. I had to. He would have never forgiven me if I didn't," Beth paused for a moment, "Remember Kate, Richard made me promise to take care of you and if anything happened, I had better call him." She added in her defense.

"It's okay … No problem. After all Beth, I'm not in a very good position to argue. Ahhh just how long have I been out?" I wiped my eyes. Wrong move that really hurt. *Take note touch eyes gently.* "I guess we can throw that dress. I don't believe there is a special occasion where I could where that rag. I've decided not to go to the battered wives' ball!" I tried to chuckle, grabbed my ribs instead. *Remember: it hurts to laugh.—Don't do it!*

"Six hours.—And leave it to you to make jest out of this situation." Beth replied in a matter-of-fact tone. "Oh, and the police are looking for Bill … Bye the way, there's one right outside your door. She wants to have a word with you. What should I tell her?" She asked curiously.

Could this be the police officer I met when I lost the baby? "Beth, please ask her to come in. And please don't take this wrong sweetie; wait outside while I talk to her. Will you Beth? I know I have no right to ask this right now but Please trust me on this." I patted her hand reassuringly. "It's time for me to get my life into some sort of order. I wanted to wait a bit, I guess there's no time like the present." I took a slow deep breath and know Beth was fully aware of out the breath exhaled with a tremble. I turned my head to hide the onslaught of tears.

Beth watched me for a moment. There were no words really for her to say right now. She looked at my bruised-up body softly sighed, returned my pat, "Guess I'll get rid of this rag while you speak to the officer. I don't think it should be here for Mike to see,—*if* you know what I mean." Puzzled and reluctantly Beth waited just outside the door until the officer came out of the room.

After what seemed to be an eternity, the door opened, and the police officer looked at Beth. The officer's face showed no emotion as to what the conversation was inside, her voice was just as curt as it had been earlier, "She wants to see you. She looks pretty tired.—Needs her rest."

"Well, can you tell me what happened?" Quizzed Beth. She was dying of curiosity.

"No ma'am, I can't," she answered in the same tone.

"She is going to press charges?" Beth insisted.

"I can't say. I will tell you this; she has everything under control. There will be another officer along in a few to take my place. I don't want to leave her alone even though I don't believe he'll show up here."

"What makes you say that?" Beth's eyes were wide. What in the world made her think that crazed asshole would not show up here?

"He called the ambulance," she answered flatly, then sat in the chair, picked up a magazine indicating to Beth the conversation was over.

Beth returned and sat quietly by my side. I slept until sometime in the evening and was awaken by a dispute in the corridor. "Oh God, sounds like Mike. They should be here any second." I giggled carefully. I became excited knowing Richard was so close.

The door flew open; a herd of elephants couldn't stop Mike as he bolted to my side. I could see Richard waiting patiently outside. Beth couldn't get out of the way quick enough. "That officer wasn't going to allow us in! I guess I couldn't blame her ... How ya doin' Sis?" Mike was by my side caressing my hair.

"A little banged up. I'll live," I chuckled.

"I'll kill that bastard! I told him I would if he ever touched you again ... Kate," He leaned closer to me and looked into my battered eyes, "Please tell me why? Why did you go to that house? What was there that could have possibly been so important?" Ask Mike sweetly as he could. He had a death grip on my fingers.

"My pride. Nothing else. My stupid pride ... I'm sorry so Mike ..." I could feel the hot tears flowing down my cheeks. I was hurting so badly but the words just spoken by my brother filled me with terror. I had to do something. I knew Mike well enough to know this was not a simple threat. I want you to listen to me as you never listened before,"

I appealed, "Mike, I want you to leave Bill alone. I will take care of it. Leave him to me.—Please?"

"Damnit Kate, he beat the hell out of you. I can't stand by and allow him to do this.—Not again." Mike looked at my battered face and broke down, "Sure, if that's what you want. But why? I hope you are going to send him to jail!"

"That's my business and never mind why. I've taken care of everything," I took a slow deep breath, "Now that you've seen I'm alive and well, could I please see Richard?" The anticipation was overwhelming.

"Sure." He looked at my battered face with sad eyes. I knew the memories of our childhood filled his mind as they did mine over and over during this ordeal, "I love you Sis," he choked, "You scared the hell out of me. I knew—No. I'll leave it alone. I'll get Richard." He kissed me on the forehead and stormed out of the room before the rage over took his senses.

Beth smiled, "I think I'd better leave you two alone and take care of mine. I'll see you in the morning. Take care of you," she blew me a kiss and went after Mike.

I watched as the man of my dreams came to my side. He knelt next to me, carefully picked up my hand and lightly kissed it. I traced his face with my fingertip. All the lifetimes I had seen this man come to my side. The happy lifetime. They all melded together into this moment. He was here.—Finally. Richard gently kissed my bruised lips then gathered me in his arms and held me tight. The tears poured as I returned the embrace. I wanted to pass right through him and become one.

"Kate, my love. My love," he choked. "I have been crazy with worry. I knew something was wrong early this morning when Maggie was on the phone. As I drove here, I sort of pieced it together. Bill must have told her what happened. Maggie wouldn't tell me. She was frantic all morning. I knew I felt something wrong, I doubled over, falling to the floor this morning as I got out of bed. I couldn't understand," he babbled, "I should have … I should have known if you were in trouble. It was as though there was a block. I–I couldn't tap into you. I–I can't explain it. When the phone rang again, I had to pry the receiver out of Maggie's hands. Beth tried to explain, I didn't hear everything, and I left without saying a word. I had to get to you." He held me at arm's length as he spoke. He was trembling.

"Yes sweetheart, you were not supposed to be with me today. This was something I had to do on my own today. It was my ending to a long drawn out chapter of hate." I was so tired, but it did not matter. Richard was here and I was not going to let him out of my site ever again.

"Kate, I don't understand? You are my split apart. I should have felt everything."

"No, Richard, not everything. Sometimes we have to take the step forward on our own to create the need change and end of a karmic situation, as I have been told. I am now your partner, complete in her own right." I smiled. I finally got it. We are capable of walking out of our own hell and move forward into the Light. We have to do it ourselves. No one can do it for us. Jesus gave us the Christ knowledge. He showed us *how* to, but it is up to *us* to do it ourselves. I felt a deep seeded rejoice at that moment as though the Heavens were applauding an old Soul back home.

I touched Richard's face and asked, "Richard, how did you get here?—You didn't ride the motorcycle in this cold?" I laid back down. The pain from my ribs was too much.

He wickedly laughed, "No, my sweet, I took Maggie's Porsche. She had me get rid of the bike. She hated it. Little does she know, I have it in storage."

"We'll just have to get it right back out and back where it belongs as soon as it gets a bit warmer …" I became silent as he looked deeply into my eyes. I had to ask, "Richard, I have to ask you something. While I was in Arizona, I was watching a sunrise, I went into some sort of meditation, and out of the blue—there you were, standing within my mind, speaking to me! Was it real?"

Surprised, he softly answered, "For days I tried to find you. Kate, I couldn't take it any longer. I had to know how you were. Mike wouldn't tell me where you had gone. So, I went to my favorite stop and sat under this wonderful willow tree, very much like the one at our picnic. I'll have to show you sometime,—anyway, I went into a very deep meditation and asked to speak to your Highest Self. Before me stood this incredible glow—your Presence. I spoke from my heart hoping to reach you ..." He laid his head by my side and cried softly, "No one would tell me where you were ... Mike told me to be patient ... I couldn't be without you ... I was planning to leave Maggie. I–I couldn't live in that lie any longer. If I was to be without you, I was going to be alone." He looked up, there was a flash of pain in his eyes, "and I should have dragged you from that bastard's house. This would have never happened! I wish I could have avoided this."

I gathered Richard in my arms; it felt wonderful to be there for him now. "My love, you knew I could not leave Bill. And for a long time, I did not know why myself. On this trip I learned so much. I know now why I couldn't leave Bill. Why it had to be finished. "My love, hush. There was no way you could have avoided anything.—This long- standing war had to be finished ... *I* had to finish it—*myself* ... *That*'s why you were blocked this morning. This is one battle you were not supposed to finish for me." I gently caressed his face. Yes, he was really there. "Richard, if you were able to reach me in that way in Arizona, you must realize you can't just leave Maggie. I don't matter how I feel towards her; *you* have to mend this between the two of you. We can't possibly have a relationship with this hanging over our heads." I hesitated, "What I don't get ..."

"Go ahead, finish Kate,—ask me. I know what you're going to ask."

"If you are so spiritually aware, why did you ever go with her in the first place?" I finished.

"I got lonely. I know it was wrong and I tried to rationalize it in my head knowing Maggie is a user and she was using me,—I know, it doesn't make it anymore right. My love, remember, we are all on the path and we are all very much human. Sometimes we get off course a little bit and are steered back. The point is, to get back on course. You're right, I'll get in touch with her and talk to her ... Let's not worry about that now ... You look tired. Why don't you try to get some sleep?"

"I don't want to. I don't want you to leave." I couldn't take my eyes off him. Should I close my eyes this moment and he would be gone making all of this part of some wild weird dream. No, I couldn't risk that. I never wanted him away from my side again.

"Don't you worry your pretty little self about that. I have no intentions on leaving your side tonight—or ever. Now that I have you. I'll never let you go." He held my hand as I dozed off.

"Well, my dear, it looks like you've been quite busy since you left," said Praise.

"Praise! What?—Are you doing here? Am I still in Arizona having a weird dream?

Or is this my Highest Self coming in as you for some reason?"

"No, you are in a hospital in Chicago. And no, I am not your Highest Self, even though we are all connected as one in the universe. It's me, Praise." She answered. Her appearance was faint and wispy.

"Then how—?"

"I told you I'd be there whenever you needed me. So here I am. You really don't need me. I felt I needed to check up on you," she smiled.

"I wish you had done that yesterday, I needed you then." I said flatly.

"No, you didn't. You had to make the decision, Kate." Praise said in her ever-popular calm tone.

"Did I have to get beat up in the process?" I asked.

"Who knows? If you remember correctly. In one life you chose to jump off a cliff. In this life to choose to end it without having to die. If you had chosen any other way, would he have picked ups the phone and called the ambulance?—No. He would not. He would have been on the run for the brutal murder. And we need to think about the fact that he could have walked away and just allowed you to lie on the kitchen floor. You are very lucky. I told you before; the perfect time would let you know. It was your time to step forward and have Faith."

I thought back and remembered the feeling. "Yeah. I did know.

That's when I dropped the knife. As badly as I wanted to take that knife and slam it into his body something came over me—a compassion if you will, and I just could not."

"See? You're a lot smarter than you give yourself credit for." She smiled. "Is it over?" I desperately wanted to know.

"I don't know,—is it? Seems to me, Kate, you have everything in hand. However, you have to keep one thing in proper perspective. This is the beginning of a new domino. It takes time to see where the pieces fall and how. I realize we did a lot of incredible things in looking back. Please remember that it was not right then in what he did or is right in this life. It is such a waste to take life," she sighed deeply, "If we could only understand, we need to look within to be rid of these atrocities and not carry them into our everyday lives … Learn to love yourself Kate, know that you are deserving all the wonderful things life has to offer … Believe it or not, so is Bill, he just doesn't realize it yet. Everyone deserves the love and infinite wisdom God has to offer … Be happy." She watched Richard as he slept. "He's very handsome. I can feel how easy it was for you to falter. The love emanating from him is very intense."

"Yes," I responded in a dreamlike state, as I lovingly stroked his hair, "I guess I have a whole lot of work to do. Praise, I know it was wrong for me to sleep with Richard. I never looked or even thought of having an affair no matter how bad things were before Richard walked into my life. I guess, I could say that I really knew Richard first. I was aware for years about him … I just didn't know how to listen to myself … No, there is no excuse for what I did. Have I created more Karma to clear up?"

"It depends on you, Richard—and Bill. "You were told there are no wrongs.—Only ignorance. You will know within if what you do feels wrong, this is your Self telling you there is something about *you* that is wrong … This is when you must change your path. Negative Karma is created when you don't listen within … First realize, we can become confused when certain things go awry after a commitment is made. That is the purpose of the challenge. You realized after the act, this could not go on. Those were the wrong feelings to feel, then you proceeded to correct the problem on your own ... Well, maybe there was a little help ... What is done is done. Have you learned from the ignorance? That's the most important question. Look at all aspects with love, see all you have done was and is perfection; this is true forgiveness."

Praise seemed to fade. She closed her eyes and became brighter than before, "You have accomplished what most people can only dream of doing. They settle in life. They truly believe they are not worthy of all the wonderful things—including love. They settle for comfort, stability,—and or pain. Very few find love as you have found it. It's out there for everyone. It all starts here," she pointed to my heart, "Remember Kate, once you have worked this out, and decide to forgive, you must let it go. Then and only then will you be free from the bondage of ignorance and live in equanimity. Should you and Richard forgive—and Bill decides not to, that's his problem. Have I totally confused you?" Laughed Praise.

I laughed lightly, "Not really. It's going to take some time. I understand mentally I should forgive Bill, it's very difficult to do it physically and emotionally. Give me some time, I will. I guess it sounds simpler than it is. Or maybe it's the other way around."

"It's pretty simple. We can all make commitments. Just understand, commitments can come to an end; they are not written in stone. Once you accept this, you will know that you can either stay—or leave ... Ask within, and you will be given the correct answer ... Trust." As she said the word trust, she became brighter.

"You haven't answered my question about how you are here.—And how am I able to see Richard? Did I finally—you know?" I asked uneasily.

"Die? No. Some people call it astral traveling. I don't leave my body. I call it multidimensional. We all have the ability to be in several places at once. I'll wake up tomorrow believing this was only a dream. You may or may not remember it. The stuff you've been getting lately—who knows. Give yourself time, one day soon, it will all come together. You will not only forgive Bill, but your father too. I need to get going. My body's becoming restless ... Take care of you."

"I'll be fine ... I believe it now." I glanced at Richard.

"Love yourself Kate, have the courage to be who you are. It makes life easier to forgive not only yourself, but also everyone around you. This will also aid in seeing with clarity. You have proven you can do anything for someone who has lived in such deep fear. You are quite an incredible person. See the God-Self in everything and everyone. If you don't,—then *you* are the one with the problem.—I love you Kathleen."

I watched her fade away with the largest grin I have ever seen ...

"I know ... I love you too." I said chuckling to myself. I became aware of my own presence in the room by Richard's sudden stir. I softly stroked his hair, watching my beloved. It was all-true. Our lives past present and future. I don't believe I'd say all the pain was worth the end result; I *am* grateful the worst was over. I can and will walk forward happier than I have ever been before.

CHAPTER TWELVE

The Beginning ...

After a few days I was feeling better and quite the spoiled princess. Between Richard, Mike and Beth, I was properly pampered. Rather flustered from all of my attention, the doctor gave me a seal of approval to go home. I believe he was getting me out of there before Mike disrupted the entire hospital.

Everyone was there to take me back to Beth's, including Mom. I asked them to hold on because I was waiting for one more person. Within a few minutes, the lady police officer was at the door. "Ready to go Kate? My partner is waiting in the car."

"Go where?" Mike inquired firmly.

"If you must know, I'm going to get my things. This officer told me she would escort me to get them. She is also going to serve Bill with the divorce papers." I stood before him with my hands firmly on my hips.

"Damnit, Kate, do we have to go through this again?" Exclaimed Mike with exasperation. He slammed his fist into the wall.

"Mike, you have to trust her. She needs to do this. You will have to understand that she needs to say her peace so she can move on with her life." Said Mom in my defense. "I believe she can do this. I wish I had."

I rushed to mom's side and held her tightly. "Thank you." I whispered.

Mike threw his arms up into the air exasperated with the whole thing then turned to Richard to come to his aid, "What do you have to say about this, Richard? You've been pretty quiet. Did you know about this?" Demanded Mike. "Surely you see the madness in this."

"Not really. I intend to drive her. She won't be totally alone," he picked up my small ragged suitcase and laughed, "I believe we'll have to get you a new one of these. Oh, and Mike, you may want to see a nurse about that fist."

"Ha-ha. I'm fine," said Mike rubbing it, "Well then we'll follow." Beth held her man in comfort and nodded in agreement.

With my entourage, we followed the police car to the house. I nervously got out of the car, took a deep breath, told Mike and Richard to wait by the car. Richard had to hold Mike back with Mom and Beth's help.

The police officer knocked, and Bill flung open the door. He looked worse than he did when I last saw him. "Mr. Sawyer, I have a court order that allows Kate Sawyer to enter the premises' and retrieve her things. I'm asking you to allow her to this," the officer instructed.

Bill stepped away from the door as we entered. He didn't say a word. The police officer then handed him the divorce papers. Bill stared at them sadly. He looked at me as he snapped the papers out of the officer's hand. His words turned into that well-known venom tone, "I guess this is what you want … It doesn't matter. I don't have to give it to you. The church won't give you the—"

"Stop right there, Bill." I held up my shaking hand. "I don't want to hear it. I am not here to listen to you. You will listen to me." I stood steadfast; "Here's the deal. You will grant me my divorce without any hassle." Again, I held out my hand to stop his next words. "You will stay out of my life. I will get half of everything in the bank. Stocks, bonds—whatever. You can keep the house I don't even want a penny if you should sell it. It was yours in the beginning. In return I won't press charges. You won't go to jail. Just sign those papers and it will be over painlessly as possible. I will send someone to pick up my things; there's a list enclosed, those are the only things I want," taking another deep breath,—You will not destroy anything!" I stepped away as the police officer stepped forward handing Bill a pen.

He snatched the pen from her hand and laughed hysterically, "You're pretty damned stupid if you believe for one moment that I will give you shit!" He threw the pen at the officer and lunged towards me, grabbing me by the throat. Fear enveloped my body. His eyes were wildly glazed, his breath was rapid, and the smell of stall beer lingered as he breathed. I didn't know what was about to happen. Sheesh *he has been on one long drink fest!* I tried to move away, this only tightened his hold.

Mike bolted for the door with Richard not far behind. The officer drew her pistol and pointed it directly at Bill. Her partner intervened with Mike and Richard, politely asking them to stay back. Beth held Mom assuring her everything was fine. I knew she was crazed with worry but wouldn't allow Mom to see it.

Bill stared at the pistol and shouted, "You're gonna have to kill me! She's mine! That bastard stole her from me!" He seemed delirious. Bill's face nuzzled into my neck and hair breathing deeply. In a harsh tone he whispered, "Please don't leave me baby, I need you." I stood frozen afraid to speak.

"Sir! Yes sir, I will shoot! You will step away from Kate … Now!" She stepped closer, cocking the hammer of the gun, making sure he understood her demand.

I got the nerve to speak up and allowed my head to rest against his shoulder and spoke as gently as I could, "Bill, please listen, let me go. This will only make things worse. I–I need to go … They will shoot you,—don't you understand this?" Sobbing tears caused me to violently shake in Bill's grasp. He realized I was just as afraid as he was. My voice grew softer, "Look deep into your heart Bill and listen … You know this is for the best."

Beaten, Bill stepped away glaring at me, "Katie, please don't do this …—I can't," he sobbed, "I can't live without you. He dropped to his knees and continued to profess his love. All I could do was stare into his pitifully sad face. I felt that old weakness flooding my body. I knew I had to get out of here. *Please let this end,* I prayed.

The officer stepped over to Bill to hand cuff him, she saw the look on my face saying please, no. Instead again, handed him the divorce papers as he crumpled to the floor sadly, signing them, "I–I still love you Kate." He looked so tired and drawn.

"No, you don't Bill. You just think you do …" I answered with a heavy heart, "Please, please get some help. "

"Ma'am, we need to get going." The officer looked at Bill and I could see the same pity in her eyes.

I nodded at the officer and looked at Bill one last time. "I don't hate you Bill. I never could … I'm going to work very hard to forgive you … Please try to forgive yourself."

I walked out the door with papers in hand and looked into the beautiful morning feeling a great weight had lifted from my shoulders. By the car stood the man of my dreams. Here. Waiting for me. I ran to him. There were no words. I felt his love so passionate against my lips as we kissed. I looked into his eyes as he gently cradled my face his hands, as he returned my gaze … Our lives would now be complete. I looked into my future's eyes …

We are so much alike he and I.

The beginning …

A few last words...

I waited until the end of this book to say thanks to everyone who was involved. While writing this book I encountered on going experiences aiding in this endeavor. My own personal growth changed some of the views. This book in itself has been one monumental hurdle to overcome. This proves anyone can do anything that they set out to accomplish—if it comes from the heart.

I wish to dedicate this book to all of my lives and people in them. I thank you all for assisting in my growth as a Spiritual Being.

In this life, I thank my parents, Maria and Eldridge Fedrick for the challenges aiding in who I am today. I love you very much.

My sister Karen Lee, for being who she is. No matter what she is confronted with, she is her own woman.

To my children Joshua and Bret. I want you to know I love you so very much and my pride in you is more than you could ever imagine.

My friends who assisted in my growth: Eileen, a special thanks you, she was there in the beginning, putting up with most of my antics and personality changes.

Bevann, my teacher and mentor.

Kelly, a dear friend, whose persistence motivated the development of this book.

Nedra, not only with her art work, for her Divine Inspiration when needed

I love you Nick.

The most important thing we need to remember about love.

Real love, healthy love, restores;

it fills you to the brim and over flows.

Love encumbrances all things. It surpasses all feelings.
Within Love, you are clear, light and happy.
You *can* deal with All things that happen within life.
Within the depths of anger, the center of chaos is love and it heals.
Within a relationship, love assists in the growth and moving forward without fears.

Knowing should a fear develop, love easily forgives and once again heals. Fear is merely a tool to aid us to look at that part of us that needs to be healed. Fear is a most honest teacher. Embrace it when it is felt, when you do this, it will fade.

Love is what makes us whole. Love is what makes us one.

We are in some very special times. We as humans are about to experience some very incredible things. We were chosen to be here to accomplish a task beyond tasks.—To remember our Enlightenment.

We will be able to see everything for what it is,—one huge illusion called drama. We are all the players and only we can decide the outcome. Believe me, it will be spectacular! When we are able to look at each other with love, we will see the route to all misunderstanding is merely ignorance only then we will see the pettiness of things we argue about and hate. Hate will no longer be fed so that it will grow. If we are standing in love, our egos will grow with us and blossom along with the rest of us. Then we can all live in equanimity. We all have the capabilities to live life this way and grow as we choose.

Remember that your obligation in life is to be true to yourself. Do not accept anything less ...

One last comment I wish to share. I read this on a bumper sticker:

> *We are not humans having a Spiritual experience, We are Spiritual Beings having a human experience.*

In Happiness,

Shananda.

www.ingramcontent.com/pod-product-compliance
Lightning Source LLC
Chambersburg PA
CBHW021424070526
44577CB00001B/45